My Cup Runneth Over

by

Paul H. Johnson

Interior design and cover art: Ragont Design

Printed in the United States of America

ISBN 13: 978-1492870173
ISBN 10: 149387017X

CONTENTS

PREFACE

WHY WRITE A BOOK?

As a retired building contractor and real estate developer, over the years people have asked me how certain events and various projects in my life came about and why I was sure that God had orchestrated all of them. Sometimes the conversations were during the social times at board meetings or maybe during dinner with friends or family. Sometimes the person would say, after I told them a story or two, "You should write a book." I must have heard that suggestion dozens of times over the years from various friends and family. My reaction always was, "It will be a lot of work and, besides, who in the world would want to read it?"

One day, when I said that to my daughter Karen, who has five children, she said emphatically, "Your grandchildren! [I have fourteen in all.] And maybe more people than you think." Recently the pressure has been increasing. In fact, one of my friends, Ron Hagelman, a retired medical doctor, went so far as to provide me with an opening outline for the book. My family, in a nice way, reminded me recently that if ever I was going to do it, I had better be about it. They didn't need to remind me that I am now in my eighty-fifth year.

One granddaughter who is a creative writer said to me, "Papa, just make some notes and I will help you." Others have said, "Just sit down with a tape recorder and start talking and others will put it all together."

When I started the process, I didn't know exactly how to proceed. I just started writing. Anyway, what you hold in your hand is the result.

So my main purpose in writing this book, is to help you, my children and grandchildren, to know more about Papa's life, and it is to you that I dedicate the whole thing.

In chronological order, to you dear Colleen, my oldest, who is a lot like her dad, and your wonderful husband, Drew, and to your five great kids. To dear Meghan who was the first grandchild and she will always be a No. 1 with me. Then to Michael, Ian, Sheena, and Lauren. I could write a book about each of you. And to my one and only son, Kevin, who has so much of his mother and her wonderful traits in him and to his delightful wife, Cheryle, and those four great kids, Camden, Graham, Brigham, and their little sister, Claire, who is the youngest of all of the fourteen. And then to my sweet daughter Karen, who seems to have gotten a good mixture of the best of both her father and mother, and to her husband, Scott, who is so dedicated to his family, and their five fantastic children, Meredith, Drew, Ginny, Kirsten, and Clayton Paul. As I said, I could write a book about each of you, but I guess I had better wait awhile as I'm sure there will be many more good things to say about all of you in days to come as your lives progress and as you follow the Lord Jesus and let Him take you through some exciting experiences. My advice, as always: just trust and obey. There is no other way.

And then, of course, to my longtime friend and helper and now my dear wife, Pamela, who worked so hard in typing up all these words that I wrote down longhand on so many pages of yellow pads, and who was such an encouragement to me and kept saying, "Don't forget to tell them about so and so or such and such." You are the very best, and I love you so much.

So, to all twenty-one of you, I love you all, and I hope this book will be of some help to you. It is because of you and for you that I wrote all these words, and I dedicate them all to you. I hope it is, indeed, of some benefit to you.

1

MY EARLY YEARS

My dad, Lawrence Johnson, was born in 1905 and brought up on a farm near Benton, Kentucky. Benton is not far from Paducah, which is at the western end of Kentucky where the state narrows down to where it is only about fifty miles from Illinois to Tennessee.

As he tells it, he was full-grown when he was about fourteen years old. Seeing his size and physical ability, his dad encouraged him to quit school after the eighth grade and go to work on the farm. He said it was hard work—planting, plowing, harvesting from sunup to sundown. His brother, Kenneth, two years younger, was also made to help out as best he could.

At age twenty, in 1925, my dad heard about Henry Ford in Detroit and that Mr. Ford was paying his workers five dollars a day. This information spread all across Indiana, Ohio, Kentucky, Tennessee, West Virginia, and who knows how far. It was like a magnet that attracted many able-bodied young men to the Motor City. My dad was among those that heard and went to Detroit. The story is that someone asked Henry Ford why he was paying that much when the going rate at that time was three dollars a day. He said there were two reasons. "First, I want to attract the healthiest, strongest men I can find; and, secondly, I want to pay them enough so that they can afford to buy a car."

After my dad got his job and a few paychecks, he went back home and got my mom, his sweetheart. They were married and moved together into a small apartment in Detroit in 1925. My mom's maiden name was Daisy Edna Cox. She disliked the name Daisy and became "Edna" from an early age.

The custom in those days was as soon as one got a job and got established, he would help bring his other family members to the big city and to enjoy a better life. On the farm in those days it was a life of work, work, work, and with just enough money from the crops to survive. In a bad year, with crop failures and other hardships, times really got tough.

My dad was the oldest of six children (two other boys and three girls), and he helped the entire family, except for one married sister, to come to Detroit. They rented a house three doors down on the street from where my mom and dad lived. The brothers and my grandfather all found work in the big city. Three years later, in 1928, I came along, born at home with the help of a midwife. As the first grandchild in the family, my dad's twin sisters, Edith and Edna, who were twelve years old at the time, said I was like a "new toy." They became my babysitters and spoiled me. They have had a special place in my life as long as they lived. They were both in their nineties when they passed away.

My mom's brother, Roy Cox, and his family also came up and rented a flat on the other side of our house and next door. He and his wife had four children. With cousins on one side and grandparents and uncles and aunts on the other side, we were all very close. To top it off, my mom's sister, Eunice, and her husband moved directly across the street from us with their two young daughters, Donna and Judy. Other friends and relatives also came up from Kentucky, found work, and settled within a few blocks.

Our family was not alone in this migration, as the auto industry attracted thousands of families much like ours. Then came the years of the Great Depression, which began with the crash of the stock market in 1929. Some investors committed suicide, unemployment was 30 to 40 percent, breadlines were blocks long. Henry Ford took pity on his workers. Instead of laying off half of them, he let them all work three days a week, which, at five dollars a day, gave my dad and others fifteen a week. The two-family flat that we lived in rented for twenty-five dollars a month. It was owned by Fred Hossler, an electrical contractor who had lived in the house and still had his shop and office in a garage behind the house. He made a deal with my mom. If she would answer his phone when he was not there, we could have the flat for eighteen a month. The fringe benefit was that we also had limited use of the phone, something very few people had in those days. Funny how I remember that number: Garfield 5919.

Many of the folks from the South became homesick in the big city and couldn't wait to "go home" for a visit. After they got their first car, my folks would sometimes "go home" for a long weekend. They would leave on Friday after work and drive all night, nonstop. There were not many "filling stations," as they were called, so they strapped an extra can of gas onto the back. Then they would leave Kentucky Sunday afternoon and get home early Monday morning. In the early days, there was so much demand for travel for those without cars from Detroit to Paducah, Kentucky, and back, that several entrepreneurs bought the biggest car they could afford and would take five passengers with them, for a fee of course. The travel experience was miserable. Poor roads, six people in a tight space; but the folks went anyway. A new business was born. In fact, one fellow named Brooks was so successful that he eventually bought a bus and opened Brooks Bus Line. His only route was Detroit to Paducah.

During the summer, it was the custom for the auto plants to shut down during parts of July and August for "model changeover time." With school out and my dad laid off for three or four weeks, we were bound for western Kentucky. My mom's folks were still there. They were too old to come to Detroit. They had a small farm, and I learned all about chickens, pigs, cows, and all other kinds of farm animals. It was summer camp for me and a whole new way of life. They grew corn, tomatoes, potatoes, and all kinds of vegetables, but the main crop was tobacco. They had one or two "hired hands" to help them. I remember picking strawberries as a kid and putting them in little square boxes, ready for the market.

From the farm to the city in those days was a whole different way of life. My grandmother and grandfather had never been off the farm or farther away from home than Paducah. They had no idea what a streetcar looked like or probably even a bus, for that matter. No electricity. No running water. And surely no car. It was horse and buggy for travel to town.

I learned a lot at a very early age and how to be thankful that we enjoyed so many conveniences and blessings. Even then I thought, "Why am I so blessed?"

Our neighborhood on 23rd Street, just north of Warren Avenue, was made up of all kinds of ethnic groups who had also been attracted to "a better life." Our next-door neighbors were African-American. Across the street was a Greek family. Two doors down from us was a Mexican family. Down on Warren Avenue, living above their dry-goods store, was a Jewish family. In the next block were Scottish, French, Irish, and just about every nationality you could think of. When I went to kindergarten, they were all my classmates, and we were all good friends. It was there that I learned that while people were from different backgrounds, they were all the same in so many ways with the same need to be accepted.

When I think of life on 23rd Street during the Depression years of the thirties, my mind is flooded with memories. There didn't seem to be any zoning laws back then. Single-family homes were mixed in with two-flats, four-flats, and small three- and four-story apartment buildings with six to twenty units, along with a small corner grocery store, all in what one would call a residential neighborhood. Across the street and down a few lots from us was a small creamery. It was built on about two residential lots and extended back to the street behind, separated by the alley. Many of the buildings came right out to the sidewalk property line. Most of the two-flats and single-family homes had small front yards of grass. Our grass front yard was about fifteen feet square. All the garages were accessed from the rear alley.

As kids, we played baseball and marbles in a vacant lot next door to my grandparents' rented two-story single-family house. In the winter it became a small ice-skating pond. We played "kick the can" in the alley and kick ball in the street. Most of the houses were heated with coal. The coal truck would dump the coal in the street at the curb in front of the house. For a dollar or two per ton, they would wheel it in a wheelbarrow to a basement window, usually along the side of the house, and dump it into a coal bin. The homeowner would then shovel it into the furnace. Most families couldn't afford to pay to have it wheeled in and did it themselves, like my dad and me. It was hard work, especially in the winter if the coal pile was left outside for a day or two and snow fell on it and froze. Not everyone even owned a wheelbarrow. We had a community one, used by all the families. It had a steel wheel and was a real chore to push uphill especially for older folks. As a result, neighborhood kids, including my dad's younger brother and two friends, would wheel the coal in for fifty or seventy-five cents a ton—about two to three hours' work.

I used to shovel snow off the sidewalks for ten cents per house. The doctor on the corner of 23rd and Warren had a big house and a big walk. He paid me a quarter. I always went to his house first to get his business.

Warren Avenue was a wide main street with streetcar tracks down the middle. The buildings along Warren, as I've already noted, were a real mixture. There were a few larger-than-average single-family houses, along with apartment buildings, retail stores with apartments above, a movie theater three blocks down, and five blocks west of 23rd Street on the corner of Warren and McKinley was Columbian Elementary School where I attended up to the sixth grade. Like our entire neighborhood, the student body was made up of a wide mixture of ethnic groups. I learned a lot about different cultures from my schoolmates and visiting in some of their homes. Some of their customs and foods and values (and lack of values) I can still remember. Suffice it to say, I got a broad cultural education at an early age.

Most all of us were poor but we didn't seem to notice it. We were all in the "same boat" and got along fine. There was one exception, the Wedler family who lived across the alley from us. They had two boys, Bobby, my age, and Junior, two years younger. Mr. Wedler had his own business. He had a small, refrigerated truck that he kept in his two-car garage. Very early each morning he would go to the meatpacking house and load up his truck with processed meat, such as bologna, various lunch meats, bacon, etc. Then he delivered it to various retail stores throughout Detroit. He was always home by 2 or 3 p.m., about the time we got home from school, giving him a lot more time with his family than most other dads. Their house was nice but not elaborate. Their furniture was way above average and they always had a new car. Bobby was in my class and we became good friends. We walked back and forth to school together and later with his brother Junior.

The way I knew they had extra money was because Mr. Wedler on his travels around town would come home and tell us about a carnival that he saw. He was always ready to go to the carnival with his wife and two boys, and very often they invited me to go along. I was amazed at how he would say to us, "Now just pick out the rides you want to go on and I'll get the tickets." We rode every ride and played every game, shot at every shooting gallery and ate all the ice cream and popcorn we wanted. He paid for everything and never seemed to be stingy about it. We always came home with a carful of stuffed animals and prizes. The money just kept coming out of his pockets—a whole different attitude and lifestyle than I was accustomed to. Over the years we probably went eight or ten times. Such extravagance! As you might guess, I made sure that I stayed good friends with Bobby for a long time.

One of the other things that Bobby and some other kids and I did was to walk to Tiger Stadium, which was about two miles away. Naturally, none of us had any money. So we would go and wait outside, asking people if they had any extra tickets. They seldom did; but if so, they usually wanted something for them. After the game started—and they were all afternoon games, no such things as lights—we would hang around and try to get friendly with one of the ticket takers located at the various entrances to the stadium. We always looked for one with a soft heart, and we finally found him. About the third inning, when no one else was coming to the game and we were all alone, he would say, "Now look, boys. I have to go to the bathroom. If you guys happen to walk in while I'm gone, just be sure and take the first vacant seats you come to and don't move until the game is over. I may come looking for you."

It was a great way to see the famous Detroit Tigers play baseball. They were also pretty good back in those days. On the way home we would stop by the factory of "Better Made" potato chips. For five cents, which we could usually scrape up between us, we could get a good-sized bag of broken chips, which actually gave us more than if they were whole chips because they packed in so well. By the time we got home, there were no chips left but we had full stomachs and a wonderful summer afternoon for one or two cents each.

We tried the same procedure with the ticket takers at the old Olympia Stadium where the Red Wings used to play hockey. It was only about five blocks from my house and was located on Grand River and McGraw. We didn't get in very often. In fact, we didn't try very often, as most of the games were at night and my mom wouldn't let me go out. They did have a few afternoon games on Saturday or Sunday. The Red Wings always had a good team, and most of the games were sold out. We did get in two or three times, but only after the first period was over and the ticket taker had left his post. We always wound up in the "standing room only" section. It was a challenge, but we persevered and celebrated our accomplishments.

There were other activities on 23rd Street. Albert was my cousin and my next-door neighbor. His dad was my mom's older brother. Albert was a year or two older than me, but we spent a lot of time together. Albert had an older sister, Calistine, who was a very pretty girl and about two years older than Albert. As a teenager, Calistine loved to go to the movies, but her mother wouldn't let her go out at night alone. The theater was on Warren Avenue, about three blocks from 23rd Street. My mom wasn't fond of the movies, but sometimes she would let me go on a Friday night with Albert and Calistine as her "bodyguards." In those days, the admission was ten cents and included two films. On Saturday afternoons, when my mom would let me go, for ten cents we could see lots of cartoons and a Western film or two, often about cowboys and Indians. Maybe four hours in all. I can remember when in the movies a bad guy was sneaking up on a good guy from behind, the kids in the show would shout out loud, "Look out!" As if the good guy could hear them. Wednesday night was dish night, when everyone got a free dish. If you came every Wednesday night for long enough, you could get a whole set of dishes.

Saturday night was a real deal. As I said, all showings consisted of two movies called the "double feature." The films lasted one week only, from Sunday morning at 12:05 a.m. until Saturday at midnight. So if you went to the show on Saturday evening about seven or eight o'clock, you could see the last showing of that week's two films and, if you wanted to stay, you could see two more films, which were the beginning of the next week's showing. It was called the "midnight show." Four movies for ten cents. So if you went to the movies every other Saturday night, you could see the whole month's showing, eight movies, for ten cents each night, or twenty cents for the entire month. My mom would never let me go to the midnight show, but Calistine and Albert and their older sister, Earline, went quite often. My dad often asked how they liked the movie. They always said they were good. My dad joked that they never saw a bad one. It was a major blow when the US government instituted a 10 percent entertainment tax and the price went up to eleven cents!

Lawrence and Edna Johnson, My Mom and Dad,
on Their Seventieth Wedding Anniversary

Papa's Fifth Birthday

Cowboy with Gun

2

OUR CHURCH

While I was still a baby, maybe two years old, my mom became interested in finding a church to attend. She had become a believer in Jesus Christ when she was a teenager back in Kentucky. But with all the activity of a marriage, moving to a new city and finding her way around, and having a baby, she had sort of put church attendance on the "back burner." Now, however, she thought it was time to look for a church. There was a small church about three blocks from our house. She went there a few times and decided that it wasn't for her. Five blocks away was a bigger, more stately Congregational church, but that one didn't suit her either. One day she was talking to a lady friend that she knew back in Kentucky, and she told my mom about the Highland Park Baptist Church, where she attended with her family. It was a long way for us to go, but we went anyway. My mom said, "This is it." She said that this is a church where the gospel of Jesus Christ is preached and where the Bible is taught as the Word of God. The folks at the church were friendly, and that was a new beginning and turned out to be a wonderful "find" for us as a family.

In those days, my dad worked the "swing shift." It was two weeks of days, two weeks of afternoons, and two weeks of the midnight shift. As a result of his work schedule, he could not always attend church with us. But my mom and I went to church every Sunday from the time I was two years old. We had to ride two streetcars, a trip that took forty-five minutes to an hour. But we went, rain or shine! I can remember standing on the corner in the dead of winter, waiting for the Woodward streetcar, shivering while my mom wrapped her coat around me to keep me from the blowing wind and snow.

My mom was always the spiritual leader in our family. My dad was a good man, hardworking and honest. I was nine years old when he came to Christ and began to study the Bible regularly. But my mom was the one who set the Christian pace. She was quick to share her faith. Most all the family knew what she believed and how she lived out her faith. Many of the family members sort of tolerated her, and only a few of them became believers.

The church had started a few years earlier in the Highland Park Theater on Woodward Avenue, about three blocks north of Davison in Highland Park. As the church grew, it moved around the corner and across the alley and behind the theater to 25 Ford Avenue, where a new church building was erected. It seated about four or five hundred people and was a two-story building. The auditorium was on the top floor, about twenty steps above ground, and the lower floor was about five steps down in a partial basement, which housed the fellowship hall, kitchen, and Sunday school rooms.

In 1971, the church moved to Lahser and 12 Mile Road in Southfield, Michigan, but retained the name "Highland Park Baptist Church." I came to know the Lord in that old church on Ford Avenue (more about that later), and at this writing I have been an attendee for eighty-two years and a member for seventy-three years. My entire life has been centered on the teachings of the Scripture that I learned in that church and the encouragement that I experienced from pastors, teachers, youth leaders, and fellow believers in Jesus Christ.

I think the church is (or was) unique in many ways. First, for its faithful teaching of the Word of God without compromise; second in its form of government. The founding pastor, William G. Coltman, was not only a faithful teacher of the Scriptures but a wise leader.

When I was growing up, people told me of the early days of the church and how when it was time to make decisions, Pastor Coltman would call the official board together and put before them the issue to be decided. Then he would go around the room, one by one to each person, asking them for their opinion. After everyone had given their advice or suggestion, he would point to one of them and say, "I think John's idea is best and we should follow through with his suggestion." This, of course, made John feel special. Obviously the pastor agreed with John and maybe several others had the same opinion, but the pastor wanted them to feel like they were making the decisions and not him. The result was that it became a member-led church and not a pastor-run church. Naturally, he and they were very careful as to the qualifications and spiritual maturity of those elected to leadership positions.

Over the years a most unusual form of church government developed. The church grew to about two thousand members, a number that remained the same for about sixty years. The congregation was governed by five or six autonomous boards. When a person indicated an interest in the spiritual welfare of the church, he would probably be elected to the board of deacons who were concerned with, among other things, serving communion, assessing the qualifications of Sunday school teachers, the order of the worship services, examining prospective candidates for membership, and more. If one had a business background and indicated a desire to be involved in the affairs of the church, he would likely wind up on the board of trustees who were responsible for the financial affairs of the church. They took care of the money, paid the bills, looked after the church building, hired the custodial and office staff, etc. If one expressed an interest in missions and ministries outside of the church, they would likely be elected to the board of missions. The members of that board could also include women, unlike the deacons and trustees who were all men. Then there was the Christian education board that concerned themselves with the Sunday school program, the youth program, and approved the curriculum and materials that were taught in our various classes and programs. The board of deaconesses, all women, was concerned with the sick, the poor, and families in trouble. They met personally with the members, prayed with them and for them, and did what they could to help. They were sort of God's compassionate ministers or "angels of mercy." Later, a sixth board was added, overseeing the Christian school.

Each board was composed of ten to twenty members, all of whom felt their involvement made a difference, that they were part owners of the church and had a voice in its ministry. At one point, we had on the boards two vice presidents of Ford Motor, the general sales manager of the Cadillac division of General Motors, the general manager of the Dodge division of the Chrysler Corporation, plus doctors, lawyers, CPAs, insurance executives, as well as bankers and business owners, but mostly just ordinary people, all working together for the cause of Jesus Christ and His kingdom and nobody seemed to care who got the credit. A most unique arrangement!

After Dr. Coltman passed away with a heart attack, we have had some outstanding men as pastors, some known nationwide in evangelical circles including Lehman Strauss, George Slavin, and Joe Stowell, who, after nine years with us, went on to be the president of Moody Bible Institute for seventeen years. In later years, the entire governmental authority fell into the hands of an elder board of nine or ten men, including two pastors. I think the jury is still out as to which system works best.

The church has been very special to me. Not only did I grow up in the church, but it was there in a boys Sunday school class that I gave my heart to Jesus Christ and accepted Him as my own personal Savior. In those days, it was not uncommon to have a special week of meetings every year or so. Sometimes they were evangelistic in nature. Other times they were called "Deeper Life" conferences and every year we had a two-week, three Sundays, missions conference when we would bring home several of the seventy or so missionaries that we supported to tell us in detail about their work and show pictures. In those days there was no TV nightly news that took us visually around the world. During the annual missionary conference, with dinner and meetings every night, we all learned among other things a lot of geography, and how people lived around the world. Missionary Conference was the highlight of the church year.

It was during one of the evangelistic conferences in 1939, when I was eleven years old, that my mom insisted that we attend every night of seven nightly programs. Each night I listened (more or less) as the visiting evangelist explained how God loved us and how we could have our sins forgiven and receive the gift of eternal life simply by acknowledging Jesus Christ as Lord of our lives and by faith trusting Him—in other words, to just take Him at His Word, simple belief. Later in the week the sermons got more personal, and by Saturday night I was becoming more uncomfortable, especially when he talked about eternal life in hell as an alternative. Even so, I resisted and I did not go forward to make a commitment to Jesus Christ. I must confess I was very happy to see that guy go! That was Saturday night.

The very next day, Sunday morning in a boys Sunday school class, the teacher, a businessman, said to us eight or nine boys, "I want to be sure that every one of you knows that if you die tonight, that you are absolutely sure that you would be with God in heaven." With that, he went around the class, looking at each of us sitting in a circle and looking into our eyes and said, "How about you? Are you sure? How about you? How about you? Are you sure?" When he came to me, I had to confess that I wasn't sure. Another boy said the same. The teacher said, "Okay. The rest of you guys can go. Paul Johnson and [another boy named] Paul, you fellows stay a little while. I would like to talk to you."

I don't remember the exact date, but I remember the time and place very well. We were in the lower level of the old church at 25 Ford Avenue in a cubicle formed by curtains that were used to divide up the larger room into small classes. And on my knees, leaning on a folding chair and with the help of a faithful, dedicated, and caring Sunday school teacher who explained so clearly how that by simple faith in what Jesus Christ had done for us on the cross two thousand years ago, that by confessing our need for Him and trusting in Him, that we could have the gift of eternal life (John 3:16), I believed both in God and in the teacher's explanation and prayed to receive Jesus Christ. Looking back over my life, it was by far the most important decision I ever made.

I didn't see any lights flash or experience any chills running up and down my spine. But I must say that that night, when I put my head on my pillow, it was a wonderful thing to know that all was right between me and God. I had a sense of peace that I never had before with the firm belief that if I died, that I would be in heaven with God forever. Mr. Auld, the teacher, had made it clear that it was not because of any good things that I had done. But it was simply because of God's love and mercy to me and because I had just believed in Him and, in effect, "taken Him at His Word."

3

SCHOOL DAYS

Back to my life at 5093 23rd Street. Although I was born in an apartment around the corner, we moved to the 23rd Street house when I was still very small, and we lived there until I was seventeen years old. After six years at Columbian Elementary School, I went to McMichael Junior High School, located on Grand River at the corner of West Grand Boulevard. It was a little longer walk and was on a large campus of three schools. They included Northwestern High School, which was a popular and prestigious school and had a winning football team for many years. That should have been my local high school, but an interesting series of events took place. During the three years (six semesters) in junior high school, I signed up for the elective course called "mechanical drafting" all six semesters. I guess not many kids took the same elective for all six semesters because in the sixth one the teacher said they only had curriculum and workbooks for five semesters. There were only four of us still in that class, and the teacher didn't know exactly what to do with us. So he said, how would you guys like to do a little architectural drafting? We said okay. Our assignment was to draw a plan of the first floor of the school building. So, armed with a one hundred-foot tape measure (which I think he bought with his own money) and a shorter one and a large sheet of paper, in teams of two, we set about to measure the building and put it down to scale on paper.

I think this was a win-win for both us and the teacher as he had little or nothing to do while we were out measuring the building. We drew the outside walls showing all the doors and windows and then the inside walls of all the classrooms, stairways, and bathrooms. We thought it was fun to get into the girls' washroom. Too bad they were all in class! We tried not to disturb the ongoing classes while we measured their rooms. Our teacher had told the other teachers what we were doing. We became very special and privileged students during the process. As we returned to our classroom to do the drawing, our teacher would help us with how to indicate the various details like the windows and the swing of the doors, toilet partitions, fixtures, etc. At the end of the semester, we had a detailed drawing of the first floor of McMichael Junior High School.

The teacher took a liking to me and said, "You have a gift for architectural drawing. How would you like to go downtown to Cass Technical High School? They have a course called Architectural Drafting and Building." I said, "Tell me more about it."

"I'll do better than that," he said. "Next week there will be a representative from Cass Tech here to see if we have any students that will qualify for Cass Tech. If you want to go, I will recommend you."

The rep came out and explained that Cass was a very special and unusual school, mostly for gifted students. Many specialized in music and art, and their graduates often went directly into fashion designing or other jobs in that field. They also had courses in electrical, automotive, science, aeronautics, and architectural drafting and building, among a few others. I said okay. My mom and dad said okay, and I signed up.

It was a decision that affected my entire life. The school was in downtown Detroit. The school was big! I had to ride two streetcars to get there. School started at 8 a.m., so I had to get up extra early to get there on time. I had to transfer from the crosstown car, which ran on Warren Avenue, to the Grand River car at the corner of Warren and Grand River. The Grand River car was always full of people going to work in downtown Detroit. It started way out northwest of the city, picking up more and more passengers as it got closer to downtown. Warren was only about six or seven stops from downtown. So by the time the car got to Warren, it was jampacked with people. In those days you got on at the front door of the streetcar and about halfway back, by the exit door, sat the conductor. He collected the five cents for the ride or a transfer ticket from another line that cost an additional one cent. Very often the motorman who stood up front operating the car would not even open the front door, as there was no more room. Or, if he thought that one or two more could get in, he would give it a try. Under those circumstances, most people would just wait for the next car, which would be along at that time in the morning about every five or six minutes. But not Bobby and me. We would rush in until the door would barely close behind us because we couldn't afford to be late for school. Incidentally, you could ride all over town in those days on the streetcar system for five cents for the first ride and one cent extra for a transfer that would let you go on unlimited additional lines.

The school covered an entire city block, and it was eight stories high. It had two huge elevators to move the kids up and down. The lunchroom was on the eighth floor. You could not ride the elevator if you were only going up or down one or two or three floors. When the classes changed, riding the elevator was bedlam. When the elevator unloaded, the operator got out too. He would stand over out of the way and when the incoming crowd pushed in and packed themselves in like sardines and there was not room for one more, he would point to the kid standing closest to the controls and say, "You. Out!" And when the kid got out, it made room for him to get in and operate the elevator.

The school was the finest of its day. The classroom for the building class was two or three stories high, and we actually built a small house in it. The next semester we put in the plumbing, and the next the wiring, and so forth. We had one course in building and one class in architectural drafting each of the six semesters. One class was in materials. Four of us were given about twenty-five or thirty small pieces of different types of wood: pine, oak, spruce, and hemlock. Each piece was labeled. We could look at them as long as we liked, smell them, etc. Then, after two or three classes of study, we were given the same pieces back but with numbers but no labels. That was the test—identify the types. During the six semesters we were required to draw a complete set of plans for a house—a house that could actually be built using those plans.

I think the administration thought that there were some kids that weren't really serious about their education and didn't belong at Cass. Therefore it seemed to me that they were trying to weed them out during the tenth grade. I barely made it through grade ten. But after that I either "caught on" or they eased up, and I graduated with highest honors. We went to school from eight to four. Most other high schools got out at 1 or 2 p.m. We had lots of homework besides. I remember sitting at a small drawing board in the small bay window of our living room at 5 or 6 p.m., watching the other kids playing out in the street. It wasn't much fun at the time, but it paid off. When we graduated in 1946, there were only eleven of us left in our class, which started out three years earlier with twenty-five or thirty.

During those high school years, three things dominated my life: school, church, and part-time jobs. We have talked a little about school. My social life centered around church and the activities of kids my age. We went mostly in groups—very little boy-girl dating. In our Sunday school classes and even in our young people's meetings, we usually sat boys with boys and girls with girls. After the formal meetings the boys and girls mixed, but in groups at someone's house or at a local ice cream parlor. The youth leaders, who were mostly volunteers and just a few years older than us, kept us occupied with wholesome activities like roller skating, bowling, retreats, summer camps. The church had both a softball team and a basketball team. We played in a church league. While I was not very good at either one, I played on both teams. The girls would come and watch the games, and then we would all go out for ice cream or cold drinks as a group. I was involved with some church-related activity almost every Friday and Saturday and Sunday nights.

It was our practice to attend church three times a week; Sunday morning and evening and Wednesday night for prayer meeting. The young people's group met at 6 p.m. Sunday evening before the Sunday evening service. We sat with our parents until we were teenagers and then in groups with our friends. Most of the kids my age lived in Highland Park and walked to church. A few lived a few miles away and came on the bus. I probably lived the farthest, but I went regularly to the many activities at and around the church.

One of the events that we as teenagers and young twentysomethings enjoyed were the bimonthly meetings of the Youth for Christ rallies. They were held every second and fourth Saturday night at the Masonic Temple near downtown Detroit. They were usually held in the smaller auditorium that seated about two thousand. It was packed with kids at most meetings. There was singing and musical groups, and always a speaker that appealed to youth, with both a challenge to receive Jesus Christ as Lord and to live pure and holy lives. The speakers encouraged us to reflect the attributes of Jesus Christ as given in the Bible in our everyday lives. It was part of a national youth organization. Every once in a while, with the coming of a special well-known speaker, like one time Billy Graham when he was very young, they would fill the five thousand-seat auditorium. The rallies attracted kids from all over metropolitan Detroit, with many coming on church buses from churches from Mt. Clemens to Grosse Isle. Our church was always represented, sometimes with fifty to a hundred kids. It was a very popular and effective ministry. Later in life, I had the privilege of serving on the local board of directors.

My other activity was part-time jobs. Saturdays and school vacations were filled with them. At age fourteen, I worked on Saturdays at a local shoe store. Saturday was a busy day. My job was to pick up the shoes that the salespeople had left on the floor and to pair them up, put them back in the box, and put them back in the stockroom. Later, as I learned a little more and when things got really busy, the boss and owner said to me, "See if you can help that lady. She has been waiting a long time." She said that she would like to see model so and so in a size 6. I took one look at her foot and thought, she will be lucky to get into a size 8, maybe even a 9. I could hardly keep from laughing. I guess it made her feel good to try to impress me. Vanity! Vanity!

I also worked during the summer at the local C. F. Smith grocery store. Of course those were the days before supermarkets. The customer stepped up to the counter and became the clerk's special and only customer. As she read off her grocery list, I would go get the item from the shelf behind me or in the back at the meat counter. The produce was in baskets on the floor, and she could pick out her own apples or potatoes or whatever and bring them to the counter to be weighed. Cereal boxes were always fun. They were on the top shelf, way up high. We had a long pole with a hook on the end, and we would hook the box, pull it off the shelf, and catch it on the way down. When her list was complete and all the items were in front of us on the counter, I would reach under the counter and pull out the proper size paper bag or bags, and with the pencil that I kept in my white apron breast pocket, I began to write down on the bag the price of each of the items. Then in our heads we would add them up, with her watching closely. Then I'd take the money, make change, and bag the groceries. Being able to add accurately was one of the tests to qualify for the job. In those days you could buy two big bags of groceries for three or four dollars. My, how times have changed!

Between my junior and senior year in high school, I worked in downtown Detroit for a big architectural firm, Smith, Hinchman, and Grylls. I was a messenger boy, running between several large office buildings where they had offices. I was always looking for shortcuts. I learned how to go out the back door, cut across the alley and into the back door of another building to keep from going out the front door, around the block and in the other front door. It saved a lot of steps. There was usually a security guard at the rear door to help with deliveries, etc. They weren't supposed to let people in the back door. But it's amazing what a nice young boy with a candy bar or an apple as a gift could accomplish. In those days I knew many security guards at the back doors of many office buildings in downtown Detroit.

I learned a lot about different kinds of people in many different types of jobs during those days. I was impressed by how many people had jobs that they didn't like. Life seemed like such a drag for so many. No joy. No purpose in life. Just living day by day in a routine rat race without getting any satisfaction from their days, weeks, months, and sometimes years of living hopeless lives.

When I was fourteen and we were still living on 23rd Street, I think my mom got a surprise. She found out she was pregnant. I had been an only child for fourteen years. With the coming of my little sister, Linda, on May 15, 1942, things changed a little. Now I had to help look after her on some occasions. She now demanded some of my mom's and dad's attention, which I had exclusively enjoyed. But she was really very little trouble, and as she grew she was a delight for all of us. She was three years old when we moved to Garden City and four years old when I started college. My mom and dad had two children who each could just about be called their "only child" because of the big difference in our ages. At that time, fourteen years was a lot of difference. But as time went on, the difference in age didn't make nearly as much difference; and the older we became, the closer we also became. I'll tell you more about her and her family later.

While I was in my senior year of high school, my folks bought a small house in suburban Garden City, which is west of Detroit, about twenty miles from downtown. This meant about a forty-five minute to one hour bus ride for me to get to school. This also meant getting up a lot earlier in the mornings and getting home much later in the afternoons. In the winter it was dark by the time I got home. Then it was no time before I was back on the morning bus. The only good part was that I could get most of my homework that involved reading done on the bus. I loved history, mostly because of a very dedicated history teacher who made the old stories come to life. He walked around the classroom giving the historical details and their implications and how, long after, they affected all of us. He made it all so interesting. I so enjoyed reading the history book, going and coming to school on the bus. The education I received at Cass Tech was a great help to me and put me way ahead of the average high school graduate.

4

COLLEGE DAYS

I applied and was accepted to the University of Michigan College of Architecture and Design. Between what I had saved from my various jobs and with a little help from parents, I was able to afford the first year's tuition and room and board.

In high school, I had developed a friendship with Ervin Kamp, one of the eleven architectural graduates. As a matter of fact, because of our names, Johnson and Kamp, J and K, we were seated next to each other in many classes all the way through high school. Erv was also accepted to the University of Michigan and we became roommates as well as classmates. On the first day of Architecture 101, the instructor passed out the textbooks that we would be using that semester. I took a look through it and said to Erv, "We've already had all this back in high school." I said we should tell the instructor because this whole semester will be a waste of time. Erv was of a very mild and quiet temperament. He said, "You'd better be quiet. You will get us in trouble."

At the end of the class period, we sheepishly and humbly went to the instructor and said, "Sir, we don't want to seem proud or pushy, but we have already had the instructions and lessons as outlined in the book." He said, "Where did you go to high school?" We said, "Cass Tech in Detroit." He said, "Take a look at this book," which was No. 2. We looked through it and almost apologetically said, "We've had this too." He said, "Take a look at this," and handed us book No. 3. Again, after looking through it, we said, "We have had almost all of this one too."

He said, "Go home this weekend and get your drawings." We did, and when he looked at them, he gave us thirteen hours of college credit and saved us a lot of time.

Because the architectural work was done mostly in the classroom from 1 to 4 p.m., three days a week, we didn't have much homework from that study, but we had plenty from the other classes like math, English, and a language. We did not have time to take a language in high school, but it was required for graduation from the University of Michigan. I chose German, which was a big mistake. I was not cut out for foreign language study and especially not German. I really struggled and barely passed.

To help with expenses, Erv worked in the cafeteria for sixty cents an hour and I got a job in a local gas station for a dollar per hour. I worked a lot of hours, mostly nights, coming home at 10 or 11 p.m. with overalls that smelled of gasoline. Erv put up with a lot. Our other roommate was Neil Duff, a kid I had grown up with at church. He was studying pre-law.

I had an old 1929 Model A Ford coupe with a rumble seat. Neil and I went home many weekends to keep up with our friends at church, coming back to Ann Arbor late on many Sunday nights.

College was not much fun for me, as it was and should be for most students. For me it was go to class, study, go to work, study, go to school, and work some more. I never had a date or attended any social activities in Ann Arbor. I didn't even go to many football games at the famous "Big House" even though tickets came with our tuition payments. After a year or so, in order to save money, Erv and I moved home. His family lived in Dearborn, only about two miles from my house, and we commuted to the university.

My social life continued to be at home and at church. From my home in Garden City to Ann Arbor was about a thirty-minute drive. What was then farmland on both sides of Ford Road is today the bustling city of Canton, well built up with nice homes, schools, and commercial areas. The distance from our home in Garden City to church was maybe another thirty or forty minutes with very little traffic on Sunday mornings.

5

A DOOR-TO-DOOR
SALESMAN

While I was living at home but still a student at University of Michigan in Ann Arbor, my folks invited some friends, Glenn and Louise Baker, over to our house for dinner. Glenn was a Fuller Brush man. They lived in Madison Heights, and his territory was in that area of the Detroit suburbs. The Fuller Brush Company had a wonderful reputation for quality products, including mops, brooms, all kinds of brushes and other household products, all sold door-to-door by salesmen.

Glenn told us how much money he was making and said it was so much better than working in the factory. He was a very personable fellow and quite likeable. He said that I should give it a try, and in my spare time I could make some extra money. He contacted the company located near Boston, and they gave me the entire territory between Garden City, where we lived, and Ann Arbor. It was about fifteen miles wide and about three miles from north to south, all rural. There were hardly any places where you could walk from one house to another in less than ten or fifteen minutes. So all the calls were by car, house by house. I made a lot of stops on my way home from school and on Saturdays and during vacations.

It was most interesting! The game plan was to show the lady a sample of a few brushes from my case, and from a catalog with pictures of the larger items and take the order. I gave them a copy showing how much they would owe. No money was paid at that point. Then, once a week, I would send in the order; and when it came back to my house, I would deliver the items and collect the money and send it to the company. The profit was about 30 percent. The company allowed one order on credit.

Every product was guaranteed and everything was on the "up-and-up." It was a good company!

My experience was varied. As you might expect, many doors were quickly closed; and I was rejected. I think this is where I learned to deal with rejection. I determined that they were not rejecting me. I was a "good guy," and they didn't even know me. They couldn't be rejecting the Fuller Brush Company. They had the best reputation in the industry for quality products. So what were they rejecting? I didn't know for sure. Some people are just negative and unhappy, I guessed, and didn't like interruption.

But for everyone who rejected me, I had two or three or more who welcomed me into their house. After all, it was not every day that a polite young man stopped in an out-of-the-way place to call on a person, and sometimes a very lonely individual. They didn't have many visitors, and there were no Home Depots or Targets or any store nearby; and I was providing a nice, convenient way for them to shop, if I had what they needed.

I did fairly well. Like in a lot of cases, the more I worked, the more calls I made, the better I did. I made enough to pay my tuition and more. It was a good experience, as meeting new people often is.

6

A CHANGE IN DIRECTION

During my third year in college, I got a job working for an architectural firm in Ann Arbor. The principal in the firm was also an adjunct professor at the university. It was a relatively small firm with only four or five employees. One Saturday morning, when there was only the boss and I working, he suggested we stop and have a cup of coffee. His drafting board was directly behind mine. I stopped working and turned around to face him. Rather philosophically, he said to me, "What are you going to do when you get out of school?"

I said, "Get a job working for an architect, I guess." I thought to myself maybe he was going to offer me a job. Then he said something to me that changed my life. He said, "Let me give you a suggestion. Get a job working in the construction industry." His exact words were, "Get acquainted with a 2 x 4 and a cement block and some bricks. Learn what a Romex wire looks like and maybe get your feet into some wet concrete. Find out how a building goes together. And you will be a better architect."

I began to think about that. I was really getting tired of working over a drawing board. I had been doing it for three years in junior high, three years in high school, plus now college. As I thought of a career in architecture, I realized that in all my years I had never known anyone who had hired an architect. Only wealthy people hired architects, and I didn't know any wealthy people. My whole family and everyone I knew were blue-collar folks, and they don't hire architects. If I wanted to ever be my own boss and have my own architectural firm, the chances of success were pretty slim. Besides, leaving school early was also becoming more interesting to me because the university had recently decided the architectural requirements for graduation were going from four years to five. I was finishing my third year, looking forward to only one more, when they said it would now be two more. I thought about it and decided I would try to get a job with a contractor for the summer and see how things turned out.

There was a small contractor in our church, and I asked him for a job. He asked me only one question. "Can you read blueprints?" I answered, "Can I read them! I can make them!" I was hired on the spot. The pay was a hundred dollars a week. I was twenty-one years old.

The work was not what I hoped it might be. He put me in the office, estimating jobs. I knew nothing about the price of various materials. He said, "That doesn't matter. Just tell me how many 2 x 4s, 2 x 6s it will take and how many bricks and blocks, how many square feet of concrete and how thick it is, and I'll tell the prices." In one sense we were like the blind leading the blind. I knew nothing about the construction business, and I soon found out he didn't either. He knew a couple of guys who could do cement work and two bricklayers and a carpenter, and almost overnight he was a general contractor. He had only been in business a year or two and, like many contractors (I later found out), he was greatly undercapitalized and overzealous. In other words, he had no money, but he had big ideas. I did not go back to school that fall because he said he needed me to stay and help him get established. I soon realized that this was no way to run a construction company. His men did fairly good work, but he was a poor businessman. I worked for him for eighteen months, and I received a wonderful education of what not to do!

After eighteen months, he announced that he was going out of business and going back to selling windows, which is what he did before he went into the construction business. He managed to pay everyone off, and as he was laying me off, he said, "You might want to stay on in the business. If you do, you can have it." I said, "Jim, that's very nice of you, but what do we have?" He said, "Out in the shed there are a couple of wheelbarrows, some scaffolding sections and planks, and a few tarps. If you want them, you can have them." As I was thinking about my future, I was wondering what I should do. I surely didn't want to try continuing on using his business name. And starting on my own would require some cash that I didn't have. As I was thinking about it, the carpenter that worked for us, named Earl, who also got laid off, said to me, "You should try to stay in the business. With your background in architecture and your pleasant personality, I think you could do very well. We could work together."

My response was, "Maybe so, but I don't have any money to pay you." He said, "I think we can work it out. You go sell the jobs. I'll do the work and you can pay me when you get paid. I have saved up a little money, and I can get along for a month or two without pay, and I trust you." He was one of those fellows who could do a little of everything. He could do cement flat work, lay blocks and bricks, and do electrical and plumbing, as well as drywall work. He was also an excellent finish carpenter. I had built up a good relationship with a lumber company, and they agreed to give me credit. So away we went. I sold my car and bought a pickup truck. I had maybe $500 worth of construction equipment. I had one employee and one helper, and I was the helper.

I was single, living at home with my parents and twenty-two years old. I figured what did I have to lose? My mom and dad were in neutral. They had no idea how to advise me except to pray for this young guy and ask God to bless him and keep him out of trouble.

7

A HELP IN GETTING STARTED

About the time Mr. Davis went out of business and laid off Earl and me, my uncle Lester Marshall, who was married to my mom's sister, Eunice, came to me with an offer. He knew I was out of a job. He was in the chrome plating business in downtown Detroit in partnership with his brother Chester. Lester and Chester. In those days (the early fifties), chrome on cars was a big deal. The more chrome, the better. Bumpers, moldings, grilles, and all kinds of trim. Lester and Chester did okay, but it was a tough and hazardous business. The tanks that the products were dipped into for plating gave off toxic fumes. Employees wore masks, and adequate ventilation was of paramount importance. Uncle Lester didn't like the business. He wanted out and, in fact, wanted to go back to Kentucky.

One day he came to me and said they were going to sell the plating business and that he wanted to take the money and build a small factory building in a small industrial park. His plan was to rent it out or sell it. It was a speculative investment. Actually, it was not a bad idea, as the car business in Detroit was booming, and there was a shortage of industrial buildings for their many suppliers and subcontractors.

Uncle Lester wanted me to be in charge of the planning and construction of the building. I formed a new construction company, and we started out. Actually, my pay amounted to a small salary, but I was able to establish credit and buy materials in my own name. He gave me the money to pay the bills and the subcontractors each month. I hired Earl to help, and at the end of the job, he promptly sold the building, made a nice profit and, soon after, moved his family back to western Kentucky.

The reason I include this little episode is that, while I didn't make much money on the job, I was glad to have the work, and it helped me to get established as a building contractor with one successful completed project. I will forever be grateful to my uncle Lester who took a chance and gave me a nice start and helped me to get established as a young building contractor. Another early blessing from the Lord.

8

BEGINNING THE BUSINESS

Some of our first jobs were finishing off attic rooms or basements in single-family houses. In northwest Detroit there were hundreds of two-bedroom, one-bath bungalows with an unfinished attic and basement. They were sort of starter homes for many middle-income families. With my architectural background, I would make a sketch showing them how we could go up into their attic and insulate it and build one or sometimes two additional bedrooms. If the plan worked out, we could often build a second bathroom upstairs over the first floor one. Sometimes we would push up the roof on the backside and make a big dormer with windows. In short, we could take a two-bedroom, one-bath house and make it into a three- or four-bedroom, two-bath house. It was a relatively inexpensive way to accommodate a growing family without having to move to a larger house.

Early in the morning, about seven o'clock or so, or as soon as the lumberyards opened, I would go with my new pickup truck with the list of materials that Earl and I had prepared the day before. There was no Home Depot. The lumberyard people would load up my truck, and I would drive to the job site and Earl and I would unload the truck and carry the materials up to the second floor. Most all of the houses had stairways already built that went to the attic. They were usually located in the center of the house above the basement stairs, which were near the side entrance off the driveway. Carrying material to the second floor was more difficult because we had go through the house and to be careful not to damage any of the furnishings. Going down to the basement with materials was much easier. Anyway, we did it. After we got all the stuff upstairs, I was ready for a rest or at least a coffee break or maybe even a nap! But then the work began. Earl was the boss and I was the helper. I learned a lot from him. His skills were amazing. Little by little we got the job done, and the homeowners were delighted.

With the truck with our name on it parked outside of the house for several days, the neighbors would get curious and would come over to see what was going on. Some of them were amazed. They said, "Our house is just like this. How much would it cost to do this for us?" As a result, we got several jobs on the same street doing the same or similar work. It was a great feeling to see all these folks so happy with their extra living space. We also finished off basements, giving folks extra space for game rooms or television rooms and the like. This is how Paul H. Johnson, Inc. got started in the construction business.

Earl stayed with me until he retired. I always paid him 10 percent above the union wage because he was willing to wait for his pay in those early days. Later on he became the foreman on some of our smaller jobs. But as we grew and got into larger buildings, we needed superintendents who were engineers. Earl didn't have the skills for those jobs, and he became too old to work as a carpenter. So he just retired. A good and faithful man.

9

A NEW VENTURE

One day I saw in the newspaper that a fellow was offering a free lot in a subdivision that he was starting. The lot would be free, if the buyer would agree to build a house, or at least start construction on a house within ninety days. The subdivision was way out in the suburbs near Northville, and he wanted to get a few houses built to establish the viability of his subdivision. The lots were selling for $1,000 each. I went to see him and there were no houses yet. I told him that I would take him up on his offer of a free lot and start a house immediately but that I would like to have an option on two other lots at $100 each. He smiled but we agreed that the price would be $500 each for lots two and three. That year I built three houses and sold two of them. The third house was finished, and I was asking $14,000 for it. It was coming winter and the lookers were few. A fellow came along and offered to pay the full price of $14,000 but he said he only had $3,000 to give me as a down payment and he wanted me to accept the $11,000 in monthly payments on a land contract. At that point I still owed the subcontractors about $3,000. So I decided to accept his offer. I took the $3,000 down payment and paid off all the subs. I had all my bills paid and a piece of paper that said a fellow owed me $11,000, which was my pay for a whole year's work.

One day I was talking to my friend Fred Byers, who owned Byers Lumber Company on Plymouth Road just west of Telegraph. This is where I purchased most of my materials. I told him of my situation. No cash, only paper. He said, "You know, that piece of paper is worth money." He said, "Come with me." He took me in his car to his bank. We told the banker the story. He said, "Give me a day or so and I'll get back to you."

After a few days, after checking up on the credit of the purchaser of the house, he said, "We'll give you $10,000 for that piece of paper." I sold it to him and now I had $10,000 for the year's work. Most people I knew, including my dad, made about $5,000 a year. When I told my mom the story, she couldn't believe I had that much money. She said, "Are you sure what you are doing is legal?" I assured her that it was, and she just walked away shaking her head. You should know that she had received a few phone calls when I wasn't home from subcontractors or suppliers wanting to know when they were going to get paid. I told her not to worry. They were all now paid in full.

Fred Byers, the lumber dealer, and I became good friends. One day he called me into his office, which was in an old converted farmhouse. His lumber operations were out back in what used to be barns and other outbuildings that were built for farm operations. Knowing of my architectural background, he said he would like for me to help him design and build a new office and showroom and retail store in front of the old house, which was set back a ways from the road. So we did it and kept it connected to the old house for storage space. It was a very attractive building now, with a real nice showroom with all kinds of samples of materials and hardware. His business began to grow considerably because the new store was so much more visible. Over on one side in the new building, we built three new offices. One was Fred's private office and one was for his bookkeeper who was his daughter, Carly. He said I could use the third one until such time as he needed it. We put in a door that opened to the outside. It was about nine feet by twelve feet and was my first office at 20154 Plymouth Road.

10

PAUL'S RESTAURANT (BUT NOT MINE)

After I moved my office to the Byers Lumber Company location, I would often eat breakfast or lunch at a restaurant on the corner of Plymouth and Telegraph called "Paul's", just down the street from my new office. I got acquainted with the owner, Paul Panaretos, a nice older Greek man who was always at the restaurant and often worked in the kitchen. He was very friendly and from time to time he would come out into the restaurant to speak to his customers. Most of us were regulars.

One day he told me of his dream to expand the restaurant and build an addition that, among other things, would house a banquet room. He showed me his property and asked me if I would make some sketches for him to look at. I did, and I wound up building it for him. But here is the interesting part. During mealtime he was so busy he couldn't talk to anyone. So he made all of his appointments at either ten to eleven in the morning, or from 3 to 5 p.m. in the afternoon. I always went by just before five o'clock on my way home to see him and usually to get a check for the work we had done the previous month. We became friends, and one day he shared with me a dilemma.

He said his wife, Catherine, who was about ten years younger, was worried that he would die, and all he had to leave her was the restaurant business. She was often there and worked part-time as a hostess, but she didn't know much about the business. So she was gently pressing Paul to buy an insurance policy on his life so that in case he died she would have some ready cash. He asked me, "What do you think?" I said, "Paul, at your age and under the circumstances, it's probably not a bad idea." He asked me if I knew any insurance men. I asked around and a friend of a friend gave me a name, and I gave it to Paul.

One late afternoon, as I stopped by the restaurant and went in the back door to his office, as I usually did, I noticed there was a fellow in the office with Paul. Paul saw me and motioned for me to come on in and sit down. The other fellow was the insurance man, and he was explaining all about the insurance program to Paul. When the salesman stopped for a second, Paul said to him, "When I give you the money each month, what do you do with it until I die and then give it to my wife?" The insurance man said, "We invest it mostly in real estate. We find good properties and invest in them and sometimes we make mortgages. A lot of it goes into apartment buildings and things like that." Paul said, "Thank you very much. I'll let you know."

The guy left. Paul and I finished our business, and I left. A few days or weeks later, I went in to visit him again. He said, "You're just in time. Sit down a minute." With that he got up and went out to the restaurant and brought back his wife. As she sat down, he said, "I'm happy to tell you that I bought you an insurance policy." She was so happy she stood up, went over to him, and gave him a big kiss. I know she was dying to ask him how much it was for, when he pulled out a photograph of a twenty-unit apartment building. He said, "Sweetheart, this is all yours. I put it in your name and I have a manager for you. I figured that if all those smart guys in the insurance business invested in real estate, it must be a good deal. So I decided to cut out the middleman and go direct. It will not only pay you when I die, it will start paying you now."

She looked at me with the funniest look as if to say, "Okay. Whatever!" I thought Paul was pretty smart, and I remembered that; and it served me well in days to come.

11

A VERY PROFITABLE JOB

Kitty-corner across the road from Paul's was Coon Brothers' gas station and garage. One day in the restaurant I met Stan Coon, one of the owners. He was telling me how he had been offered the opportunity to become a dealer for Nash cars. I said, "Great! You should go for it." "Yes," he said, "I think so too, but I have a problem. The Nash Company requires that I have a service garage that can handle fifteen cars at a time. I have a building out back that would probably be big enough, but it has a block wall down the middle of it that holds up the roof. I got a price from a contractor and he wants $75,000 to take off the roof, remove the wall, and put back a new roof, and I can't afford it. Do you have any ideas?" I said, "Let's take a look." I did, and a few days later we met for lunch at Paul's and I asked him if he could live with three columns located twenty-five or thirty feet apart down the middle of the building. I showed him a sketch as to how the cars would be able to come and go and park for service and how I didn't think the columns would be a problem. He didn't think so either, and he asked how much it would cost to do it this way.

My friend Earl said that before he knew me, he used to work for a contractor who did a lot of that type of work. Between the two of us, we came up with a plan. We said we could do it for $38,000. Stan said, "Let's go." Our plan was to prop up the existing steel joists that were resting on the center wall that was holding up the roof, then knock out the center wall and install three columns with a steel beam down the middle and let the roof joists back down on the new steel beam. The trick was how to get the steel beam (or beams, they were in sections) up into place. So, after the middle wall was down, we cut a hole in the end wall of the building large enough to get the beams in, and we slid them in on rollers to where they were ultimately going to go, but up on top of the columns. Then we hired a crane, cut three holes in the roof, and dropped the cable down through the holes, one at a time, and lifted the beams up into place on top of the columns. The entire crane operation took about four hours. We patched up the holes in the end wall and the floor where the old wall used to be and the holes in the roof. Stan Coon was one happy camper. He got his franchise to sell Nash cars and was very successful for many years.

Now for the best part. When I added up all our costs, they came to $19,000, and remember, our contract was for a firm $38,000. At the time that Earl and I were figuring the cost, we didn't know for sure how it would all go. So we made ourselves safe. This was a win-win situation for both Stan Coon and Coon Brothers Nash dealership and us.

The following incidents took place. First, my mom. I told her about making $19,000 on one job in about thirty days. She was sure there had to be something wrong some place. This just couldn't happen. When I told her the Lord was answering her prayers and was looking after me, she was still skeptical and again walked away shaking her head. The other interesting incident was with my accountant who came out once a month to help us with the books. He said, "Where are the rest of the bills on the Coon Brothers job?" When I told him that he had them all, he was flabbergasted. "You mean you made 100 percent profit on that job?" "Yes," I said, "that's just the way it turned out."

Percentage wise, it was indeed one of the best jobs I ever did. The Lord was looking after me at a very early age and has continued until today, as you will see as you read further in this book. I'll tell you more about my business life a little later, but first let me tell you another very interesting story.

12

ANOTHER LIFE CHANGE

One Sunday morning after church, a lady approached me with a request. I knew her vaguely. Her name was Mrs. Glines. She was in the same Sunday school class as my mom. She said that her daughter, Marilyn, who was a high school senior, had taken the bus to East Lansing for the weekend to visit a friend who was a student at Michigan State University. Marilyn was considering going there to college. Then Mrs. Glines said Marilyn was coming home that afternoon and would be getting off the bus stop on Grand River at Lahser at 5:30 p.m. She also said that she and her husband, Johnny, had been invited out to dinner at his boss's home, and they felt like they should go. All that to say, would I be so kind as to pick up Marilyn at the bus stop and take her to church for the young people's program at 6 p.m.? She knew it was basically on my way to church. She was sure that I would be going to church as well. I said, "Sure. I'd be glad to do it."

I knew Marilyn only from a distance. She was one of the cutest girls in church, but she hung around more with girls her own age. I was four years older. When she got off the bus, she looked all around for her parents' car. I was parked across the street. I got out of my car and waved to her. She looked a little bewildered, but she came across the street carrying her small suitcase. Her first question was, "Is something wrong with my mom or dad?" I said, "No, they're fine," and told her the story and how her mom asked me to meet her.

Well, she was furious and somewhat embarrassed. "How could my mom do that?" she said. I said, "It's okay. No problem. It's not much out of my way. I was going to church anyway." I was happy to help. She fussed all the way to church. She was sure that her mother did this just to get me to meet her. She already had a part-time boyfriend. I was naive and just thought I was being a nice guy to help her mom with a logistics problem. Well, as we got to church and she started to get out of the car, she reached for her suitcase. I said, "If you want to just leave it in the car, I'll take you home after church," which was also very little out of my way.

By the time church was over and we were on our way to her house, she had warmed up considerably and was very nice. There was something going on at church a few days later that we were both going to, and I offered to pick her up and take her. She said that would be fine, and I did. That was the beginning of the relationship that resulted in marriage about a year later on April 19, 1952. She was nineteen and I was twenty-three. Her mom was very happy. Marilyn was not only beautiful, she was very bright and far more mature and sophisticated than most girls her age. Her mom worked in the office of an S. S. Kresge store; and sometimes she couldn't get all the work done at the store and would bring it home. Marilyn would help her, and she learned to be a bookkeeper at age eighteen. The more I got to know her, the more I liked her. We fell in love and by Thanksgiving 1951, I asked her to marry me. She said yes, and, as they say, the rest is history. I'll tell you more about her later.

Her mom really liked me, and we became good friends. When I heard all the bad jokes and stories about mothers-in-law, I couldn't relate. Mimi was the best! I guess I should tell you that, like my mom, she didn't like her name, which was Maizie Irene. She was born up near Chatham in Ontario, Canada, about an hour's drive from Windsor, which is right across the river from Detroit. As a teenager, she left home and moved to Windsor to live with her older sister. She then got a job in the Kresge store in downtown Detroit and came to work each day through the tunnel on the bus. At her job at the "dime store" as they were called in those days, she met and became good friends with a girl from northern Michigan whose name was Hulda. She, too, disliked her name. So they decided to call themselves "Pat and Mike." Maizie became Pat and it stuck with her all her life. Everyone thought her real name was Pat. Some even called her Patricia.

When our first baby, Colleen, was born, Pat did not want to be called "grandmother" or anything close to it. So she decided on "Mimi," which someone told her was French for grandmother. That name stuck, and from then on all of us and many of her close friends called her "Mimi."

Let me tell you a little about her. Those of you who are older remember some things about her because you knew her quite well. She was very attractive and very smart and a diligent worker. Her husband, Johnny, died at age fifty-four with heart problems that could probably be easily fixed today. She and her younger daughter, Ginny, who was about fifteen, moved to a smaller house about a block from our house. Mimi became a part of our family and was the number one babysitter, with the help of Ginny and Pam Callam who lived across the street from Mimi, and Ginny who later became "Gigi." (More about Gigi and Pam later.) When we moved from Detroit to Birmingham in 1965, Mimi moved in with us in a special "mother-in-law wing," which we constructed when we built the house.

A lot of stories come to mind about Mimi, and maybe they will come into play later as we progress, but one in particular is interesting. She always told our kids when they asked her age that she was thirty-nine. Well, this worked for a while until her daughter, my wife, Marilyn, was approaching thirty-nine. Obviously the kids were skeptical and wanted to know the truth. She would never tell. She would say to them when they asked, "Can you keep a secret?" They would say, "Yes." And when they would lean in closer waiting for this special disclosure, she would say to them, "So can I." And they would say, "Aw, Mimi!"

One day, as we were all getting into the car, someone closed the door on Mimi's fingers. She was in a lot of pain, and Marilyn said we should go to the emergency room and get them X-rayed and make sure nothing was broken. So we did. As we approached the receptionist with Mimi holding her throbbing fingers with her other hand, the lady asked Mimi's age. She looked down at her granddaughter Karen, who was about seven or eight and standing next to her, and said, "Sweetie, come with me," and took Karen over to a chair about twenty feet away so she wouldn't hear Mimi give her age. Little by little the kids figured out her age, but by that time she didn't care. She was a very special mother-in-law. Marilyn used to say to me, "I think my mom likes you more than me." It wasn't true, but I loved them both very much and so did everybody else.

13

A STEPPING-STONE TO OUR FIRST HOME

When Marilyn and I were married, we rented a one-bedroom apartment on the second floor of a complex on West Chicago Boulevard, west of Evergreen near Rouge Park. By that time, I had made enough money to buy a new car, a bright-red Ford convertible. At that time, we still had the office at Byers Lumber Company. As the business grew, Marilyn became the bookkeeper, and she was very good at it. And she did it for almost three years when two things happened. We grew to the point where she needed more help, and the problem for her was solved when she became pregnant and quit working.

By that time, in fact a little before that time, we were thinking about building a new house for ourselves. We had saved up $15,000, which would be enough for a good down payment, and we could probably get a mortgage for $50,000 or $60,000. In those days, $75,000 was enough for a good-sized and lovely home. The problem was that the construction business was unpredictable. So far, we were doing okay; but there were no regular paychecks for very regular monthly mortgage payments. So we were a little cautious, if not a bit concerned, about taking on debt with no guarantee as to how to repay it.

A year after we were married, we took a long winter vacation, because in those days in the wintertime the construction business was mostly "on hold." It was in the days before admixtures that are used today that help cement get hard before it freezes, and all the other methods used today, such as temporary heat and the procedure of tarping in buildings. Most of us smaller guys just shut down. The vacation plan was to drive along with another couple who were our good friends (and later an employee), Joe and Ardella Guthrie, to California to visit Ardella's sister and her family. The arrangements were to leave Joe and Ardella in Southern California, and we would continue on up to Palo Alto to visit Marilee and Bill Dufendach. Marilee was Marilyn's dear friend and Hulda's daughter. (You remember Hulda from Mimi's story of "Pat and Mike.") Marilyn and Marilee were born a week apart, and their moms named the girls Marilyn and Marilee. They, too, became lifelong friends. Along the trip we went south as quickly as possible to avoid the bad weather, arriving into Texas at Texarkana and driving the southern route to California. As it turned out, we took a detour and drove all the way to Mexico City, but that's another story.

During our drive across Texas, I noticed a very interesting building. We took pictures of it, and when we got home, I made a sketch showing how we might build a similar one. It was a two-story office building that was "L"-shaped and built on a corner with the open part of the "L" facing the corner of the two streets. It had a nice landscaped area out in the front yard, with sidewalks that ran along the inside of the "L" with entrances to the various offices. Both sides had a lot of windows facing the open landscaped area. Those were the days when just a few business-people were starting to move out from downtown Detroit. There were no full-service buildings for them to rent, so a few businesses were housed in one-story buildings built on commercial lots much like retail stores, but used as offices with parking for three or four cars in the rear off the alley. Some doctors were building their offices in a smaller configuration. Their problem was that there were no janitor services or maintenance personnel to call on like they had in their downtown buildings. Some put up with the inconveniences and had their nurses or others help with the details of cleaning every day and heating, air-conditioning servicing, etc., and they were willing to put up with these inconveniences in order to be closer to their clients and closer to their own homes. I thought that if we could build a building and offer these services, we would be a welcome solution for these kinds of tenants.

So I took the $15,000 that we had saved up for a new home and bought five twenty-foot lots on the corner of Six Mile Road and Freeland, in northwest Detroit. The bank agreed to loan me $65,000 to construct the building. So we did, and it was one of the first complete service buildings in northwest Detroit. It only had about eight thousand square feet. We filled it in no time with doctors' offices on the first floor and general offices on the second. They all had a nice view of the landscaped front yard, and they loved it. It was a big hit!

14

THE ACTUAL HOUSE

We were still living in the apartment but now had no money to build a house. But we had a steady income from what was left over after we paid the bank and taxes and other operating expenses from our new office building. We called it "cash flow." The building became known as our "Freeland Building." The income was pretty secure for five years, which was the term of the leases.

So I went back to the bank and said I wanted to borrow some more money—this time to build a house. I think the amount was $50,000. I said I wanted the monthly payments to be such that the loan would be paid back in five years. The bankers liked that idea because the leases on the building were for five years. They agreed and felt pretty well assured that they would get their money back.

We bought a wonderful lot on Minock Street in northwest Detroit. It was an unusual find and just perfect for us. It was only forty-two feet wide. It was at the end of the street, three houses south of Outer Drive. The beauty of it was that it bordered on Stoepel Park, which contained twenty-nine acres of land. There was a forty-foot easement between our lot and the park proper, which was a landscaped area. Our lot overlooked the outfield of the baseball diamond, which was beyond the easement. At our location we were in extreme center field. Prince Fielder or Miguel Cabrera probably could hit a ball that could reach our house, but the kids playing in the park seldom got one even to the easement. So, with our $50,000 we started construction. My architectural training was all about contemporary designs with a lot of glass and flat roofs, so our twenty foot by fifty foot house of two floors was all glass on both floors facing south, which was perfect for the sun and overlooking the beautiful park.

My longtime friend Erv Kamp and I designed the house, and he made the actual working drawings.

After we finished the house and moved in, the *Detroit Free Press* sent a reporter out and took a lot of pictures and featured it in the home section one Sunday. She called it "a forty-two-foot lot with a twenty-nine-acre view." With all the glass and the southern exposure, we had a perfect arrangement for the sun. We had a four-foot overhang, which kept the hot sun off the glass during the summer months when the sun goes over the top. But in the winter, when the sun makes a lower arc, the sun came streaming in the windows. There were many sunny days in the winter when the furnace would not come on because the sun was heating us very nicely.

We had a one thousand-square-feet house, but with a second floor and a finished basement, we had three thousand square feet. Among other things, we had all large double-glazed windows from floor to ceiling on two floors and motor-operated drapes that completely covered the windows as necessary. We had a built-in music system, like a jukebox, with speakers in every room. We had the latest in kitchen appliances with stove burners that folded down for use and back up off the counter. We had a small dumbwaiter that went from the kitchen to the basement. We had three bedrooms upstairs plus a playroom with a cork floor. The main floor had a nice sunken living room with a fireplace, a marble foyer, an open stair to the second floor, a dining area, and a nice den and television room. Every room, except one bedroom, had a twenty-nine acre view.

We lived there for nine years and sold it for $45,000. It was so different that it took a special buyer to appreciate it. We lost $5,000, but it was worth it. While it was a great house and served us well, it had limited appeal to most people. In fact, when the building was under construction and began to take shape, some of the neighbors came over out of curiosity. There were only five of them, two on one side of the street and three across the street. The street dead-ended at the park. The house didn't really fit in with the style of the other houses. At first they were a little concerned, but as we got to know them and they got to know us, particularly dear sweet Marilyn and a cute little baby, they warmed up considerably and we became good friends. In fact, a couple of them said when they saw the finished house, "What a great idea to take advantage of the twenty-nine acre view." By contrast, the house directly across the street from us had its driveway on the park side with only two small windows facing the park, one in the kitchen and one in a bedroom.

Our lot was the only one not built on for many years after the others were. My guess is that most people were afraid that the activities in the park would be a disturbance. We never had that problem. I'm satisfied that the Lord was keeping it vacant until we came along with a house that took advantage of all of its amenities. Another blessing from God.

LIVING Section

HOUSE on a 42-foot lot has a deceiving amount of living space: 2,300 square feet plus carport and basement. Residence of Paul H. Johnson.

Free Press Photos by Ray Pillsbury

GLASS AREAS are almost entirely on park side, to the south. Privacy wall shields elevated patio from street. Note four-foot roof overhang and balcony for sun control. Trim is redwood.

A 42-Foot Lot But a 29-Acre View

BY LILIAN JACKSON BRAUN
Free Press Living Section Editor

For those who prefer urban living but despair of finding a location within 42-ft. lot. The secret of its success: It borders on the 29-acre Stoepel Park No. 1, use — but it proves that ideal locations still exist in the city.

In summer the four-foot roof overhang shades the glass-walled bedrooms on a privacy wall. It's reached through the sliding walls of the living area

Our First House

15

LIFE IN THE NEW HOUSE

W e moved in in 1956. Colleen was one year old. We had lived in the apartment about three and a half years, two and a half by ourselves and about a year with a baby. In the meantime, our business was growing and we were now building good-sized custom homes. I'll tell you more about that later but let me tell you about some of the activities that went on while we lived on Minock by the park. We were very active in church-related activities and in a Sunday school class of young married couples like us. When it came time for parties at someone's house, we were selected most of the time; and we loved it. Marilyn was a great hostess, and everybody loved her. She was so sweet, and our house was perfect for entertaining. It had an open plan and a full basement with a Ping-Pong table, a full-sized pool table, plus an open area where fifty or sixty people could sit in folding chairs and we had plenty of them. Our two popular helpers were Marilyn's sister, Ginny, and our friend Pam Callam, who was Marilyn's Pioneer Girl pal and good friend of our family. Mimi was often the babysitter for both Colleen and her younger brother, Kevin, who had come along two years later. Ginny and Pam were perfect and like real professionals. They helped with coats and serving the meals in all kinds of configurations and settings, picking up plates, helping with dishes, and more. They knew most of the guests and they were both real cute teenagers. They were great! I offered to get them those skimpy black and white uniforms like French maids wear, but nobody liked my idea!

16

A SHIFT IN PRIORITIES

Let me tell you another story of God's faithfulness. When Colleen and Kevin were about four and two years old. I was quite busy building single-family custom homes. We would have two or three going at the same time. In order to communicate with both husband and wife, it necessitated evening meetings. I would often go to the church for a board meeting on a Monday evening and meet with a client on Tuesday evening. Wednesday night we usually attended the prayer meeting at the church. On Thursday night, I would often meet with another client. We usually kept Friday night as family night, going out to dinner or to visit my folks who had now moved back into Detroit near Six Mile Road and Hubbell, or to Marilyn's folks. On Saturday morning, I would tell Marilyn I was just going over to the office to open the mail and catch up on things. Very often I would get a call or start working a little or talk to someone, and I wouldn't get back home until two or three in the afternoon.

After a few months of this routine, Marilyn gently reminded me that I was neglecting my small family and not spending enough time with those precious kids whom I loved so much. I listened to her and replied something like, "I know, dear, but what else can I do? If I'm going to be successful as a custom home builder, I have to meet with these couples when they are both available, and that is in the evenings." I had helped most of them with the design of their house, and they felt closely connected to me personally, and they were often very receptive to ideas I gave them and were depending on me more than most people did to the average home builder. I rationalized and said, "Dear, I know you're right, but I'm caught. Maybe later, when I can afford to hire other people."

After a few months, she said, "I don't think you are being very wise with your priorities and your time with the children." I'm sure she would have liked to have said, "And with me," but she didn't. She did say, "I've told you how I feel, and I'm not going to say any more. It is your decision."

Well, I began to think more seriously about the problem and, more importantly, I began to pray. One Sunday afternoon, as I was planning for the coming week, I became overcome with the feeling that she was right. One hundred percent! As she usually was about everything! I remember saying to the Lord, "Okay. No more evening business meetings." I thought to myself, these little kids are growing up and I really should be spending more time with them. "I don't know what all this will do to me. It may even mean no more construction business. But, Lord, I want to do the right thing. I may wind up back on a drawing board, but I want to follow what I know You would have me to do. I want to be Your kind of father and husband. Amen."

It was sort of a scary decision. My mom had told me again and again, "You'll never go wrong if you do the right thing." I knew what the right decision was, and I made it.

At that time, we were almost finished with a nice home, when the owner said to me, "You seem like a decent guy. Would you be interested in helping me put an addition on my factory?" He was in the tool and die business, and his shop was about forty feet wide and eighty feet deep. He wanted to add forty feet onto the rear of his building, making it forty feet by 120 feet. I said, sure I would be glad to help. He asked if I could make the drawings, etc. I said, sure, no problem. I got my friend Erv Kamp. He made the plans. We got the building permit and did the work. It was really quite simple to build three walls and a roof and floor along with a few windows. We knocked out the existing back wall, and his building was now 50 percent larger. He was delighted.

While we had his building under construction, the man across the street saw all the activity and came over one day to see me and said, "I own the lot next door to my shop and I would like to expand sideways." So we did a job for him.

All this was in a small industrial park. Down the street were three or four vacant lots owned by a company that made kitchen cabinets. I knew them and had purchased several cabinets from them. When they noticed that we were building in the area where they were planning to build a new factory, they asked me if I was interested in helping them. And I did.

The house I was building was finished, and for some reason we didn't get any more calls for houses. In fact, that was the last house we built. From then on, it was all commercial buildings with each job getting bigger.

At some point it dawned on me how the Lord had honored and blessed my decision to give up evening meetings. People who want commercial buildings designed and built don't want to meet in the evening. They want to meet in the daytime. What I thought was going to be a detriment to my business turned out to be a nonissue. I was afraid my business was going to fail. Instead, God not only solved the problem of night meetings, but He started me on a path of building commercial, industrial and institutional, structures of all sizes and varieties.

The lesson was one that my mom taught me from an early age. "Always do the right thing and you'll never go wrong." Or, "You'll never go wrong if you do the right thing." At first I thought that it was a little clichéd, or a nice, self-evident saying. But the older I got, the more I remembered her advice and I took it. I found it always to be true. When I decided to give up night meetings, I knew it was the right thing. But I had no idea how God was going to change my business and life as a result. And all for the best.

17

MARILYN BARBARA

I told you Marilyn's mom set us up to get us acquainted. I don't know what her ultimate plan for us was, or if she even had one. But, looking back, I am sure it was another case of God's direction in my life. Soon after our first meeting, as you've already seen, I was impressed with Marilyn. Not only was she beautiful on the outside, she was beautiful on the inside. She had a deep love for the Lord Jesus. She displayed so many of the fruits of the spirit that are mentioned in the Scripture. She was kind and thoughtful and faithful. She was twelve years old when her little sister, Ginny, was born; and she already had motherly instincts, and at an early age she helped to care for her. She was far more mature than most of the girls her age. She already had a part-time job working in the S. S. Kresge dime store, helping her mother who was the bookkeeper.

I liked what I saw in her from the beginning, and it wasn't long until I fell in love with her. Our first meeting was in the spring of 1951. By Thanksgiving time I gave her an engagement ring. I was sure she was the one for me. I was so happy when she said she felt the same way about me. At the time, my mom and dad had gone back to Kentucky for the Thanksgiving holiday. They knew nothing of our engagement. I called them on the phone to say that I was coming down for the weekend and to meet me at the airport in Paducah. When they saw Marilyn was with me and we showed them the ring, my mom was so happy. She later said that she thought that Marilyn was the perfect person for me. How right she was!

While we were engaged, she got a job working in the office of the Brabant Brass Company on the east side of Detroit. It was a family-owned company that made brass fittings for the plumbing industry and others.

Their offices were in part of an old warehouse building. She heard them talking about remodeling the old building and making some new, modern offices. She told them about me as a possible contractor to do the work. As you might guess, they were pretty skeptical about dealing with a twenty-three-year-old in such an important and sizeable project. But they agreed to meet with me. Their skepticism showed loud and clear, and they were not about to turn this sizeable project over to a kid who only had a pickup truck.

They were ready to terminate the meeting when I made a suggestion. I said, "Look, I know how to get this job done. It is not all that complicated. I have a background in architecture, and I think I can save you some money. Just let me be your planner and advisor. I will make the plans and get the building permit. Then I will get the various subcontractors for you. You make the individual contracts with each of them. We can get as many bids as you want for each trade. I will coordinate and supervise the work. As the work progresses, you pay the subs directly so you will know what each part of the job costs. For my services, you pay me $1,000."

They were two brothers. They looked at each other and said, "We'll let you know." When they asked Marilyn what she knew about me, she said she was going to marry me. I don't know all that went on, but they called me a few days later and said I had the job. So, even before we were married, she became part of the business. We did the work, and they were very pleased and said that they had saved a lot of money over another bid they had to do the work. It was a messy job with a lot of demolition, but it turned out fine.

Since the job sort of came out of the blue and because of Marilyn's "selling job," I thought I should spend it on her. So that is the money that we used to pay for our honeymoon trip. After the wedding night at a Detroit hotel, we drove to New York City and spent the night at the famous Plaza Hotel on Central Park. We stored our car in a city garage for a month and flew on Pan American Airlines on what they called a circle trip. Every day the plane left New York City and flew to Puerto Rico and then on to the Dominican Republic and then to Haiti and then to Jamaica and then to Havana, Cuba, and then to Miami and returned to New York. It was an all-day flight. For $198, you could stay as long as you liked in each place and then get the plane the next day or whatever day you wanted. We visited all the places. We were gone a month, and the $1,000 from the brass company job covered all the costs.

We had rented an apartment and purchased some furniture before we left. When we returned, her mom and dad had painted the apartment, arranged for the furniture to be delivered, moved in all of our wedding gifts, hung pictures, and had the apartment all ready for us. It was wonderful, and so was she as my new bride.

We lived in that apartment for about three years. It was on West Chicago Boulevard, a block west of Evergreen near Rouge Park. Our office in the Byers Lumber Company building at that time was only about a mile away, and she became the bookkeeper and the "office manager." The office was about ten feet by twelve feet, and she and I made up the entire office staff.

The business began to grow, and she said we needed more operating capital because sometimes we had to pay the subcontractors and the suppliers before we got paid. So I went to our local bank and asked for a loan. They sent me downtown to the main office and to see a loan officer. So I went. It was in the old stately Manufacturers National Bank building on Fort Street. The man's name was Dean Richardson. I asked him for $5,000. He said, "Give me a few days." He looked over my contracts, etc., and determined that I didn't need $5,000. He said I needed $10,000. So I said, "Whatever you say." Marilyn was delighted that she could now pay the bills in a timely fashion. Later he told me that there were "3 Cs" to consider when he made a loan. The first "C" was collateral, or what assets can you pledge? The second "C" was character, or integrity and a strong desire to pay the money back. The third "C" was capacity, or a viable plan to pay it back. He said in my case I had no collateral, a pickup truck, and maybe $500 worth of construction equipment. But, based upon his investigation of my reputation, after talking to some of my customers and business associates, he thought I had character. He also said that after looking over my contracts and history, he thought I had a way to pay it back. And pay it back I did, and I established a sixty-year relationship with the bank. That young man with his three "Cs" went on to be president and chairman of the board of the bank.

My, how times have changed in the banking business. The three "Cs" today are collateral, collateral, and collateral. Very little credit is given for character or capacity.

Marilyn worked as bookkeeper in the office for about two years until she became pregnant with Colleen, who was born April 5, 1955. I've told you about the house we built on Minock near the park, and Colleen was less than a year old when we moved in. Marilyn was the best wife and mother that ever was! She was not only very bright intellectually, she had a heart of gold. She was so compassionate for others. Everybody loved Marilyn. I don't think she had an enemy in the world. But she surely had a lot of friends. As our income grew and we could buy most anything we wanted, she was never extravagant. She realized that everything we had was a gift from God. She reasoned that if that were true, we should use these gifts to glorify the Lord—not only financially but using gifts like our home to entertain others and to hold Bible studies.

In both of our homes we had good-sized finished basements that became popular gathering places. We had a Ping-Pong table and a pool table, plus ample space for fellowship. In our Cranbrook house, we had room for seventy to eighty people. Marilyn was always quick to offer our home for church and Sunday school class parties and then later on it became a regular place for teens to hang out with our own kids. The same was true about the swimming pool. She loved having people in our home. She felt like it was a ministry and she never complained about the work necessary to get the place ready or to clean up afterward. She was the perfect hostess, and she trained our children to be the same, not only by instruction but by example. I think people liked coming to our home, not only because of the facilities but because of her and her sweet spirit and personal interest that she took in each guest. Everybody loved Marilyn, and she loved everybody with a spirit that reflected her love for the Lord Jesus.

She also agreed that we should use our vacation apartments to help missionaries and pastors and other less-fortunate folks by letting them use them.

She had a great love of books and was an avid reader. Actually, she became the church librarian, a job she loved. She had excellent taste as a decorator, and all three of our residences were beautifully decorated. She was "into" genealogy and traced her ancestors back to the year 1060 in England. I think we have been in every cemetery in England, looking for them. She believed she was the great-great-great granddaughter of King Henry II. I always knew she was like royalty.

She was the household bookkeeper, taking care of all the bills, etc., until she no longer could do it because of the Alzheimer's.

As you may know, Alzheimer's disease is one of the worst ailments there is. The best way to describe it is that it is "a long good-bye." No one ever gets better from Alzheimer's. Also, I think it is worse on the loved ones than it is on the patient. Marilyn never seemed to have any pain. One time she fell down, face forward, and split her lip. We quickly got her up, and while Colleen was putting ice on her lip, I asked her if she was in any pain. She said, "No. What are you doing to me?"

It was so painful for all of us to see her deteriorate so steadily but also rather slowly for ten years. The best the doctors could do was to slow it down by giving her different medications. I don't think anyone knows if they work or not. At any rate, she just got worse and worse.

Fairly early on, we found a wonderful lady named Faye, whose husband was a minister. She came to the house every day from 8 a.m. until about 4:30 p.m., five days a week. She was wonderful. Marilyn loved Faye, and Faye loved Marilyn. They were a great match! Later, we hired another lady named Nancy who was single and a second grade schoolteacher. Nancy came to our house after school each Friday and stayed with us the entire weekend. Both of these ladies were sent from the Lord. We had determined that, if at all possible, we did not want to put Marilyn in an institution. I know that sometimes that is the only option for some folks, but not for us, if we could possibly help it.

Those were some of the darkest days of my life to see the one I loved so much turn into a totally different person. It is hard to explain the feelings of hopelessness, frustration, the anticipation of her death, and the day-to-day experiences of living with that situation. The only good news was that she would soon be home in heaven and in her right mind with the Savior whom she so dearly loved. We can only conclude that He also loved her so much that He wanted her to be with Him sooner, rather than later.

Paul and Marilyn, April 19, 1952, a Happy Day

Here is a Christmas letter that I wrote just a few days before Marilyn passed away just after midnight on December 10, 2007.

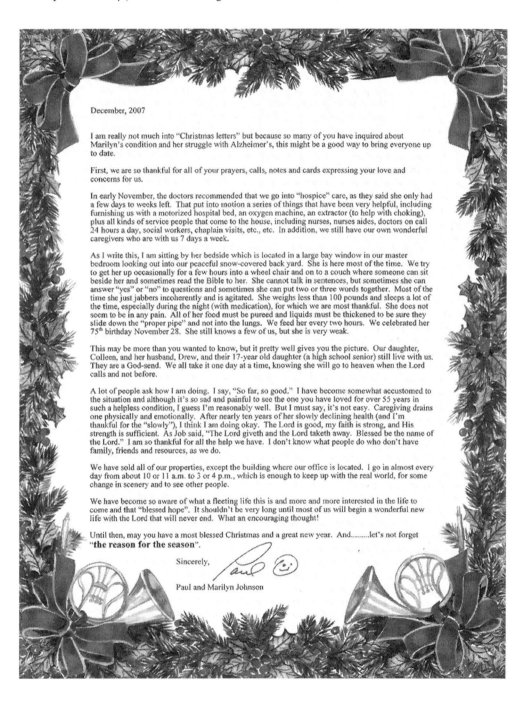

December, 2007

I am really not much into "Christmas letters" but because so many of you have inquired about Marilyn's condition and her struggle with Alzheimer's, this might be a good way to bring everyone up to date.

First, we are so thankful for all of your prayers, calls, notes and cards expressing your love and concerns for us.

In early November, the doctors recommended that we go into "hospice" care, as they said she only had a few days to weeks left. That put into motion a series of things that have been very helpful, including furnishing us with a motorized hospital bed, an oxygen machine, an extractor (to help with choking), plus all kinds of service people that come to the house, including nurses, nurses aides, doctors on call 24 hours a day, social workers, chaplain visits, etc., etc. In addition, we still have our own wonderful caregivers who are with us 7 days a week.

As I write this, I am sitting by her bedside which is located in a large bay window in our master bedroom looking out into our peaceful snow-covered back yard. She is here most of the time. We try to get her up occasionally for a few hours into a wheel chair and on to a couch where someone can sit beside her and sometimes read the Bible to her. She cannot talk in sentences, but sometimes she can answer "yes" or "no" to questions and sometimes she can put two or three words together. Most of the time she just jabbers incoherently and is agitated. She weighs less than 100 pounds and sleeps a lot of the time, especially during the night (with medication), for which we are most thankful. She does not seem to be in any pain. All of her food must be pureed and liquids must be thickened to be sure they slide down the "proper pipe" and not into the lungs. We feed her every two hours. We celebrated her 75th birthday November 28. She still knows a few of us, but she is very weak.

This may be more than you wanted to know, but it pretty well gives you the picture. Our daughter, Colleen, and her husband, Drew, and their 17-year old daughter (a high school senior) still live with us. They are a God-send. We all take it one day at a time, knowing she will go to heaven when the Lord calls and not before.

A lot of people ask how I am doing. I say, "So far, so good." I have become somewhat accustomed to the situation and although it's so sad and painful to see the one you have loved for over 55 years in such a helpless condition, I guess I'm reasonably well. But I must say, it's not easy. Caregiving drains one physically and emotionally. After nearly ten years of her slowly declining health (and I'm thankful for the "slowly"), I think I am doing okay. The Lord is good, my faith is strong, and His strength is sufficient. As Job said, "The Lord giveth and the Lord taketh away. Blessed be the name of the Lord." I am so thankful for all the help we have. I don't know what people do who don't have family, friends and resources, as we do.

We have sold all of our properties, except the building where our office is located. I go in almost every day from about 10 or 11 a.m. to 3 or 4 p.m., which is enough to keep up with the real world, for some change in scenery and to see other people.

We have become so aware of what a fleeting life this is and more and more interested in the life to come and that "blessed hope". It shouldn't be very long until most of us will begin a wonderful new life with the Lord that will never end. What an encouraging thought!

Until then, may you have a most blessed Christmas and a great new year. And.........let's not forget **"the reason for the season".**

Sincerely,

Paul and Marilyn Johnson

18

COLLEEN

As most of you know, after Colleen came Kevin on September 6, 1957, two years and six months later, and then Karen five years after that on June 14, 1962. Three wonderful children! I will not tell you too much about them, as they can tell you grandchildren their own stories. But I will tell you a little about their early years that they might not remember.

Colleen was a precocious child. Being the first grandchild of both sets of grandparents, she got special attention. From the time she was a baby, her mother always dressed her in beautiful little dresses, coats, shoes. Her two grandmothers contributed to her wardrobe. She always looked like the baby models you see in catalogs. I don't know who taught her, but by the time she was one year old and before she could talk, she could make the sounds of about a dozen different animals. For example, we would say, "What does the cow say?" and she would say "Moo"; and "what does a sheep say?" and she would say, "Baaa." And she loved to show off. One day we were standing in line waiting to be seated in an upscale restaurant in New Orleans. She was less than a year old. I was holding her in my arms, and the other people in line started noticing her and how well she was behaving. To pass the time, her mother started getting her to make the sounds of the animals. Within minutes, she had an audience of eight or ten people, and she was a performer.

Not only was she a performer at an early age, she was also a high achiever. She got mostly As in school and loved to excel. One time in junior high, the school had a candy selling contest. The money was to go to help one of the school's programs. The school gave each student a few boxes of candy, and they were supposed to sell them and bring the money back to the school and get more boxes. There was a prize for the best salesperson. Colleen brought home the few boxes and sold them in no time to family and friends. That was easy, she thought. So the next batch she sold door-to-door in the neighborhood. She thought that, too, was fairly easy but too slow. So she engaged her younger brother, and the two of them went door-to-door in an apartment building we owned in downtown Birmingham. There were fifty-four apartments in all. Naturally, when they told them who they were (and how they got into the building), sales came quickly. Still not satisfied, she and her brother set up a table in front of the main entrance to the office and retail portion of the building, which is on a main street with fairly heavy foot traffic. She kept getting more and more boxes each time she went back to school until the authorities became skeptical. Needless to say, she won the contest and the prize for candy salesman of the year.

She wanted to learn to cook and was always bugging her mom to show her how to do things in the kitchen. She learned fairly quickly and liked to help out with meals. On one occasion, when she was about twelve years old, we were expecting guests from out of town for a weekend. They were going to stay with us, along with their two children, a girl and a boy, the same ages as Colleen and Kevin. The day before the guests were to arrive, Marilyn fell ill with a high fever and other complications, and she couldn't get out of bed. What to do? Naturally we thought of taking them out to dinner, but Colleen said, "No problem. I can do it."

So, with Mom's instructions from her sickbed, she started. She was told where to find the recipes and the food that Marilyn had purchased, and step-by-step what to do. She must have made twenty trips up to the bedroom for instructions. Soon she again got her brother to help, and the two of them prepared the whole meal, not only cooking the meal but setting the table (which she already knew how to do) and cooking and serving the entire meal, complete with dessert. Well, the guest couple, as you might guess, was in awe. In fact, it was a little embarrassing when the guest children saw what Colleen and Kevin had done. They were all very impressed that a twelve-year-old and ten-year-old could prepare and serve a first-class dinner for out-of-town guests.

I have deviated a little from telling you more stories about your grandmother Marilyn and our life together. But while I'm at it, let me tell you a little more about Colleen, Kevin, and Karen; and we'll go back to my life with Marilyn a little later.

Colleen went on and lived a fairly normal life, graduating from Seaholm High School and then from Wheaton College in the nursing program. She fell in love while in college and married John ("Gibby") O'Gieblyn. After thirteen years of marriage and four children, he left and went back to Portland, Oregon, his hometown. This was three days after Colleen had given birth to her youngest, Lauren. It was awful.

They were living in an old farmhouse in Vermont at the time. Marilyn and I were there to help with the new baby, and I had just left to go home while Marilyn stayed a little longer. Colleen was all by herself in this big old house way up in Vermont with four little children. It was fifteen miles to the nearest grocery store. Meghan, who was eight years old, was the oldest. Michael was six, and Ian was four. Colleen wanted to stay in Vermont until she could sell the house. We visited her regularly, and she would come home at Christmas and for all summer to be near us at Maranatha where she lived in a condo that was available to her.

Those days were so painful for Marilyn and me. We knew life was so difficult for her, but there was little we could do except to pray for her and help her financially. Each Christmas, she would come back to our home where she grew up and where her children had spent every Christmas of their lives. Her time was flexible because she homeschooled all the children. After Christmas, when she would load up all the four kids in her van along with all the Christmas presents, car seats, and so on, Marilyn and I would stand on the front porch hugging each other with tears in our eyes as we watched her drive down the driveway heading back for a two-day trip to Vermont and to that big old drafty house. We cried ourselves to sleep that night and many others during those days, so concerned about her and those four little kids. We prayed for her fervently for years. We knew that God hates divorce, but He loves the divorcee and that He loved her. We rationalized that she was unlikely to get remarried very soon. After all, who would want to get involved with a woman with four little children? We thought that maybe after fifteen or sixteen years, when the children were all grown up, maybe she might meet someone.

One summer, about three or four years later, she let a missionary family use her house in Vermont for the summer while she and the children came to Maranatha. About late August, she called the missionaries to see how they were doing in her house. The lady said they were in trouble. Her husband had taken ill and they could not go back to their missionary post overseas. But she quickly said that Colleen shouldn't be concerned, that they would move out of her house, as planned, by Labor Day. Colleen told her, "Hold everything," and said she would call her back in a day or two. Colleen asked me if she and the children could stay in the condo after Labor Day and after the conference season ended. We could see no problem. In fact, we were delighted. The condo was winterized and she would be living a lot closer to us in Muskegon, three hours away, rather than in Vermont, two days away. She was still homeschooling the three older children, so that wasn't a problem. So she stayed, and it was great! We saw them every few weeks instead of every few months.

Later that winter, Marilyn and I went to Florida for February and March. Along about the end of March, Colleen called to say that there was someone she wanted us to meet. We said, "Sure. We'll be home in a week or two and that will be fine."

She said, "No. We're coming down to Florida this Friday for the weekend." We thought again, oh my goodness; who would want to get involved with a lady with four little children? He must either be a "gold digger," assuming Colleen was from a wealthy family, or someone who "didn't have all his marbles." Anyway, she said to pick them up at 4:30 at the airport. So we did. She introduced us to Drew Wolford, and we immediately went to a dinner at a restaurant on the way home. As soon as we had ordered dinner, he said, "Let me tell you about myself."

For the next hour or so, we listened to his incredible story. He had an eight-year-old daughter, Sheena, and his first wife had died. He lived with his mom and dad in Fremont, Michigan, where he worked. His folks looked after the little girl while he was at work. He and Colleen had met at a church in Muskegon at a single parents group. By the time he was finished with his testimony for Christ and his personal story and how much he loved Colleen and her children, I remember thinking, "This is too good to be true." Well, it was, indeed, all true; and it was a great weekend and a beginning of a whole new life for Colleen and her children.

Oh, incidentally, regarding the "gold digger" possibility, she had never told him anything about her family until they were on the plane on their way to Florida. He told me later that she was so secretive about me and her family that he thought maybe I was in jail! As most of you know, they were married and have had a most wonderful life together with a blended family. That was eighteen years ago. As I told you, God hates divorce, but He loves the divorcee. In her case, He was so merciful to Colleen. I don't know where she could have found anyone who would be better suited as her husband. He is just perfect for her—a gift from God. That's the only way to explain it. He took on the role as father to her four children, plus, of course, his own daughter, Sheena, and all of them call him "Dad" and why not? He has been a wonderful father to them for the last eighteen years.

Some of you know that when Marilyn was getting pretty bad with Alzheimer's, Colleen suggested to Drew that they sell their house and move in with us to help take care of her mother. At that point, the children were all grown and pretty well "out of the house." Some were still in college, but fortunately our house was large enough to accommodate them when they came home to visit. To Drew's credit, he agreed to accommodate Colleen and move in with us, his in-laws. I don't think many husbands would look favorably upon moving in with their wife's folks and especially to help care for the mother-in-law. But he did it. I am sure it was mostly to be supportive of Colleen and her desires. It is just one example of his caring spirit for his wife. It has now been almost six years, and the living arrangements are working out just fine. More about this later.

19

KEVIN

Kevin was born on September 6, 1957. We still lived on Minock in Detroit. He was an unbelievable child. He was almost perfect and so obedient and agreeable to most anything he was asked to do. He had a most sensitive spirit. If he did something that we didn't approve of, just a look of disapproval from Marilyn or me would cause him to hang his head and cry. I don't think he received more than two or three spankings in his entire life. He had blond hair and he wore it in a brush cut and was as cute as could be. When people wanted to show affection to him, they would often rub the top of his head, running their fingers through his hair. He hated it. He was much more "laid-back" and with a quiet disposition. He always was, and is, tenderhearted. He was never aggressive nor did he ever put himself first. He was always thinking about the welfare of others. He was so much like his mother in so many ways. He was not much into sports. He did play soccer at school; but when he broke his nose in a game, his interest diminished. He was so well organized, and in his room he had a place for everything and everything was in its place.

He soon took an interest in photography. At first, we thought it was just a hobby, but after a while and two years at Taylor University, he decided he would like to pursue it professionally. So after some investigation, he determined that the best school was Brooks Institute in Santa Barbara, California. During a visit there and his investigation, the school told him that one of their most famous graduates was from our area right here in Troy, Michigan. His name was Vern Hammarlund. So Kevin went to visit him at his studio. Vern is a commercial photographer (as opposed to a portrait photographer) and, at the time, among other businesses, he had the account for the Buick automobile. Vern liked Kevin and the idea that he was headed to Brooks Institute; and he gave him a job as a photographer's assistant. It was great training, and by the time Kevin went to Brooks, he already had a working knowledge of his proposed profession. Vern took him on several trips all around the country, photographing Buick cars with all kinds of backgrounds as scenery. In those days, Buick was one of the few car companies that still had a large fifteen- or twenty-page full-color brochure featuring all the different models available. It was a great account, and Kevin learned a lot from Vern and his staff. The day he loaded up his little compact car and headed for California was a sad day for his mom and me. That little car was packed to the brim. He even had things on the front passenger's seat with barely enough room for himself.

It was particularly sad for us as he drove away for that lonely drive all across the country to Southern California. We visited him a number of times during his time out there, and he seemed to be well adjusted. After a while, he made some good friends and got himself a dog for closer companionship. Many of the graduates were motion picture students and they often wound up in Hollywood. He worked for Vern in the summers during his schooling. After graduation, he came home and took a job with W. B. Doner Company. They are a large advertising agency. His job was a producer for radio and television advertisements.

Later on, with two other young fellows, they started a business making slide shows for industry. One of their customers was General Motors. They were often used for training purposes to show the car dealers how to repair or replace different problems or new features on the cars. They were quite successful. It was in the days before video. Slides with commentaries were a lot less expensive to produce than movies. Sometimes their setup was with multiple computerized projectors, and after watching for just a few minutes, it felt like you were actually watching a movie. Along the line, he was one of the youth sponsors at our church, working with teens. It was there that he met Lisa Whitman, who later became his wife.

He also met Bruce Wilkinson, president of Walk Thru the Bible, and

Bruce offered him a job at their office in Atlanta. Soon after that, and later on after they were married, both Kevin and Lisa went to Russia as missionaries during the CoMission program. Their job was to photograph and document the activities of the various schoolteachers and others who were there working in the schools. After that program ended, they came back to the United States, and at the request of J. B. Crouse, who was president of OMS mission society, they moved to the Indianapolis area where the main office of OMS was located. The agency needed help in the area of communication, magazine production, pictures, advertising, etc. After doing all he could to help them, he and Lisa started up a business of making commemorative slides and videos for weddings, anniversaries, and other occasions. They could take a box of old family pictures and put them together and make a video presentation along with music showing the life of a person in pictures.

Then, after about fourteen years of marriage and four children, Lisa started divorce proceedings. In the settlement, Kevin retained the house so that the children, Camden, Graham, Brigham, and Claire, could be in the same house that they were born in and sleep in their own beds. After six years of being alone, the Lord brought a wonderful lady, Cheryle Marks, into Kevin's life. She had lost her husband, Ron, about four years previously, after a long illness. Some of you know the story of how she and Kevin were high school classmates at Southfield Christian, graduating in 1975. They were married in late 2011. Incidentally, her maiden name was "Johnson." She is a lovely person who is a devoted follower of Jesus Christ. She and Kevin seem to be so happy and well suited for each other. When I first met her and we got a little acquainted, I said to her, "I'm so happy that you like Kevin."

She said, "Like him? I love him." That was a most encouraging and enthusiastic confirmation to us. She has taken to his children, and they to her. It is another direct answer to prayer and an example of God's love and provision for those who love Him and are faithful to Him. In recent years, Kevin has been with FedEx, working in their "logistics department" at the Indianapolis airport.

20

KAREN

Five years after Kevin came Karen Sue, born June 14, 1962. She was the smallest of the three babies and was such a good baby. She slept most of the first year of her life. She also had hardly any hair until way past her first birthday. She was like a new toy for her five-year-old brother and seven-year-old sister. In the daytime, Marilyn kept her in a little swinging, low-to-the-floor cradle located in our family room. There was a large pass-through to the kitchen, and Marilyn could keep an eye on her as she worked in the kitchen. After school, the two older ones would stand next to her while she slept, and it was all they could do to keep their hands off of her. She was a beautiful baby, and she grew up to be a beautiful person. We moved into the Cranbrook house when she was three years old. We visited the new house several times during the construction, and she always called it, "going to the big house." For the first time, she had her own room. Big stuff for a little girl! She was always looked after and protected by her older brother and sister.

As she began to grow up, she watched them very closely. As a result, she saw some things that worked for them and some things that were not so good and, therefore, avoided them. She learned a lot from her brother and sister simply by observation. Across the street from us lived the Hamlin family. They had a girl Karen's age, Jennifer, and she had a younger sister. Cranbrook Road has a fair amount of traffic on it, and yet those two little girls, ages three and two, would come over and ring our doorbell and ask if Karen could come out and play. We often responded by inviting them in to play with Karen. Karen and Jennifer later went to school together and became lifelong friends, even after Jennifer moved thousands of miles away. Karen was the homecoming queen the year she graduated from high school.

While she was still in high school, and with a brother and sister in college, Marilyn and I were invited to go on a trip with CBMC to the Orient. We were going to be gone three weeks. We asked the school officials if we could take Karen out of school to go with us. They thought it would be "educational" for her and would be okay as long as she kept up with her schoolwork while she was gone. We visited the Philippines, Hong Kong, Korea, and Japan. She was fifteen years old at that time. She made friends with an older single girl, Gwynn DeMoss, on the trip; and they became good friends for years to come. After Moody graduation, she became associated with Youth for Christ. She worked with underprivileged kids in Detroit and other communities.

When we finished our Birmingham Place building, she became a salesperson, showing and renting the apartments. One day she showed an apartment to a nice-looking, single guy. He rented an apartment but also became interested in Karen. He took her out several times, often to expensive restaurants and other events. I invited him to a CBMC meeting where he heard the gospel and later prayed to receive Christ. As they continued to date, something told Marilyn and me that he was not the right one for Karen. We had prayed for all our children that they would marry a person who really loved the Lord and put Him first in their lives. Somehow this young man didn't seem to "fit the bill." We told Karen how we felt, and she had a dilemma. Was she going to listen to her parents, whom she loved and respected, or continue on in a relationship where she was having a lot of fun and enjoying a lot of nice entertainment?

Marilyn and I began to pray more fervently. One night while we were sitting in the family room, about 10 p.m., she came in the front door crying. She stuck her head in the room where we were and said, "Well, I did what you wanted me to do. I broke up with him tonight." And she ran upstairs crying.

Now we had mixed emotions. We were so sad because our dear, sweet Karen was unhappy. But we were glad that she did what we believed was the right thing and in her best interest.

A short time later—looking back it seems like only a matter of a few weeks—an incident took place. Our friends from church, Dave and Ruth Penner, had a son, John, who attended college in Grand Rapids. He came home for a weekend and brought a friend with him named Scott. In church, Scott noticed Karen and asked John about her. John said that she was the daughter of his parents' friends and that he knew her fairly well. John introduced them, and after church Sunday evening, they all went out for coffee before the boys drove back to school in Grand Rapids. Scott began to come home with John more often and to see Karen. As you might guess, a romance developed. Scott Melby was a wonderful Christian young man. He had grown up in a Christian home in the Chicago area. He had gone to Wheaton College and to Harvard Business School. We liked him right away, and we were so happy for Karen. She fell in love with Scott, and he with her. They were perfect for each other, in our opinion. We thanked the Lord for His goodness in providing such a wonderful mate for her as a reward for her after she had done the right thing in breaking up with the other guy, even though it was temporarily painful but in obedience to what the Lord would have her do. God's plan is always what's best for us if we are obedient and just do what is right. He never leads us to do what is wrong. We usually do that on our own. Karen has developed a keen sense of judgment, not only about what to do what is right but about people and whom to trust. She seems to be able to meet people and, very quickly, determine their character and sincerity. She has that gift from God, I believe, and she is right most of the time.

After they were married, they moved to the Chicago area where Scott got a job with a firm owned by a friend of mine, Clayton Brown. It was a municipal bond company. After a short time, Scott was transferred to Florida and put in charge of the company's operations there, which was selling municipal bonds to banks. His territory was the entire state, so the company told him he could live wherever he wanted. They selected Boca Raton. It was there that Meredith was born. Marilyn and I went down a day after she was born. One thing I don't think I will ever forget about her was that she was the smallest baby I had ever seen. Much smaller than her mom was. And her little fingers were not much bigger than toothpicks, but she was quite normal and grew up very nicely.

After a while in Florida, the company said that they wanted to promote Scott and eventually bring him back to the home office in Chicago. However, the business path would be to put him in charge of a large section of the eastern part of the United States. This would mean travel about three weeks of the month. With a wife and a new baby, that didn't appeal to them very much, even though it might eventually have been the way back to Chicago. We talked it through with them and offered him a job with our firm. He would be in charge of showing and leasing our commercial and retail space. The problem was, even though he was very bright and astute in business in general, he had no experience in the real estate business. The job we had for him was not quite ready at that point. So he got a job with a large real estate firm, basically to learn the business. He learned quickly and then came to work for us. They moved into one of our larger apartments in our Burlington Arms projects, just upstairs from my mother and dad's apartment. That's where they lived when the second child, Drew, was born. After a while, they bought a house and later enlarged it and remodeled it into a very nice six-bedroom, five-bath, family home. Their family grew to five children, including Ginny, Kirsten, and Clayton, while they lived in that house. In fact, with five outstanding children, they became a wonderful Christian family. Karen homeschooled the children from time to time, and they started Bible studies for young parents as soon as they had moved back to the Detroit area. At first, because their apartment was too small, they used our house and then later, their own home. In fact, they grew to the point where they established a new church.

After several years of Scott working for us, we decided it was time to sell our properties and give away most of the money to the Lord's work and some of it to our family and friends. We thought it was better to do it while we were still alive and in time to help them before they got too old to enjoy it. After all, my dad lived to be one hundred, and if I lived that long and waited until I died to pass it on to my children, they might be in their late seventies. However, as we sold our properties, Scott found himself out of a job. So, to ease the blow, we offered to help him out financially if he and maybe some others would find some business opportunity that they wanted to pursue. As it happened, he and his brother-in-law, Randy Witt, decided to open a water park in the Chicago area. I'll tell you more about this later.

Top Left: Colleen
Top Right: Kevin
Bottom: Karen

21

FLORIDA APARTMENTS

Most of you know that we still own some apartments in south Florida. You may be wondering how that came to be and why we still have them. This is the story.

It began back in 1956. In those days, as I explained previously, the construction business in Michigan was very slow in the winter. It is not so bad now, as we have new and better methods available that make it possible to work a lot of winter days. But not so back then. The result was that most of us "small guys" just shut down for two or three months. That was a good time for us to go to Florida for a vacation, along with a lot of retired snowbirds. So we did. By contrast, summers were so busy that it was hard to "get away." At that time, we had no children in school, and Colleen was only a one year old.

When we arrived in Florida looking for an apartment to rent for a month or so, we were not very warmly greeted because of a one-year-old baby. It took us a fair amount of time to locate a friendly manager to give us a chance. We finally did, but it was made clear that we were "on probation" until one of the other guests complained about a crying baby or noise from the pool area.

While we were there, we noticed some new condos under construction across the street. We inquired as to whether or not they would allow children. We were told no, but there was an identical complex under construction about a block away that would take children. So we went down the block and inquired. We were welcomed, and we bought one, a two-bedroom, one-bath unit, known as Apartment #12 at 625 Orton Avenue. As most of you know, it is one of twenty units in three two-story buildings; two eight-unit buildings and one four-unit building. It has a swimming pool in a nice backyard and is located three short blocks from the ocean in Fort Lauderdale.

At this point, I think I should tell you about the developer and a very creative scheme that he pulled off. He purchased six parcels of vacant land, all the same size and all in the same neighborhood, within a block or two of each other. Some were back-to-back, facing different streets, and some were across the street from each other. There were 120 units all together. All six complexes were the same, ten one-bedroom units and ten two-bedroom units (about 850 to 900 square feet). All modest-sized and with minimal amenities. He had a contractor build them and advertised them for sale at his cost. No profit, except that he retained the land, and each unit (or complex) paid him rent for ninety-nine years. This served to reduce the cost of the units to the buyers but with a small lease payment to him. The amount of lease payment for each unit was reasonable, even though it went up slightly every five years. But, multiplied by 120 units, it gave him a nice income for life, and without any long-term investment on his part.

As the units were being finished, he advertised a "sale day" to be held in a hotel ballroom at 10 a.m. on a certain day. The prices were $10,000 for a two-bedroom and $7,500 for a one-bedroom unit. He rang a bell, and the sale began. By the end of the day, they were all sold. Several realtors and investors bought multiple units with the idea of reselling them at a markup.

It was soon after that when we came along and bought Apt. #12 from a realtor for $12,000. It was still unfinished but a very good deal at that time. It was the winter of 1956. It was one of the first ones sold in our complex, and we got what we thought was the best unit overlooking the pool on the second floor.

We were sitting out in the yard around the pool about a year or so later, and a fellow with a loud voice came into the area from one of the other buildings, shouting, "Anybody want to buy a blankety-blank apartment?" When we inquired as to the details, he said he had purchased the apartment at the "sale" as an investment and rented it out. He went on to say that his tenants had trashed the apartment, didn't pay the rent, and he wanted to sell. When we asked the price, he said, "Exactly what I paid for it—$7,500." It was a one-bedroom unit (Apt. #1). I went over and looked at it, and the "trash" was mostly the furniture, venetian blinds and some paint scratches. At that point, Marilyn's mother and dad were thinking about retiring, and I thought it might be good for them, so we bought it. Since it was only a year or two old, it didn't take much to fix it up like new.

Well, wouldn't you know? The very next winter, we were sitting out in the yard again and here comes the same guy, this time looking for me. He said, "Do you want to buy another one?" This time it was a two-bedroom next door (Apt. #2). He explained that he was a local dentist who was looking to make some extra money in the apartment rental business, but the "business" had backfired with his bad choice of tenants, and he wanted nothing more to do with the real estate rental business. The price was the same, his cost—$10,000. This one took a little more to fix up but my dad and Uncle Lester did most of the work, and it became the winter home for the two couples for many years.

That was it for about forty years. We had three apartments with a total investment of less than $30,000. Then one day our daughter Karen called me while she and her family were vacationing in our old original Apt. #12. She reminded me that they now had five children, and the two-bedroom one-bath apartment was a little "tight" for seven people, even though we had two sleeping couches in the living room. When I asked what she wanted me to do about it, she let me know that the apartment next door (#11) was for sale. Her plan was for me to buy it and knock out a wall between the apartments, and the result would be a three-bedroom, two-bath apartment with another living and dining area and a second kitchen. I thought about it and decided it might not be a bad idea. So she negotiated a price, and we bought it, but at many times the price of the original three other units; but, after all, it was forty years later!

She later called back to say that the new apartment was "the pits," as she put it. It needed a complete makeover with all new kitchen cupboards, appliances, and more, but not to worry, she knew a decorator and she had a contractor who could handle the entire project. No problem! After investigation, they found that the wall between the apartments was a bearing wall and could not economically be removed. So they put in two doors, like in adjoining hotel rooms, which could be open or closed, depending upon the need and use. The decorator's name was Bridget. And between Karen and Bridget, we spent more to "fix it up" than the unit cost to purchase. But it is very, very nice—one of the nicest in the entire complex. Karen took after her mother when it comes to "good taste."

So, that's the story. Of course, both of our parents are gone, but we still have the apartments. The cost was so low, and they don't cost too much to maintain, that we just kept them. We have made them available to pastors, missionaries, friends and family, without ever collecting one dime in the way of rent. For years now, my sister, Linda, and her husband, Dale, have occupied Apt. #1 from January 1 until about May 1, and the other three apartments are used by others during the winter months. Linda and Dale do a great job of looking after the apartments and caring for the details between guests.

22

ANOTHER FLORIDA APARTMENT

Marilyn's mom and dad (Mimi and Johnny Glines) had Apt. #1 originally, and it wasn't long until her dad, Johnny, passed away. After Mimi was widowed, she began spending more and more time at a winter Bible conference called "Bibletown." It was located about seventeen miles north of Ft. Lauderdale in Boca Raton and was something like Maranatha, except that it was operated only during the winter months. She loved to go up there to meetings, and she became acquainted with several other ladies, mostly also widows. She drove up from Ft. Lauderdale three or four times a week to visit with her friends and attend the evening meetings. Every Saturday night, they had a musical concert that was very popular, and we would often go with her when we were there.

One day she came to me with what she said was "a proposition." She had heard from some of her lady friends that a new condo building was being built just a few miles from Bibletown, and she was interested in purchasing an apartment. It was a ten-story building, and she had picked out a unit on the fifth floor overlooking the ocean. It had two bedrooms and two baths and was about fifteen hundred square feet. She showed me the brochure and the floor plan. It was really quite nice, and she would be close to her friends and to Bibletown. The cost was about $40,000.

Here was her proposition. She said that she would make the down payment, about $4,000, and I should make the monthly mortgage payments because I could deduct the interest from my income taxes. Then she would pay the monthly condo fees and I would pay the real estate taxes, also because I could deduct them from my income taxes. I said,

"Sure, Mimi, whatever you want to do." Well, she was so happy, and the deal was done. She also said that when she went to heaven, she would leave the apartment to Marilyn, which she did. It is the best of all our Florida apartments and the one Pam and I currently occupy in the winter.

One more story about Mimi. As time went on and she was living in the new apartment all winter, I knew she didn't have a lot of money, but she never complained or asked for anything. One day I said, "Mimi, is there anything that I could do for you to make your life more comfortable?" She thought a minute and said, "Maybe there is one thing." Just name it, I replied. She explained that she was getting along okay financially, but she only wished that she had a little extra money so that she could take some of her lady friends out to lunch or dinner from time to time. Some of them were not too well off, and eating out often put a strain on their budget. Some were retired missionaries or pastors' wives, etc. When asked what she wanted, it was to help others! I said, "Mimi, you got it!" And from then on I sent her a check every month that allowed her to be very generous with her friends. I told her not to say where the money was coming from, but to just go as much and as often as she wanted to. Actually, we thought it was a good investment, not only to help Mimi to be happy but also to help some others with a small pleasure that they otherwise might not be able to afford and enjoy.

It wasn't long before Marilyn and I would be at the conference center and ladies would come up to one of us thanking us for all the meals that Mimi was treating them to. Mimi could in no way be deceptive. She couldn't keep a secret! She had to have "full disclosure" in all things. She was one in a million! Another blessing to my life.

23

OLD FRIENDS

Early in our marriage, as an endearing and affectionate name, I started calling her, on occasion, "Marilyn Barbara." That was, after all, her real name. Other girls had double names; like Peggy Sue, Mary Ann, Barbara Jean, and I didn't want her to miss out. It wasn't long until a few of our close friends started calling her Marilyn Barbara. I always used it along with a compliment or as an expression of my love and appreciation for her. My sweet Marilyn Barbara.

During our life together, God brought some wonderful people into our lives. We made friends with many people at church and at various ministries and on boards, etc. Way too many to mention here. But let me tell you about a few that we met early in our lives and who have remained friends all these years. Dean and Lois Couch come to mind. Dean was already a dentist and had finished additional schooling at the University of Michigan to become an oral surgeon. He and Lois were just married, and they moved to Detroit, where he was to take his residency training at a Detroit hospital in association with Dr. Herbert Bloom, a well-respected oral surgeon. Somehow they started to attend our church when it was still downtown in Highland Park. This was about 1952 or 1953, and we had also been married only a short time. We were among a small group of young married couples who were trying to start a new Sunday school class for us newlyweds. I noticed this new young couple in our Sunday morning church services on several Sundays, but before I could catch up with them after church, they disappeared.

One Sunday I stood at the back door of the church and waited for them. I invited them to join our new Sunday school class, and they said that they would be happy to come. Incidentally, they said the reason that they had to leave church so promptly was so that they could get to the cafeteria at the hospital before it closed. As a doctor, they could get free meals. They came to our class, and we became the best of friends. We were established in business by this time and had a few extra dollars. The Couches, by contrast, were barely getting by. His salary was next to nothing, and she was working as a schoolteacher to help pay the rent and living expenses. So we invited them to dinner a good deal of the time as our guests. To reciprocate, they would invite us to the hospital cafeteria. Since Dean was the "low man on the totem pole" in his group of doctors, he was assigned to see the hospital patients on evenings and weekends. So sometimes on Sunday, after church, we would go with them to the hospital and have lunch and then sit in the lounge with Lois while young Dr. Couch visited the patients.

After a few Sundays, he asked me if I would like to go with him as he made rounds. I agreed, and he got me a white coat. He said to me, "Now just follow me and keep quiet." So away we went. We would go into a patient's room and he would introduce me as Dr. Johnson. He would say something like, "Now, Dr. Johnson, this lady was in an automobile accident and broke her jaw. We have done so and so, and she is getting along just fine and she'll be able to go home on Wednesday." I would walk over close to the bed, and as he was talking I would say something like, "I see. Uh huh!" Or "Very nice." And we would move on to the next patient. There were usually three or four patients of his at a time in the hospital. I got a crash course in oral surgery and learned about various conditions and how they could correct protruding jawbones, class two and class three, etc. After that, we would often spend the afternoons together and go back to church Sunday evenings.

They were both from the Carolinas and couldn't wait to go back. Dean was offered a position with the Bloom group here in Detroit, but they went back to Charlotte, North Carolina, where he joined an older oral surgeon who soon retired, and Dean had his own practice. Before he left, he met a missionary from our church named George Dee, who had been in Africa. George said he felt sorry for a lot of Africans who had toothaches but a dentist was nowhere near to help. He asked Dean if he could teach him to pull teeth. So he did. Not only did he show him, he took him out to a local jail where Dean went once a month to do free dental work and help the inmates with problems of the mouth. Dean got George a set of dental "tools" and taught him how to pull teeth and supervised while he pulled a few. George learned quickly, and after his next four-year term in Africa, he told us how many people had their pain removed as a result of George's dental work. That's not only servicing the soul but the body as well.

We kept in touch with the Couches for years and years, visiting them on our way to Florida; and they came up to Detroit, but always in the summer. They didn't like cold weather. We were so sorry to hear that Dean had been diagnosed with cancer and was gone to heaven about thirty days later. Lois asked me to take part in his funeral service. Lois is still with us, and we have visited her a couple of times within the last few years. Special friends for many years.

Dr. Hugh Clarke and his wife, Martha, were and are great friends. He was a neurosurgeon from Tennessee who was doing his residency at the famous Ford Hospital in Detroit. They also found their way to our church. Hugh originally came as a single person. Then he went south, got married to Martha and quickly came back. We had much the same experiences and relationship with them. Martha had a great voice, and she sang solos regularly in our church. Hugh was (and is) a remarkable fellow. He was an outstanding left-handed tennis player. I played with him a few times. It was impossible to beat him; he had a left-handed serve with so much spin on it that when it hit the ground it actually went sideways. There was no way I could return it. So I soon stopped playing tennis with him.

Hugh was also an excellent photographer, almost professional. He had a darkroom, and he could develop and enlarge pictures, and all of excellent quality. Then he taught himself Greek and could read the New Testament in its original language. We had a great few years together while they were in Detroit. Like the Couches, they too wanted to go back south, and he joined a medical group in Memphis, Tennessee. When

Marilyn was diagnosed with a ruptured disk in her back, he insisted that we come to Memphis for him to do the surgery. We did, and when the nurses in the hospital found out that after Marilyn was discharged we were going to go to Dr. Clarke's house for a period of recovery, she became a celebrity in the hospital.

He was so loved and respected by the entire staff in that hospital. Dr. Clarke was their hero, and he became one of ours. Hugh and Martha later moved to Greenville, South Carolina, and Hugh became involved at Bob Jones University as a board member. At that time, there had never been a graduate of Bob Jones University accepted into a medical school. It seems that there was a certain stigma about the school, as a Christian organization, so that their graduates were not very well received in medical schools, even though many of them were well qualified academically. Dr. Hugh Clarke determined to change that. He began to work on both ends. He helped the students, showing them how to fill out applications and how to conduct themselves at interviews, etc. Martha even got into the program by teaching them how to dress and talk, and then Hugh contacted a few medical schools, saying, in effect, you should give this student a chance, even if he or she did graduate from a Christian school. They do, indeed, meet the academic requirements and many with very high marks. Well, little by little, things started to change, and students were accepted. Most of them excelled in medical school, and many went on to be department heads and with all kinds of medical celebrity status. I was talking to Hugh last year, and he told me that he had now been successful in getting over three hundred students into medical school. Before he moved to Greenville, none had been accepted in well over fifty years. I told him he should write a book. So he contacted all the graduates and asked them to write him a one-page letter of their education and professional medical history. He then put them into a book. Most of them said that they owed Dr. Hugh Clarke a large thank-you for his help. Quite a legacy, I would say!

John and Nancy Teets came to Detroit and to our church a little later. Maybe 1967 or so. John had a background in food and had a successful time at the New York World's Fair in charge of the food service at the

Greyhound pavilion at the fair. Most people don't know that the Greyhound Corporation was a conglomerate. They owned not only the bus company but Dobbs Catering Co., which caters many airlines. They also own more airplanes than any airline. They buy the planes through their financial subsidiary and then lease them to the airlines. They owned Armour Food and Packing and the Carnival Cruise ship line. What brought John and Nancy to Detroit after a very profitable world's fair experience was the food division of Greyhound, which owned at that time all the restaurants in the bus stations all across America called "Post House" (which later changed over to become Burger Kings) and the roadside chain called Stuckey's. John was made president of those divisions, which were based in Detroit, along with the Prophet Company, which catered all the General Motors factories plus many other industrial cafeterias. John and Nancy also found their way to our church. They had two girls the ages of our children.

Marilyn helped Nancy find her way around our area and told her about doctors, stores, and everything a new resident to our area needed to know. They were both dedicated Christians. John's progress in the Greyhound Corporation was phenomenal, and he went on to help them acquire the Dial Corporation; ultimately, he became president and chairman of the board. We remained good friends even after they moved the corporate headquarters to Phoenix. He used to joke with me. He would say, "You show me how to make some money, and I'll show you how to be an executive." He didn't need any help in making money. Like my dear Marilyn, John contracted Alzheimer's and passed on to heaven in 2011. He was in his seventies.

Jerry and Dee Miller were also good friends. I told you something about how he was an executive with Texaco and quit to go to work for the Billy Graham Association. Well, one day Marilyn and I were reflecting on these special friends of ours who had come into our lives in Detroit for a few years and then moved on, but had remained such good and unusual friends. We concluded that it might be nice for us all to get together for a reunion. They didn't know each other—Marilyn and I were the common denominator. But we thought they would all enjoy one another. CBMC,

Christian Business Men's Committee, was having a convention in Miami. So Marilyn and I decided to go on down to Jamaica and see if we could find a nice place that we could all go to. I surely didn't want to invite them without knowing the details about the place. We traveled almost the whole island until we found a nice six-bedroom home with a swimming pool and a lighted tennis court. It was also on a golf course. It was a five-minute walk to the ocean. It came with a maid, a cook, and a groundskeeper. It was perfect. We contacted the four couples, and we settled on a date and booked the house for ten days.

At the last minute, John Teets called and said something had come up and he and Nancy couldn't attend. He was not yet the company president at the time. When I told the others about it, Dean Couch called and asked if they could bring a guest couple as a substitute. He assured me they would "fit in." When I said, "Sure, any friend of yours is a friend of mine," he told me who it was. It was Melvin and Peggy Graham, Billy Graham's brother. Dean said that Melvin had had some recent brain surgery and needed to go somewhere and take it easy to recuperate. I said, "Sure, bring him along." They were a delightful couple. We settled into the nice house and began a great ten days of getting to know each other. Indeed, they all did mesh together very nicely. After agreeing on the menu, the cook would go to the market in Montego Bay along with Marilyn and maybe one or two other ladies and pick out the food we needed. Then we paid for the food. We had a great time, and it was determined that we should do this again some other time. So, as usual, we got appointed as the arrangements committee; and we all went to Switzerland and Germany and a visit to the Passion Play at Oberammergau in Germany and on another trip to Austria.

While we were on that trip to Jamaica, an interesting thing happened. Due to Melvin's brain surgery, he had an open wound on the top of his head just above his forehead. It had a bandage over it, and it was most fortunate that Dr. Clarke was along to help with minor treatments and cleansing and re-bandaging it the wound. One day Peggy Graham and Marilyn wanted to go shopping in town, but they didn't want to go alone. So they talked Melvin and me into going along. We took our rental car and drove into town, about a ten- or fifteen-minute ride. The ladies were in a store, and Melvin and I were standing outside on the sidewalk chatting. A Jamaican cab driver drove up on the wrong side of the street, right in front of us, and asked if we were looking for a cab. We told him, no, that we were just waiting for our wives. With that, he got out of the cab and walked up to us and said, "Where are you fellows from?" Melvin spoke up and in his heavy Southern drawl said, "North Carolina."

The cab driver said, "North Carolina? Have you ever heard of Billy Graham?"

Melvin said, "Yes, sir. I have."

"Have you ever heard him preach?" the cab driver asked. "Yes, sir. I have," answered Melvin.

"Well, you know," the driver said, "he was just here last month for a crusade that lasted a whole week, and I went every night." "That's great!" said Melvin.

The man went on to say, "He is one of the best preachers I've ever heard." Melvin said, "I agree with you, sir. He is a great preacher."

The conversation between them went on for eight or ten minutes, all about Billy Graham and what a great fellow he was. Finally, the cabbie said, "Well, here's my card. If you need a ride, just give me a call." And he drove away. I looked at Melvin and said "Why didn't you tell him who you were?" In his down-home style, he said, "What's the use? He probably wouldn't have believed me anyway."

Melvin was a comical guy with a lot of funny stories and sayings. Once he said, "Do you know the definition of a gentleman farmer? Well, that's a fellow with white sidewall tires on his manure spreader." We had a great ten days and enjoyed a lot of stories about Billy Graham's growing-up years. Melvin said one day the two of them were out working in the field on their father's farm. An airplane skywriter flew over and made the letters in the style, "G P C." Billy said, "Look, Melvin, that's a message for me. It means, 'Go preach Christ.'"

Melvin, who was a little older, said, "Forget it. Get back to work. I think it means, 'Go plow corn.'" Melvin and Peggy are now both with the Lord.

One more couple who have been very special to us are Carole and Charlie Newport. We have known them a long time. Carole was at the church with me when we were both teenagers, and she was one of Marilyn's best friends. Charlie came up from the south, and after a tour in the Korean War, they were married. As we got established in business, Charlie worked for us, in charge of all of our construction equipment. He made sure all the equipment was in good working order and stored at our yard, ready to go out on our next job. He would then bring it out in one of our trucks. As times changed and we began to subcontract out more and more of our work and hire fewer and fewer of our own people, Charlie's duties became less and less. It finally came to the situation where we had no more work for him directly on our payroll. So, with a fair severance pay, he left our direct employment. But we hired him as a subcontractor to do small jobs for us. He had learned the business; and with his son, Scott, who became an accomplished carpenter, they did fairly well.

Both Charlie and Carole were, and are, true "people persons." For years on Sunday morning, Carole would put a lovely meal on the stove before they went to church. After church, she would look for new people and invite them home for Sunday dinner. She had the gift of hospitality and used it extensively. Sometimes, when she couldn't find new people, she would invite us. We have had many Sunday dinners at their house; and always the same menu. Wonderful!

They were also the first ones to visit folks from our church who were in the hospital. When your wife contracts Alzheimer's, it seems no one invites you to their home for a party or for a meal. Nobody but Carole and Charlie Newport, that is. As our many friends sort of forgot about us socially, and I guess rightfully so, Carole continued to invite us to their apartment in downtown Birmingham. At least once a week, and maybe more, she would have us over for a nice meal. And while Marilyn was still able, on occasion we would walk across the street to a movie. When she was no longer able to follow the story, we just spent the evening in their apartment. Then when Marilyn was no longer able to leave home, they would bring dinner to us. It was often very simple, like Chinese or Kentucky Fried Chicken. I can still picture Carole sitting next to Marilyn at the dinner table, feeding her with a spoon, one small bite at a time. Only real friends do things for others like this—especially in circumstances like ours. When they would bring dinner, it gave Colleen and Drew a night off. The Newports would stay and often help me get Marilyn into bed. There are not many friends like them. As I always say, "Friends are like silver, but old friends are like gold."

24

OUR OWN FIRST OFFICE AND EVENTS FOLLOWING

After I left college, my good friend Erv Kamp continued on and graduated. He got married to Shirley, but he had to serve some time in the army. We visited them one time while he was stationed near Baltimore, Maryland. When he was discharged, he came to work with me. He did the plans, and we did the building. At one point we became partners and started a company called "Johnson and Kamp Designers and Builders." It didn't last long because other architects saw us as competitors, and they wouldn't let me bid on their jobs. So we had to separate the companies.

It was about that time that we felt like we should build our own building. So we designed a building to fit on a forty-by-one hundred-foot lot on the corner of Six Mile and Annchester, between Outer Drive and Evergreen. It was a two-story building with all glass on the second floor. It had a small doctor's office on the main floor that we rented out and a glassed-in circular stair to the second floor where our office was located. The rest of the first floor provided parking for nine cars under the building. One of the interesting features of the building was the roof, which was designed to hold about two inches of water in the summertime. This served as extra insulation and actually had a cooling effect as the water evaporated. In the fall of the year, we lowered the drains so as not to have ice up there in the wintertime—a rather ingenious concept that helped to reduce the amount of air-conditioning required.

Erv had his own office and business across the hall from our offices. I owned the building, and he was a tenant as well as a business associate and good friend until he retired, and even after he retired. He contracted Parkinson's disease, and his dear wife, Shirley, cared for him at home as long as she could and finally had to put him in a nursing home. She visited him every day for five or six hours for years until one night in February 2012, he quietly passed away in his sleep. He was eighty-three. We had been friends since high school, about seventy years.

Along with the coming of our new office building, our business began to grow quickly. Fred Wilkinson was an accountant and a new CPA who worked for a midsized CPA firm. In the beginning, Fred came out to our office one day a month to help Marilyn with the books. Soon it was two days a month and then three days or sometimes more. When looking at the invoices for accounting services, I thought I could probably hire someone full-time for what I was paying the accounting firm. Of course, I had Fred in mind. So I went to his boss, whom I knew, and asked him if I could have his permission to talk to Fred. He said he would get back with me. A few days later he came back and said okay. "If he says yes, it will be sort of a double loss for us. We will lose one of our best accountants and probably lose you as a client. But," he said, "we'll let Fred make the choice and decide what he thinks would be best for him." So, after a few weeks of consideration, Fred decided to leave public accounting and cast his lot with me in the construction business. It was a great day for me. Although he was never an actual partner in the construction business, I treated him as one and consulted with him on all major decisions. Later on, when we began to build buildings for ourselves, I did give him, along with others, an interest in some of the buildings. More about that later.

As the construction business grew, we built buildings for anybody and everybody. We built small office buildings, more industrial and commercial buildings, several churches, and three or four ice arenas.

It was in the days when little league hockey was catching on, but there were not enough arenas. In fact, some of the kids had to practice at two or three o'clock in the morning, which was the only time they could get ice time because of the few arenas. As a result, parents began to pressure their city officials to build an arena. Soon every local municipality built one. The construction contract was always determined by competitive bidding. The low bidder got the job. Somehow, we were the low bidder and got one job. When the next arena came out for bids, we had an interesting thing happen to us, or for us. The subcontractor who installed the pipes under the concrete floor and put in the refrigeration system came to see me one day. He said in effect, I have enjoyed working with your people. They are very cooperative. They don't call me until the job is ready, and they make the working conditions such that we can get in, do our job efficiently, and get out. Therefore, we save money when we work for you, as opposed to others who call us before the job is ready for us, which costs us more money, etc. So, as a result, on this next job we are going to give you a $20,000 lower price than the other bidders. Since his contract was one of the largest on the entire job, this gave us a $20,000 advantage over our competitors. With his help, we were low bidder on several more ice arenas in the area. It was a win-win for both of us. We also built the ice arena for the city of Southfield. It was the largest of them all as it not only had a large arena with bleachers and locker rooms, but it had a restaurant and a big outdoor Olympic-size swimming pool. So they were able to use the facility year-round; hockey in the winter and swimming in the summer, using the same locker rooms and restaurant amenities. Some people would say that was a nice gesture that the refrigeration contractor did for us; but I'm sure it was just another blessing from the Lord, all orchestrated for our benefit.

25

A NEW YOUNG EMPLOYEE

I mentioned before about Pam Callam as Marilyn's Pioneer Girl pal and our babysitter, party helper, and good friend of our family along with her mom and dad, Zela (pronounced Zeela) and Gordon. Well, one day when she was seventeen years old and out of high school for the summer, I told her that we were real busy in the office and that we could use her to help us out, just answering the phone and doing general office work. She agreed and came to work for the summer. When she went to finish her senior year in high school, she worked out what was called a co-op program where she went to school until 1:30 p.m. each day and then she came to work for us from 2 p.m. to 6 p.m. She was really smart, and she learned the office procedure very quickly. When it came time to go to college, she selected Michigan State University. As she left to go to college, I said, "Why don't you take some courses in shorthand? It will be a big help to you later in life no matter what you decide to do." At the time she was planning to be a nurse, but somewhere along the way she changed her mind. When school was out in the spring, after one year at MSU, she came back to work for us during the summer. By that time we were growing and doing more and more business. Fred took her under his wing and taught her to be a bookkeeper. She expressed an interest in being able to read blueprints, and all the guys in the office were eager to help her.

At the time, Erv Kamp, the architect, had his office across the hall from ours, and he didn't have a secretary. So Pam moonlighted for him at night and Saturdays, typing the specifications for the various jobs that he was doing. As a result, she became acquainted with the terminology used in the construction business that describes different parts of a building. Within a short time she became quite knowledgeable with all aspects of the construction business and she seemed to like it and working for us. So she did not go back to college. Over the years she became my most valuable employee. Fred taught her so well that in later years he would ask her how to do certain things.

As time went on, she knew more about the details of our business than either Fred or me. She was one in a million. As some of you know, she never was married. It seemed that she just devoted her whole life to helping me. Besides all of her office skills, she became not only an excellent secretary but she became my administrative assistant. She was such a help to me with all the work I did for various organizations and boards that I served on, travel plans, and so on; she always seemed to especially enjoy that part of her job. She could (and still does) do everything.

26

GOD'S PROTECTION

We also built a number of hospitals. It seems like many of them had stories of divine intervention connected with them. One was the Oakwood Hospital in Dearborn. Our job was to add three stories on to the existing ten-story building and then remodel three of the existing floors after all the facilities were moved into the three new floors. So we had to start up at the ten-story roof level. As you might expect, we had to allow the hospital to keep on with its operations, totally unaffected by us and the complicated construction process.

One of the first things we had to do was set up an outside elevator alongside the building around the back and fairly close to a parking area we could access for material deliveries, etc. This was in the days before the big tower cranes that are used today. The elevator was in an open cage and attached to the building in several places for security. We also had a chute erected near the elevator where all the debris would be discarded. The chute stopped a little above the ground so a truck could drive under it, catch the debris, and haul it away. The elevator required a person to operate it. Its motor was located next to the shaft on the ground. By pulling a lever, the elevator would go up or down—a quite simple arrangement once it was set up. One day soon after we got the contract for the job and began setting up the elevator, the business agent for the union of the operating engineers stopped by our office. You should know that the members of their union were the men who operated all kinds of big construction equipment, such as large cranes, bulldozers, scrapers, steam shovels, etc. They were well trained and highly skilled. Every piece of construction equipment that had a motor and required an operator must be operated by an "operating engineer," according to union rules. Their pay scale was among the highest in the industry.

So, the union boss who stopped into my office came to remind me that one of his men from his union would be required to operate the elevator on the Oakwood Hospital job. He said he would be happy to help us find one. I reminded him that was seldom the practice with the operation of construction elevators of this nature because the elevator sometimes only went up or down three or four times a day, and anyone skilled or unskilled could pull the simple lever. We had planned to use one of the masons' helpers whose job it was to mix the mortar down on the ground and load the bricks and blocks on the elevator and then occasionally pull the lever and send the elevator up.

The rules are the rules, he said. I told him the difference in wages between the two rates over a period of perhaps two years, because of the future remodeling we had to do, would probably wipe out our profit on the job. The amount was significant. He said, "Too bad. This kind of work belongs to my men," and he left.

I was devastated. We had not counted on this expense. Nobody did this. This highly paid guy would be sitting around all day long and maybe sometimes pull the lever every hour or two. We were going to work for two years or more on this project without any profit, and if the job was prolonged, we might even lose money. So, as usual in times of trouble, I began to pray. I told the Lord all about the situation (as if He didn't know) and finally said, "Lord, it is in Your hands whatever You want to do. I am helpless."

Well, guess what? About a week later the union boss came back to see me. I thought he was coming to say he had the man all ready for us to put on our payroll. Instead, he said something like this. "I was talking to my wife about you and this project and our rules, and that you seemed like such a nice young man. She said, then why are you making him do this when you don't require it for others?" So he said to me, "Go ahead. We won't require an engineer for such a simple job."

As you might guess, after I thanked him and he left, I went to my desk, bowed my head and thanked the Lord for His mercy and, in this case, His intervention in my business affairs.

There were many similar incidents in various jobs over the years that were too frequent to be call coincidences.

Let me tell you about another hospital job, but a different type of blessing. We had a small job at the Veterans Hospital in Dearborn. We were building an outbuilding to be used as an animal lab where the doctors performed surgery and did other studies on animals. It was about a $450,000 job. While we were finishing up our contract, the hospital came out with plans for a major addition to the hospital. It was about a $2 million job—which in those days would be like a 15 or $20 million job today. We studied the plans and put in our bid. As in all government jobs, the low bidder wins, usually. We were not the low bidder but missed it by only fifteen or twenty thousand dollars. Our superintendent of construction on the animal lab happened to be the superintendent for the construction of the original large hospital while he was working for another contractor years before. He knew all the hospital administrators, and they were disappointed that we didn't get the job. Obviously, so were we. In fact, I remember saying to the Lord, "This is really too bad. We had a nice profit built into this job, and think of how much we could have given to the church and to missions."

One of our many competitors, J. A. Fredman Company, was the low bidder. Along with most bids, the builder comes up with what are called "alternates." These consist of questions and related prices to the work, such as, how much would it cost if we put a marble floor in place of vinyl tile floor in the lobby? Or maybe, how much could we save if the wall in the cafeteria was painted block in place of brick? Sometimes there were eight or ten or more such alternates. Some additions and some deductions. And sometimes, depending on the alternates that were selected by the owner or the architect, the low bidder on the basic job might not be low anymore, particularly if the original base bids were very close. So by manipulation and selection of alternates, the client might have a legitimate choice in the selection of which contractor gets his job. Well, this was the case on the Veterans Hospital job. There were several alternates.

My superintendent said, "Look, I know all the people, including some of their bosses in Washington, D.C. Let me go and talk to them. I'm sure they would like for us to have the job. Maybe by selecting the right alternates, we would be low bidder." So, he did. But nothing changed. We did not get the job, which is how it should have been. But now I'm really disappointed. I said again, "Lord, I don't understand," etc., etc. I finally got over it, and we went looking for the next job.

Then one day a salesman stopped by to see me. We sat down out in the lobby and began to chat. He asked, "Did you hear about United Heat and J. A. Fredman on the Veterans Hospital job?" I said, "No."

Well, he said a most unusual thing happened. It seems that United Heat and Engineering Company, which was the low bidder on all the plumbing, heating, and ventilating work on the Veterans Hospital, pulled a fast one on Fredman. "How's that?" I asked. He said he didn't know all the details, but somehow United Heat overbilled Fredman, and Fredman, therefore, overbilled the government; and when United Heat got paid, he took the overbilled money and went to Mexico. He left Fredman with more work to do than he had money coming to do it with.

I had never heard of such a thing. How could he get his overbilling approved by Fredman, by the architect who had to approve all monthly payments, and then by the government? Nearly impossible! But he did it. The amount that he stole was about $250,000. There was a performance bond on the job, supplied by a large insurance company, which basically said to the government that if the general contractor did not perform his work according to the contract, the insurance company would guarantee that the work got done. This bond, of course, cost the contractor a fee based on the size of the job. We all had to furnish them on government jobs. In this case, the Fredman Company had to either finish the job using their own money, or, if they couldn't, the insurance company would do it with another contractor and go after Fredman for whatever it cost them. Nobody ever wanted to have a bonding company take over and finish your job. It was usually bankruptcy. In this case, $250,000 was involved.

As the salesman was telling me this story, I had such mixed emotions. First, I felt sorry for Fredman. But then I quickly realized that it could have well happened to us, if we had got the job, because United Heat was the low bidder to us; and if we had gotten the job, we would have used them and likely been put in the same disastrous situation. $250,000 at that time would have put us out of business.

This time when the salesman left, I remember going into my office, closing the door and saying, "Lord, I will never again question anything that happens to me. It was Your hand of protection that kept us from getting that job. I didn't understand it at the time, nor was I able to see future events like You can. Thank You, Lord. I am so sorry that I questioned Your actions." Another coincidence? I don't think so.

27

SOME "Ps"

Speaking of protection, perhaps this is a good time to tell you about all the "Ps" that God provides for us as His children that I have come to appreciate over the years. One time I was on an airplane coming into Detroit. In a gentle way, I had been sharing my faith with the fellow sitting next to me who seemed interested. As we got off the plane and were standing together just inside the terminal, he said something like, "I'm interested in what you have been talking about, but I only have a couple of minutes to talk as I have to catch another plane. Can you tell me in two minutes what would happen to me if I asked Jesus Christ to be my Lord and Savior?"

I stumbled around the best I could, trying to be concise, but I'm not sure I did a very good job. I promised to send him some written material.

On the way home in the car, I was thinking about what had just happened; and I asked the Lord to help me and maybe to give me a little track to run on that I could use in two or three minutes to explain the benefits of the true Christian life and to answer the question, "What would happen to me if I became a follower of Jesus Christ?" As I was driving, the Lord gave me an outline that I have used for years. Four words that all begin with "P" that I could tell someone in two minutes. First, you would have "peace." As I said earlier, when I had prayed to receive the Lord and I put my head on my pillow that night, I had a sense of peace, knowing that all was right between God and me. I had a clean slate with him. Real peace of heart and mind.

The second "P" is "pardon"—knowing that God has forgiven me

for all my sin and shortcomings. In fact, pardon may even come before peace. Jesus Christ has pardoned me by His own promises and what He did for me on the cross. I am clean before Him.

The next "P" is "power." Scripture says that when we become a believer in Jesus Christ, the Holy Spirit comes into our lives and gives us power to live just a little above the mundane circumstances of this life—sort of power to cope.

Next is "purpose"—a new purpose for living. To reflect the attributes of the Lord in our daily lives, such as love, joy, peace, patience, gentleness, and so on.

So the four "Ps" that came to me on that drive home were Peace, Pardon, Power, and Purpose. Since then, several other "Ps" have come to play in my life. The one that brought all this to my mind was *protection*. I believe God protects us as His children from things and circumstances that we cannot foresee. This was the case with the Veterans Hospital job. God protected us by not letting us get the job. That became very clear to me when I heard the bad news about United Heat and Fredman. There are other "Ps" that I have also experienced like "priorities." I think God helps us sort out what is best for us. There are a lot of good things in life, but we sometimes have to choose. God helps us with priorities.

I could go on and on about the "Ps." There are several more, like perseverance and patience. But that's enough about "Ps." Maybe you can think of some more that have been helpful to you.

We built a number of buildings of all kinds, and the business grew. At one point, we had fourteen superintendents supervising the jobs all over southeast Michigan. We went as far east as Mt. Clemens, where we built the main post office and a hospital. Our farthest-north project was to Lapeer where we also built the Lapeer County Hospital. We went northwest as far as Lansing where we built an office building for Michigan Bell Telephone Company, and to the west in Ann Arbor, which was the site of an apartment building complex that I will tell you more about later. To the south our limit was to Monroe, where we built a warehouse and utility building, also for the Michigan Bell Telephone Company.

28

LET'S BUILD MORE CARS

In the mid-1960s, the Plymouth assembly plant was located on the east side of Detroit in what was known as the Lynch Road Assembly Plant. The bestselling cars were Chevrolet, Ford, and Plymouth, mostly because they were the least expensive. They were all very competitive. There was only one final assembly line at the Plymouth plant, and they wanted to install another one. The line ran down fairly near to an outside wall. Our job was to enlarge the building so that a parallel line could be added. The construction work was quite simple—building three walls and tying the roofs together. The challenge was to remove the former outside wall that now separated the buildings and not disrupt the production of the cars. Each summer, as I already mentioned, the plants have "model change-over time." It's usually about three to four weeks in July and August. During this time, the assembly line shuts down and is retooled for the new model. So during these three weeks or so, we had to work three shifts around the clock, knock down the old wall, remove the block, brick, and windows, and haul it all away and patch the floor. We did it, and all went well and they could now assemble twice as many cars as before.

During the course of construction, we would meet with several supervisors in the office of the plant manager. Above the door to his office were a red light and a clock with a large sweeping second hand. Any time the assembly line stopped for any reason, the red light would come on. When it did, he would look at the clock and notice the position of the second hand. At that point he was preoccupied and not paying attention as to what was going on in the meeting. If the light went off within a few seconds, he would mentally rejoin the meeting. If it was on for sixty seconds, he was up out of his chair and out into the plant to see what was wrong. In those days one car a minute came off the assembly line. A minute lost was one car that they could never sell and make a profit. After we finished our work, the new conveyors were installed and started up. Now they were able to build two cars per minute.

As a stark comparison, a few years later we had the privilege of taking a tour of the Rolls Royce plant in England. They also had a final assembly line, but you could hardly see it move. They built one car per hour, or eight cars per day. A cute story. While on tour of the plant, there was a man inspecting large leather skins that were going to be used to cover the seats. He had a strong light and a magnifying glass, looking for the smallest blemish. Now and then he would toss one aside as a reject. One of the tourists asked him what they did with those rejects. With a wink, he said, "We sell those to Mercedes!"

29

A LOGISTICS PHENOMENON

It's not always the buildings that we built that were so interesting. It's what went on inside the building that was often of interest. We got a job for the Kmart Corporation to build their regional distribution center in Melvindale. The building itself was not difficult, but it was quite different and the operation that went on inside was amazing, at least to me. The building was large enough to hold four railroad cars on two parallel tracks across the rear of the building, making a total of eight railroad cars inside the building. The entire building was about four feet above grade except for the area where the railroad cars were. Other walls of the building consisted of about thirty overhead doors, side by side, large enough to accommodate thirty semitrailers that were backed up to each door. Each door had a hydraulic leveling device that allowed the floor to be pretty much level with the various-sized trucks. The balance of the large building was vacant except for a small office and a washroom.

Each railroad car had come from a single manufacturer and was loaded with one type of merchandise. For instance, one car might be full of toys, another might be from a textile mill and contained all towels and sheets and soft goods. After we finished our work, another contractor working directly for Kmart came in and installed a complicated system of overhead conveyors onto the extra-heavy steel beams that we had installed. The system went from each railroad car to each of the trucks. The trucks were each going to one or two stores with a variety of merchandise. An employee would open the railroad car door. Then with a forklift truck, they would lay down a large steel plate to bridge the gap (about two feet) between the railroad car and the floor of the warehouse. Then, using the forklift, he would go into the car and remove the merchandise, usually on pallets, and bring it outside of the car and just onto the floor of the building. From there, through the complex conveyor system, it was picked up using straps or cables and hooks and taken to the appropriate truck. Then another load to a different truck, until that railroad car was empty. Then they would open the door of the railroad car next to it and drop another plate between the two railroad cars. The process was started again, working through the empty car. The second car with a different kind of merchandise was unloaded and distributed to the various trucks. No one ever handled one box or package in the entire eight cars. At the end of the day, all eight railroad cars were empty and thirty trucks were on their way to the various stores, all with a variety of items in them that they had ordered; and the big warehouse was completely empty.

I had occasion to visit the building after they had begun operations. I was amazed at how clever and efficient the operation was. They had very few employees. Most of the conveyors were automated and went by themselves, crisscrossing the building and doing the work of probably twenty or thirty people if it had to be done by hand. Once in a while a load would be directed by a person walking alongside the load with the control in his hand hanging from a wire. But it mostly ran by itself. I'm sure that today, with the technology that is available through robots, etc., there are more interesting operations going on; but at the time, this was one of the most interesting that we were a part of.

30

OTHER JOBS

Some of the other jobs were the airport terminal for the city of Pontiac, as well as the immigration center in downtown Detroit for the justice department of the federal government. It was on that job where I met Robert Kennedy, who was the Attorney General. I have pictures of us shaking hands at the groundbreaking ceremony. We built schools, and several churches where we often donated our services or worked for a very small fee. Contrasted to churches, we built the jail for the city of Dearborn. An interesting job! Out in Bloomfield Hills, we built an addition on to an existing nursing home. It was privately owned by a doctor. When it was time for our monthly payment, he would tell me to come out, and he would meet me on the job about 10 a.m. After we inspected the new construction, he would say, "Okay, come with me up to the office and I'll give you a check." To get there, we had to walk down the hall of the existing nursing home. As we did, he would stop at each room and say, "Hello, Mary. How are you today?" At the next room he would say, "Hello, Fred. How are you today?" The reply was usually, "Okay, Doc. I'm doing fine." By the time we arrived at the office, he had put his head into ten or twelve rooms. He then said to me, "You know I can legitimately bill the government for a consultation fee with each of those patients." I was learning how some people abused our government and made enough money to build their own nursing home and even put an addition on to it so that they could cheat even more and make even more money.

In those days, we also had five people in the office estimating and running the jobs from the office. At one point, we had about two hundred employees, including carpenters, brick masons, reinforced steel workers, cement finishers, laborers. Bookkeeping in those days was a nightmare for Pam. Not only did she do the payroll and write out all the paychecks by hand, she had to send reports to all the various unions about each employee. In those days, we had no computers, everything was done by hand. We did have typewriters, so when billing the owners monthly, they often required four or five copies. Pam had to put four or five sheets of carbon paper in her typewriter to produce the copies. Although she was very young and had no experience with all of this, she learned quickly and was a "whizbang" at her job.

Bobby Kennedy, Attorney General, at Groundbreaking Ceremony

31

BIRMINGHAM'S FIRST SKYSCRAPER

One day, the president of the Chamber of Commerce in Birmingham became very concerned. He was also the owner of a real estate company, and he had heard that the B. F. Goodrich Company was planning to build a tire store on one of the main corners in town on Woodward Avenue and Merrill Street. His office was right across the street from the site, and he had visions of people vulcanizing tires in this garage building with ten or twelve garage doors facing Merrill Street. He went to the city and complained. The city people said, "What can we do? The property is zoned commercial, and they want to build a commercial building. They have that right."

The realtor, whose name was Andy, was very upset. He went to the mayor, who was a Ford Motor executive. He told Andy the same thing. "While we don't like it, there's not much we can do."

One of the offices in Andy's real estate firm was occupied by Gordon Callam, who had his own small insurance agency. Andy was complaining about the situation one day to Gordon, and they agreed that something nicer and better should be built on that prominent corner. So somehow they decided to call me out for lunch. Gordon had told Andy he knew me as a potential developer of the lot. When they told me the story, I said, "What do you want me to do? Goodrich is perfectly within their rights."

Well, they went on and on about how it was not right and Goodrich was going to destroy the town. As I thought about it and began to pray, I said, "Have you ever told Goodrich how you feel?" Andy said, "No." I said,

"Let's give it a try. We have nothing to lose." So we made an appointment with the local boss of Goodrich and went to see him. He listened very intently as Andy was explaining his position. Finally, the man said, "Okay. I understand. If you don't want us there, just give our money back and we'll find another location."

I thought Andy was going to fall off his chair. But what an unusual answer to prayer. That was the beginning of God's hand in this whole project. Andy said, "How much do you want?" The gentleman said, "I don't know. Just a minute." He called in his secretary and asked her how much money they had invested in the Birmingham location. She said, "Just a minute." A few minutes later she came back with a list. She said, "This is how much we paid for the land. This is what we paid the lawyer and the realtor and the architect and city, etc." She said the total came to $245,000. The boss said, "Give us $250,000, and we will move on." We thanked him profusely and went outside.

Andy said to me, "There it is. It's all yours. See what you can do with it." I said, "Andy, I don't have $250,000. It will take time to design a building that will fit on the lot and to figure out how to make it profitable. $250,000 is a lot for that size piece of land. We will probably have to have more than a two-story building." Andy said, "Oh my goodness. What are we going to do? We have to get Goodrich the $250,000 pretty soon or they are going to build a tire shop on that corner." So Andy came up with a plan. He said, "We will form a company called the Birmingham Community Development Corporation. We will sell stock at $1,000 per share to all the businesspeople in Birmingham to get the money." He knew everybody in town, since he was president of the Chamber of Commerce. "Then we will hold the land until you can get your ducks in a row and plan a development."

"Good idea," I said. "I'll buy the first five shares." Andy went around to all the merchants in town selling the stock. If anyone hesitated, he would say, "Would you rather have a tire shop on that corner?" He was quite successful, and he sold 150 shares. With that, the local banker said they would put up the last $100,000 and take the property as collateral. Andy said to me, "There it is. Go to work." We soon discovered that with the rent structures in Birmingham, we would have to build a multistory building to make it work financially.

We prepared a plan for a six-story building with the top four floors containing fifty-four apartments and with retail stores on the first level and a basement for parking. The second floor was a problem. The city would not allow apartments on the second floor. So we decided to make it into a mini-mall with small spaces for retailers and others that wanted just a small space. We had about fifteen thousand square feet to rent out to probably fifteen or twenty tenants. It would be serviced by an escalator. When we presented our plans to the city, you would have thought we were asking for a skyscraper. All property in Birmingham was zoned two-story at the time. In 1966, nothing over two stories existed. It was a struggle. There was a lot of opposition to this tall building right in the middle of town. The Chamber of Commerce and the mayor were on our side. Again, if anyone objected, they would say, "Would you rather have a tire shop there?"

We finally made it. The city had to write a whole new zoning ordinance. The state got involved, as it was the first mixed-use building in Michigan. We planned for retailers, residential space, some service shops, and a few offices, including our own, all in this one building.

We had one more problem. The city required more parking than we could provide in the basement. The lot next door to us was owned by a lawyer in town. A tough old guy! There were four stores on the front part and vacant land in the rear. We asked him if he would sell us the rear part of his vacant land. He said, "No." I asked, "Would you like to invest in the project by putting in your land as equity?" He said, "No." I began to pray more fervently. "Lord, if we can't get this additional land, the whole project is doomed."

One day when telling Andy my problem with the lawyer, whom Andy knew very well, Andy asked, "Have you talked to him lately?" I said it had been about two weeks prior that I had been flatly turned down. He said, "Go try him again. Maybe he has mellowed a little." I did, and he seemed very nice and said, "I won't sell you the land, but I will lease it to you for ninety-nine years." Well, a ninety-nine-year lease is tantamount to ownership except that the rent was to be adjusted every five years according to an index. I quickly agreed and asked for one condition. That if he ever decided to sell the four stores, I would have first option to buy them and the land. He agreed, and we were friends for many years until he passed away and we bought the stores and the land from his family.

With that extra land, we were able to make the building larger in the basement and on the second floor. The added space in the basement and the first floor area behind the four stores gave us the required parking. The second floor gave us six thousand more square feet of commercial space. It was at this point that we decided to move our construction company offices from Detroit to Birmingham, on the second floor of the building.

The Merrillwood Building had many obstacles to overcome where, I am convinced, the Lord intervened. In retrospect, it was exactly what the city needed: fifty-four people living in the downtown area who were built-in patrons for the shops and restaurants in town. I think the city officials and merchants also saw this, and they loosened up the zoning restrictions to allow taller buildings. Our cup of blessings was filling up.

The Merrillwood Building

32

ANOTHER CHANGE IN DIRECTION

Not only did we build a lot of commercial and industrial buildings, we built some apartment buildings. We had one customer who would have us build him an apartment building, and after he rented it up, he would sell it and we would build him another one. I concluded that the fellow buying the completed building with it full of tenants and a steady stream of income was the smartest of all of us. In those days he was able to get long-term financing for most of the cost, and with a relatively small down payment, he could easily make the mortgage payments, with some cash left over. Besides every month, his mortgage became less and the value of his building was increasing with inflation. So year by year the value of his investment was looking better and better. If he could keep doing this, he would soon be wealthy, and many did. So we thought maybe we should try one on our own. We knew everybody that had to be involved such as real estate brokers, bankers, etc., and we sure knew how to design and build buildings.

Marilyn's uncle Ray had inherited his mother's old house on Highland Avenue in Highland Park. In those days the street had a variety of buildings on it. There were three or four apartment buildings and a telephone company building mixed in with a few single-family houses. Uncle Ray said, "Why don't we tear down the old house, and I will put it into the deal and let's build an apartment building on the site." He said to me, "You get a mortgage for the construction and do all the work, and we will be fifty-fifty partners." We built a nineteen-unit apartment building and rented it up fairly quickly, and we were now not only builders, we were landlords with a small but steady stream of income; and it didn't take up much of our time.

It was about this time that I started to think that's what we should do more often: build for ourselves. The problem was that we didn't have much cash to be used as down payments. We needed all our cash to keep operating the construction business. So we continued to build for others.

We got a job to build a substantial addition on to the existing Mt. Clemens General Hospital. The existing building had a basement, and the addition was also to have a basement. We dug the big hole and began to lay out the job for the foundations for the outer walls and for the steel columns inside that would support the building. Somehow in the process of the layout, our superintendent got the new building out of square. The foundations didn't properly line up with the existing building. This was discovered by the architect's representative who also had an office at the job site. He supervised our day-to-day work and gave regular progress reports to the owner. We always tried to have a friendly relationship with them and always do the right thing. Fortunately, the error was discovered while we were still putting in the foundations, but the structural steel was already being fabricated; and that process had to be temporarily stopped. The bottom line was that it cost us $40,000 to make the corrections and to make the two buildings fit together properly. This was our projected profit. We wound up building the building for nothing. The superintendent was one of our best and most experienced employees. I determined that if he could make such a costly mistake, imagine what I was exposed to with thirteen other guys out there working on all kinds of complicated structures!

So as I thought about all the risks involved in our type of business, I thought more and more about investment construction. When I approached my two senior officers, Fred who was vice president of finance and a fellow named Chuck who was vice president of construction, with my thoughts, I received two different responses. Fred thought it might be a good idea. But Chuck thought that to make money in investment construction would take a long time. They both worked on a bonus system (along with their regular salary), and Chuck said if the construction company didn't make a significant profit, there would be little or no bonus for him. He didn't like that idea. He wanted to make money now. Not later. I offered to give him a part ownership in each building that we built. And I did. We built another sixty-unit apartment building, and I gave both him and Fred a 15 percent interest in it. He did not like the whole idea, and he quit, taking his secretary and one of our superintendents with him. He started up his own construction business in a different area of Detroit. He was never any competition to us. Interestingly, I heard that a few years later he started to build some buildings for himself. Also, he was quite happy to receive his 15 percent share of the proceeds when we sold the building a few years later.

33

A BAD DECISION TURNED OUT FOR GOOD

One day two young entrepreneurs came into the office with a set of plans for a twenty-four-unit apartment building to be built on West Jefferson in St. Clair Shores. They wanted a price from us for constructing it. After examining the plans and figuring the job, we gave them a bid of $180,000. They said that was too high and that they could get it done for $160,000. I remember explaining to them that was about our cost and that we really didn't want to do the job for nothing. I said, "If you want to talk about $179,000 or $178,000 perhaps we could talk, but not at $160,000. So they thanked me and left. It was all very friendly. They seemed like nice guys. Actually they were brothers-in-law. A few months later they showed up again at the office. They said, "We've got trouble. The contractor that took our job for $160,000 has gone broke. The building is partway up. Many of the subcontractors haven't been paid. The bank won't release the money, and the work has stopped. Can you help us out?"

First, the fact that they came back to see me is remarkable. In most situations like this, the owners would be too embarrassed to go back to the original bidder. They would have looked for a third party to help them out. But they came back to me and said, "You seem like a decent guy. Can we work something out to get the building finished?" I said, "Okay, but it will be a lot more work and trouble now with these disgruntled subcontractors and trying to figure out how much of their work is actually done and what they are entitled to be paid, etc. We will help you, but it will be on a cost-plus basis. You pay us the actual costs plus the same $20,000 that we figured to make in the first place." They said okay, and we started. As it turned out, the bank that was loaning the money was our bank as well. When they found out we were taking over the job, they released the money right away, and we went on and finished the job. There was only one problem. The loan was for $160,000, and that's about what the building cost. And the guys said that they had no money to pay us our $20,000 fee. They were very up front about the whole thing and said they were trying to do the job using the land only as the equity for which they had not paid very much. In other words, they were trying to build the building for little or no money. The fact is, in those days and with generous loans that was sometimes possible. So they were quick to say, "We have no money to pay you but we are willing to give you a 50 percent interest in the project."

This is not exactly what we wanted or needed. We needed the $20,000 to keep operating our construction company. Actually, a 50 percent interest wasn't worth $20,000; but I figured it was better than waiting forever for the $20,000. So I said, okay, under two conditions. You also own the lot across the street where you plan to build twenty-two more units. We will become your partners on this one if we can be your partners on that one too. They had arranged adequate financing on that one already. And, second, that we will become the managers and handle the money.

So, an unholy alliance was formed. I knew better than to become partners with unbelievers. The Bible says very clearly to "be ye not unequally yoked with unbelievers." Most people think this pertains to marriage. But I think it has to do with any kind of "close hookup" or partnership, whether it be marriage or in a business arrangement. In another place it says, "How can two walk together unless they be agreed." But I rationalized and figured I was in a tough spot and had little choice. When the apartments were finished and we started collecting rent, those guys came to the office asking if there could be a distribution and could they get some money out of the project. When they would go to Fred or Pam, they would tell them, no! The few dollars that they saw that we had in the bank was for upcoming taxes and not available. They "bugged" us constantly. At one point I had to loan the partnership a few dollars to pay some bills, and they were constantly wanting to take money out! What's wrong with this picture?

34

HOW ABOUT SOME BIG APARTMENT UNITS?

A s time went on, these guys were good "bird dogs." They found several good pieces of land for development, and they would bring them to us to see if we could make a deal as partners. We said no, but in several cases we agreed to pay them a "finder's fee" and tell them goodbye. They kind of liked this because they were high livers and it took a fair amount of money to live up to their desired lifestyle. They didn't have an office. They pretty much operated out of the trunk of their car where they kept their plans and business papers.

One day, they did us a big favor. They came into the office and told us of an unusual opportunity. They told us about a choice piece of land on Woodward Avenue in Birmingham. It was owned by five partners who began to squabble amongst themselves and couldn't agree as to how to progress with a project of seventy-seven luxury apartments. They had the plans all made and a building permit ready to be picked up at the city hall. All we had to do was pay the fee to the city. The partners were so mad at each other that they wouldn't sell to each other. The only way they could settle their dispute was to sell the entire project to someone else.

There was a mortgage loan available from an insurance company for the construction. The mortgage broker became the central contact and was anxious to keep control of the deal for fear someone would buy it and go elsewhere for the loan and he would lose a commission. We assured him that if we got the deal, we would use his financing arrangement and he would get his commission. So I think he went to work with the owners to try to get us the deal. The plans were for apartments larger than we had ever built. They were of a French provincial design, with very large units. As a result, the price for the land was quite high, $5,000 per unit. Most of the apartments we knew about had a land cost of about $1,000 per unit.

The mortgage broker who was really very nice and quite knowledge-able said that the mortgage company believed that the project would rent up very quickly, even at much higher than existing rents for smaller units. That's why they had offered to loan $1,350,000. The rents for a two-bedroom, two-bath unit would have to be about $200 per month to make it work. The average rents in Birmingham were about $95 to $100 per month, but for smaller units. In fact, there were no apartments in Birmingham large enough to accommodate a dining room table and a buffet. The living rooms were so small that only the minimum amount of furniture could fit. The same was true of the bedrooms. And very few had two bedrooms and none had two baths. So if we went ahead with this project with these big apartments, we would be breaking new ground and charting new waters. But I thought the insurance company was right. I figured that there were a lot of people in the big houses in Bir-mingham and Bloomfield Hills who would like to retire and move into an apartment to avoid lawn work, home maintenance, and all the problems that went with home ownership. The problem was there was no place to go that was big enough to accommodate even a scaled-down amount of their furniture. Nobody ever heard of condominiums at this time. This was 1961 and 1962. So we decided to take the plunge. We paid the two "bird dogs" a small fee and took the plunge. We only had one problem. No money! The total cost was estimated to be $1,500,000. So I needed $150,000 cash. I began to pray. Where was I going to get $150,000? I told some of my Christian friends about the project. They seemed interested. So much so that they told me to go ahead, make the deal, and they would furnish the $150,000. An amazing answer to prayer! Our deal was this: the four or five of them would guarantee the money, and I would do all the work. We would be fifty-fifty partners with the understanding that the first cash that came out of the project would go to them until they got their $150,000 back. After that, when no one had any cash invested, we would split fifty-fifty from then on. We were to be builders and managers and keep all the books, for which we would be paid a fee and have full control and make all the decisions. They would be "silent partners," just supplying the front money.

They came up with $100,000 very quickly, and we got started. The project was very successful. In fact, we had just put up a sign with a picture of the buildings; and as we were tearing down an old house, the big cars began to slam on the brakes and turn into the driveway. They were mostly ladies wanting to see a brochure. The construction super-intendent, Ernie Ryan, who was a real personable fellow, told them that the project was so new that we didn't have brochures yet. Well, they said they wanted him to show them the plans, which he did. They would say, "I want this one right here. Put my name on it." He began to make notes and send them to us in the office to follow through with the applications and other paperwork. So many people were stopping to see him that one day he called me and said, "You've got to get someone out here to help me. These prospects are taking up all my time, and I don't have time to build the buildings."

Pam's mom and dad, Zela and Gordon Callam, were slated to be the resident apartment managers. But they were not planning to start for another year or so, after the project was completed. So I called Mrs. Cal-lam and said, "I need your help now," and told her the problem. So Ernie fixed up a small office for her in the back of the construction trailer, and she went to work. She would meet the prospects (mostly ladies) and take them into the construction trailer office and show them the plans. If they were interested, she would help them to select an apartment and fill out the application. As time went on and the buildings progressed, she would take them out into the construction site with only framing in place and climb up into the actual apartment and show them the view that they would have. She went through dirt, mud, and sometimes snow, doing her job. She was about sixty years old at the time and most of her prospects were also mature ladies and they hit it off real well together.

By the time the buildings were finished, we only had three units left—a one-bedroom, a two-bedroom, and a three-bedroom. So the last prospect still had a choice of units. Mrs. Callam had such a delightful personality that as she was showing the apartments, many of the ladies asked her where her apartment was to be located. She had told them that she was also going to be the resident manager. When she told them, many of them wanted to be located near her apartment. She was much more than a resident manager. She took care of them by taking in packages for them, letting people into their apartments, and taking them chicken soup when they were sick.

There were lots of interesting stories regarding Burlington Arms. When the first building was nearing completion, we furnished three apartments as models. One of the five original owners was an interior decorator named Wallace Newton. Most of his clients were quite wealthy. He was an older gentleman and we had kept in touch with him. He still liked the project a lot, even though he was no longer an owner. He asked if he could furnish and decorate the models at his own expense, hoping to get some business from the tenants. We said, okay. And he decorated three of them. We paid for the carpet and drapes. I think he emptied out his store and his warehouse. He had so much furniture in them that we could hardly get through with prospective tenants. What it did do, though, was to show how much furniture one could get into the apartment. It wasn't all bad, as many of the tenants were coming from big houses and with a lot of furniture.

One day a little old lady came through the models and expressed an interest in renting. She looked at both the one-bedroom and the two-bedroom models. I happened to be there, and I was helping her make up her mind. She said she was a widow. She finally said she had better call her trust officer and see which one she could afford. She asked me if I would be willing to meet with him and explain the details. She was quite elderly. Her name was Mrs. York. So an appointment was made, and the trust officer came out to the apartments. I was in the model with her when he drove up out front. She said, "That's him." I went out to the parking lot to meet him and introduce myself. As he was getting out of his car, he looked all around at the entire complex and he said to me, "How much are you asking for it?" I said, "For what?" He said, "The building." "Oh," I said, "the building is not for sale. Mrs. York just wants to know if she can afford to rent a one-bedroom apartment or a two-bedroom apartment."

He chuckled and said, "She brought me all the way out here from downtown Detroit to ask me that? She could afford to buy the whole building." We went into the models, and she showed him the two options. Of course he advised her to take whichever one she wanted. The rental price was of no consequence. She finally settled on the one-bedroom and wound up actually renting the model apartment. Her trust officer told me as he was leaving that years ago her husband owned several small telephone companies in several communities in Ohio. He sold them to AT&T for stock; and before he died, he was one of the largest stockholders in AT&T. But his dear widow had no idea that she was a multimillionaire. She lived in that apartment until she passed away in her nineties.

Well, as I said, Burlington Arms was very successful. It was the first apartment development in the area where people could come and live in an apartment and enjoy life with room for many of the items that they had come to enjoy in their homes. The kitchens had room for a small table. The living room could accommodate a fair amount of large pieces. The master bedroom was thirteen by seventeen and had a small dressing area and private bath. They all had nice balconies. We seldom had a vacancy, and often we had a waiting list. One day I met a lady who said to me, "I'm going to become one of your tenants at Burlington Arms." I said, "Really? I think we have a waiting list to get in." She said, "I know. But last week we were playing cards with my friend, Mrs. So and So, and she told us that in November she is moving to Florida. So she took me to meet Mrs. Callam, and I will be taking her apartment."

The partners got their investment back in about three years; and from then on we split everything fifty-fifty. We kept the building for over forty years and sold it for many times what it cost. My mom and dad lived there the last thirty-five years of their lives. My dad lived to be a hundred. It was the largest living quarters that they had ever lived in during their entire lives.

One day, the "bird dogs" came into the office all excited. They had found a wonderfully located thirteen-acre parcel of land in Ann Arbor. It was about a mile from the University of Michigan and just off of a main road. It was zoned for 160 units. They really wanted to be partners with us, as this would make a great development. I saw two things: one, the potential of the property in Ann Arbor; and second, a chance to get a divorce from these two guys. So I said, "Look, you guys need income. I need vacant land to keep my construction company busy and to develop a long-term income. So I'll give you my interest in the forty-two unit finished apartments out on the east side" (which were by now producing a nominal cash flow), "and you give me your rights under the option on the thirteen acres." So they thought that was a good idea, and we did it. What began as a wrong decision to become partners with these fellows, out of what I thought was necessity, actually turned out okay. I am sure the Lord knew my heart and provided a way out, as He often does.

We continued to be friends with those two guys. They were always good-natured and sometimes even funny. One day years later, I ran into one of them in a store, and I inquired about an office building that I knew they were developing. I asked how it was coming along. He said, "It's great. Everything is wonderful. We finished the building about three months ago, and we're doing fine except for one thing that we forgot." I said, "What's that?" He said, "To get some tenants!"

Burlington Arms Apartments, Birmingham, Michigan

35

A BIGGER HOUSE

The Lord has worked in so many ways and at so many times throughout my business life and the various projects. Let me tell you another story as to how He provided the location for a new home for our family. We were thinking about moving from our Detroit home out to the Birmingham-Bloomfield area. It was 1963. There were a number of factors at play. The Highland Park Baptist Church had started a branch in Southfield, and they had purchased twenty-eight acres of land on Lahser Road at Twelve Mile Road. The long-range plan was to move the entire church to that site. We thought it would be convenient to live closer to the church. We now had three children, and the two girls were sharing one bedroom. Mimi was at our house a lot of the time, and we thought that if we had a house big enough, she and her daughter, Ginny, who lived with her, could live with us. Ginny was in college and wasn't home very much. With all of these thoughts, we began to look for a house to buy.

I really didn't want to go through the process of building a house. At that time we were real busy in our commercial business, and I was sure that there would be a house available that would meet our needs. Another criteria was that we needed a space for the sixty to seventy women to meet at Mothers' Club on Monday nights. We also needed a three-car garage for our two cars plus one for Mimi. We looked and looked. Nothing was available in Bloomfield Hills that met our needs. During the search, the kids said that there were no sidewalks in that area. They said, "We won't have anywhere to ride our bikes." They were ten, eight, and three years old.

After one frustrating day with the realtor, we were on our way home, driving south on Cranbrook Road. As we crossed Quarton Road, we noticed a vacant lot on a corner where there was a bulldozer on the site pushing up the topsoil to save and use later for the lawn area. There was a sign on the lot that read, "Lot for Sale or Will Build to Suit." The kids got real excited because there were sidewalks. It was in one of the nicest subdivisions in the area called Bloomfield Village. I called the number and made an appointment with the owner/builder. He showed me the plans of the house he was planning to build. I asked him if he would just sell the lot. He hesitated a minute and said that he guessed he would. He gave me a price, and we agreed; and we bought the lot. His name was Ralph Scheel. He lived just a couple of blocks from the lot, and we met at his home. As I was leaving his house after we had closed the deal, he said rather wistfully, "I think I made a mistake." I said, "Why's that?" He said, "You seem like a decent guy. I should have insisted that I build the house for you." I said, "Well, maybe it's not too late. Perhaps we can work together." I had found out that he was a good builder with a reputation for building quality houses. So we made a deal. I would pay him a fee, and I would pay all the bills. He might get some of the subcontractors and I might get some. He would be on the job all the time and supervise the construction. We moved a small construction trailer on the site and put in a telephone. He never had anything like that. He was so pleased. The house that he had approved for construction was a Southern Colonial style with four big round columns on the front porch, two stories high. It was about as different in style from the house we then lived in as it could be.

We changed the floor plan somewhat and made the house a little larger and added another bay to the garage. He was a big help and made a lot of good suggestions. He got all good-quality skilled workmen. As I got acquainted with Ralph, one day I asked him a question. "How come this lot was still not built on after the whole neighborhood was built up years before and with mature trees?" I found out later that the house next door to us was twenty-four years old. We were sure that somehow the Lord had saved this beautiful corner lot just for us in this lovely subdivision with its winding streets and all those nice trees.

He told me the story. The entire subdivision, which is about a mile square, was owned and developed by a man named Judson Bradway. He was very particular about the kind of houses that could be built. For instance, no garage doors could face the street. All the houses had to pass his personal inspection as to exterior design. As a result, Bloomfield Village was one of the nicest areas in all of Michigan.

On this particular lot the setback requirement was eighty-five feet from Cranbrook Road and seventy-five feet back from the cross street, Tottenham. Incidentally, all the streets were named after towns in England, which Marilyn liked as all her ancestors were from England. The lot size was about three hundred feet by two hundred feet. When you excluded all the land required out front for the setbacks, it didn't leave too much room for the house to have a decent backyard, especially with the garage door requirement. Also, he required that the house face Cranbrook Road, which was the main street. The lot had fallen into several different hands over twenty or thirty years, with each one failing to figure out how to place a decent-sized house on the lot and meet all the restrictions, and especially facing Cranbrook Road.

Judson Bradway was Ralph Scheel's uncle, and Ralph convinced his uncle that if ever that lot was to be developed properly, he should modify the restrictions and allow the house to be built on an angle, facing the corner. Ralph showed his uncle his plan, and the old man finally agreed and allowed the modification. It was just about that time that we came along. Another coincidence? I doubt it! The way the house sits on the lot and its exterior design is one of the most attractive houses in the whole subdivision. At this writing, we have lived there over forty-seven years.

36

OBSESSION

Ralph and I became good friends and after a while I asked him why he was willing to sell me the lot. It turned out to be a story about obsession with material things—and I learned a lot from that story. Ralph said that he had recently built a big custom home up in Bloomfield Hills, and the owners had refused to pay him the last $50,000. They complained about things not being done right or defects. As a result, Ralph had to sue them. The dispute had gotten so bad that the owner would not let Ralph's workers into the house to make any adjustments or repairs. It was coming to court soon, and Ralph asked me if I would be an expert witness on his side. When I asked what I had to do, he told me that there was going to be a meeting at the house the next week with the two attorneys and two experts from each side to go through the house and give an opinion on the three typewritten pages of complaints.

We all met, and the lady of the house showed us through the house, pointing out all the defects. It was ridiculous! A carpenter and a painter could have fixed everything on the list in about three or four hours. There were doors that were slightly sticking and spots that needed to be touched up by a painter. One item was a scratch on the window in the breakfast room. I couldn't find it, and I asked the lady to point it out to me. She said, "It's down there about six inches from the floor." When I still couldn't see it, she said, "Well, you can only see it at about seven o'clock in the morning on sunny days when the sun hits it just right!"

We were alone for a moment, and I asked her, "Ma'am, what is really the trouble here?" She replied, "I'll tell you! My husband and I both worked for over forty years, saving up our money for this house. We bought this lot years ago. It's one of the nicest lots in the area, and we have been saving all this time for our dream home. We hired the best architect, and we thought we had the best builder. We wanted a perfect house. It has been our lifelong project, planning for a perfect house, and it is not perfect!" I tried to tell her that there never has been a perfect building but that hers came about as close as any I had ever seen. She was not satisfied. She was obsessed with a dream that was impossible to attain. And to think her obsession was with a "thing." Her whole life was out of whack. I tried to convince her to "let it go." "It's not worth all the agony you are causing yourself and others."

I learned a new lesson: don't get obsessed with things or perfection of things. It can ruin your life. It had hers. To end the story, they went to court and her lawyer made a big deal about the defects, and we tried to show that they were minimal. But, as usual, when the judge doesn't know who to believe and what to do, he just splits it down the middle. He ordered them to pay Ralph $25,000. As a result, Ralph probably built the house for nothing. He didn't want to run the risk of that kind of a situation with us, so he just sold us the lot. As it turned out, it was good for both of us and very good for us. By the way, I heard later that the lady passed away about three years later with a heart attack. I'm not surprised. She put a lot of strain on that heart. What a shame! All that work, saving, hoping, dreaming about a "thing."

37

OUR NEW HOME

O ur house has not only been a wonderful home for our family, but it continued to be the place for many more parties and gatherings of our friends; and, later, our children's friends and even later our grandchildren's friends.

The grandchildren were always inviting their friends to sleep over. Of course, young people come and go at all hours and just recently during a school break, I came into the kitchen one morning. There was a young lady whom I didn't know sitting there having breakfast. She looked up at me and said, "And who are you?" I said, "I live here. Who are you?" Of course, I knew she was one of my granddaughter's friends who had come in with her late the night before from college. Wonderful!

Marilyn continued her hostessing, even more so with a bigger house. We even had a full kitchen in the basement when the dinner parties were too much for the upstairs. Not only was it a warm and comfortable family home, the layout made it very nice for entertaining; and entertain we did! It had a mother-in-law area on the first floor, plus four bedrooms upstairs. Each child had his or her own room, with the girls sharing a tub and toilet room. They each had their own sinks and vanities. We even had a room for Ginny, Marilyn's sister. Ralph had insisted that the house have a maid's room. We told him we didn't have a maid. He said it was necessary for resale. It became Ginny's room and later Marilyn's office.

We put in a pool after the first year, and that helped to attract even more young people to our house over the years. We thought it was all just perfect for us. And oh, the cost? You might be interested. We paid Ralph $20,000 for the lot. He built the house for $65,000. We went to a local furniture store to buy all new carpet, drapes, and furniture, as the furniture in the old house was all of contemporary design and would not fit at all in this new Colonial-style house. It all cost $15,000. So, for $100,000 in 1964, we were able to build and furnish a wonderful new home. What a blessing from the Lord!

Just another word about our dear friend Zela Callam. We had just moved into our new home on Cranbrook Road. It was January 15, 1965. I guess we could have moved in before Christmas, but it would have been a "push" and at a busy time of the year. So we decided to wait and do it more leisurely, two weeks later. Any move is hectic. But this one was major for us, with three children, getting into a new school plus all the details of the move itself and, of course, a new house. So, as moving day ended and the movers left, here comes Zela Callam with her husband, Gordon, and daughter, Pam, with a wonderful, fully prepared dinner. It was like a second Thanksgiving with turkey, stuffing, and all the trimmings. She, along with help from Marilyn and Pam, set the dining room table after finding the boxes with the tablecloth, dishes, and silverware, and served a sumptuous meal. That's just the way she was—always thinking of what she could do to help someone else, and then going about it with a loving spirit.

1400 N. Cranbrook Road

38

BEFORE YOU CALL,
I WILL ANSWER YOU

Let me tell you a quick story how the Lord confirmed the "divorce" from our former partners and blessed the Ann Arbor project. But before I do, I should tell you that in all of the thirteen projects that we developed over the years, every one of them had at one point some incident or a hurdle or situation that seemed insurmountable and threatened the viability of the project. Arbor Village was one of them where God had a better answer.

As I said, when we purchased the property, it was zoned for 160 units. We closed the deal naturally expecting to build 160 units. However, when we had our preliminary discussions with the city, they informed us of a problem. They said that there was a fairly large subdivision of homes behind our property and there needed to be another ready access to the main road. The city believed the best plan would be to cut a city street right through the middle of our property. When I complained that the city couldn't do that, they, in effect said, "We can do anything we want." When I also told them they would be lowering the value of our land because we wouldn't be able to get as many units as we had planned, I thought perhaps now we could get only one hundred units, if we were lucky.

I was very upset, to say the least. I remember thinking, "I'll bet those guys who sold me the land knew about this and were trying to pull a fast one on me." The city assured me that was not the case, that this was a new city development plan, and that they were sorry.

"You're sorry," I said. "My land has just gone down in value because of your decision. Why don't you put a road through someplace else?"

While I was both praying and fuming, my landscape planner, Carl Johnson (no relation), said to me, "Take it easy. Calm down. Let's see what we can do."

There was a section in the planning ordinance that referred to something called a PUD, or Planned Unit Development. It basically says that if you have ten or more acres of land, you can go to the city with a PUD, and if the city likes it, they, in effect, will throw the zoning book away and you can build that development only and with that developer only. Carl knew of this and said, "Let me see if we can work something out." Carl was a fine Christian gentleman and was well liked by the Ann Arbor city officials. He was also an adjunct professor at the University of Michigan and a good friend. We had used him and his firm before.

After a little time, he came up with a plan showing the street going right through the center of our property, just as the city wanted. The plan was to build our project in two phases: eighty-six units on one side of the street and 156 units on the other side, for a total of 242 units. It was eighty-two units more than we originally planned. The city thought it was great and issued the permit. We were off and running. It turned out to be one of our finest projects. Again, the Lord provided things that were above and beyond our expectations. As a future bonus, the city decided to have a city bus come down the street with a bus stop on our property. The bus went by the university and to downtown Ann Arbor, making our apartments a very desirable place to live. Because we built the apartments in phases, I was able to handle the down payment myself, and I wound up as the sole owner of the project. We did not have any students as tenants except for a few grad students, but we had a number of professors and university personnel. We also had a number of retirees. It also was a very successful project. More blessings in my cup.

39

AN UNUSUAL OPPORTUNITY

A nother thing that I think that confirms God's hand in the direction of my life is that I never went out looking for projects to build. Every one of them was brought to me by someone else. I don't remember ever getting in my car and going out looking for a piece of land for a potential development. I'm convinced the Lord brought them all to me. A lot of opportunities came along that we did not take, but all thirteen that we did develop were brought to us by someone else. Very interesting!

One day a fellow came into the office with a set of plans for three hundred units in Westland, just a few feet north of Hudson's Westland shopping center. He represented the owner of the land, who was out of Toledo, Ohio. How he came to me, I have no idea. Only God knows. The owner was a company that manufactured prefabricated homes and components for apartments. They made roof trusses and prefabricated walls that would come to the job site and be erected by a crane. For some reason, they wanted to sell the land to someone who would purchase the components from them. The buildings as designed were very attractive Colonial design of red brick with pillars on all the porches and white trim, really very nice. The price was $300,000, which was $1,000 per unit. A fair price and a very good location. The problem was their condition that we buy the prefabricated components from them. So I said, how about this: we will get some bids from some carpenter contractors and lumber dealers to build the buildings conventionally and compare the costs with what you want to charge us for the same work. And if our prices are lower, then we don't have to buy from you. They said okay. And they were sure they could beat our method of conventional on-the-job construction.

As it turned out, our prices were considerably less. They didn't know that the construction methods in the Detroit area were much like the ones used in the automobile industry, which were, therefore, very efficient and cost-effective. When they verified our costs, they couldn't believe them. But they accepted them, and we were free to build the buildings our own way. We decided to build the project in three phases of one hundred units in each phase. Here again, we had a slight problem. No money. We had used all of our funds to build Arbor Village. We were able to get good financing for the Westland project, but we still needed cash.

I didn't want to look for partners for the project, as I was not sure of its success; and I didn't want to have disappointed investors. So, to raise cash, I decided to sell a portion of Arbor Village. Because it was a proven project, and I was sure the partners would get a fair return on their money, I decided I would sell shares at $12,000 each for a 1 percent interest and that I would sell no more than 45 percent so I could retain control. I promised the investors a 10 percent guaranteed annual return for five years. If there was ever not enough cash flow to give them 10 percent, I would just take it out of my 55 percent share. As it turned out, there was always enough without using my shares. This raised over $500,000 and we proceeded on the Westland project as 100 percent owner.

The first one hundred units rented up really fast, and the mortgage company and I decided to build the balance of two hundred units all at one time, in order to save money even if it took awhile to fill up two hundred more units. We did, and we soon filled up and within a few years we had a waiting list. They were more modest apartments in size: 150 one bedrooms and 150 two bedrooms, with one bath. It was a very attractive project and proved very successful.

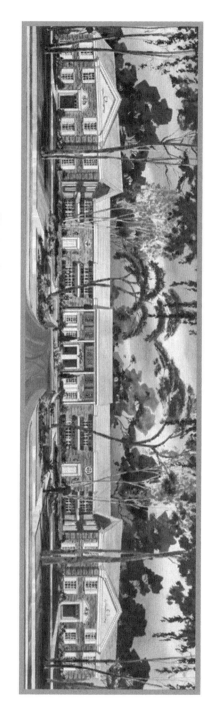

Westland Colonial Village Apartments, Westland, Michigan

40

TAKING TIME-OUT

After developing all these apartment complexes, all of which were doing quite well, we developed a small strip center in Southfield with about twenty stores. I'll tell you how that turned out later on—how it became a legacy for our three kids. We built a few other buildings for other people, but mostly on a cost-plus basis. We weren't very aggressive about seeking new work. We just did what came our way.

With all the properties producing a steady income, I was forty-one years old, and we had enough income to retire except that we had to manage the properties, which was much less stressful than developing them. I figured I was about halfway through my productive life, with twenty years behind me and maybe twenty years ahead of me. And maybe it was time to reevaluate my life and see if the Lord had something different for me to do with the rest of my life. Maybe we should get away from the business for a while and just sit down, pray, meditate, and give the Lord time to give me some direction. At that point, the business, with the good people I had, could just about run itself. Also, we had a desire for our three children to be in good Christian schools, and there were none in our area.

So we bought a home on the water in Ft. Lauderdale, Florida, and took our small boat and a few personal things and moved. The home was furnished. We put our three children, Colleen, fifteen, Kevin, thirteen, and Karen, eight, in Christian schools. Colleen went to a Christian prep school near Orlando. I came back to Detroit for a few days each month for meetings, etc. We lived there for an entire school year. After all the Bible reading, praying, and meditating, I received no word, no message, no indication of any changes I should make in my life. So we sold the house and came home. My mom and dad lived in our house while we were gone. One indication for us to come back was that our church started a Christian school, and we enrolled Kevin and Karen in the opening year. Colleen was still in a Christian school near Orlando, Florida, where she was in high school.

The year we lived in Ft. Lauderdale was interesting. We had heard of the Coral Ridge Presbyterian Church and Dr. D. James Kennedy. It was their Christian day school that Kevin and Karen attended. We started attending the church and became acquainted with "Jim," as he told us to call him. His daughter, Jennifer, also attended the school. She was in the same class as our Karen. They became good friends. With last names that started with J and K, they were often seated together. After a while, Jennifer was at our house or Karen was at their house one or two nights a week. We became good friends with Jim and Ann Kennedy.

Jim had come to Ft. Lauderdale to establish a Presbyterian church. It was like a missions church. He started with a very small group and eventually saw it grow to a very large church with a well-known television program. The reason for the growth was largely due to a ministry of evangelism. The church grew because of new believers. If anyone visited the church, someone from the church would call on them in their home. They were encouraged to ask two basic questions. First, they would ask, "If you were to die tonight and stand before the Lord tomorrow morning and He asked you, 'Why should I let you into My heaven?' what would you say?" Most responses were something like, "Well, I think I have been a pretty good person. I think I am better than a lot of people. I never killed anyone. I've been a good husband or wife . . ." and so on. Then the visitor would ask, "Just how good do you think you have to be to qualify for heaven?"

With this, most people didn't know what the standard was. Many said there is no way to know until you get there, and God will decide. Then they would ask, "Don't you think that's kind of scary to go through life not knowing whether or not you are going to heaven?" Many would say, "I just don't think about it." Then the question was asked, "Wouldn't you like to know for sure that you were going to heaven?" As you might guess, many would say, "Sure, but how can that be?" At this point the visitor would share with them the basic gospel message: that it's not what we do; it's what Jesus Christ has already done. All of us are sinners from birth. Everybody has done something wrong. No one is perfect or deserves heaven, which is a perfect place. So God, knowing that, sent His Son, Jesus, to pay the price for our sin by dying on the cross. All we have to do is to acknowledge that and, by faith, trust Him; and the by-product is eternal life in heaven. Most people would say, "It's that easy?" And with a simple prayer of confession and sincere belief, the Bible, God's own Word, says we are made clean before God and become His children with the gift of eternal life. It is not what we do. It is all by faith!

As you might guess, many people prayed that prayer and began attending the new church where they were fed spiritually and their faith began to grow and become stronger. As a result, the church grew and grew with new believers. In fact, Jim wrote a book called *Evangelism Explosion*, and many churches used the program to train their people how to simply share the gospel with others.

One other story about one person who was a member of the church. There was a group of five guys who played cards every Friday night. They played at their different homes. Sometimes the game would go on until two or three o'clock in the morning because they didn't have to go to work on Saturday. One night they got carried away, and the game went on until 5 a.m. When they finally finished, one of them said, "Why don't we all go out for breakfast?" Then someone reminded him that most restaurants didn't open until 6 a.m. Sort of in jest, one of them said to the fellow in whose home they were, "How about you wake up your wife and ask her to make breakfast for us?" He said, "Are you kidding? She would kill me." Another one said, "You know, I bet if Bill here called his wife, Ann, she would get up and do it for us." Another one said, "Are you kidding?" as he looked at Bill. Bill said, "Yeah, she probably would." He said, "I don't believe it. I dare you to call her."

So Bill went to the phone and called his wife, Ann, and asked her. She said, "Okay. Give me about forty-five minutes and come on over." They did, and as they walked into Bill and Ann's house, they could smell the bacon frying and the coffee brewing. They all sat down to a lovely complete breakfast. As Ann was pouring additional coffee, the skeptical guy said, "Ann, I have to ask you a question. What on earth would make you get up at five o'clock in the morning and serve a bunch of bums like us such a lovely meal?"

With that, she put the coffeepot down and walked over beside her husband, Bill. She put her arms around his shoulder and said, "You know, Bill here is not a believer in Jesus Christ. Therefore, he is not going to heaven to enjoy all the benefits that God has promised for us for all eternity. The only joy and pleasure that he will ever know is what he experiences in this life. I love him very much, and therefore I want to do whatever I can to make his life here on earth as comfortable and happy as I can, because this is the best he'll ever know." With that, the table went silent. Finally, Bill said, "That's just the way she is."

The story has a good ending. Bill plus two others became believers in Jesus Christ because they saw demonstrated a life that reflected the love for people that can only come from having a proper relationship with Him! Ann's actions for an hour or so were so unusual and unnatural that they spoke volumes to those guys about real love, more than a four-hour lecture or an entire book on the subject. Remember: "Nobody cares how much you know until they know how much you care!"

41

BIRMINGHAM PLACE

After we all got home from Florida, I didn't have much to do, except I was still the chairman of the board of CBMC of U.S.A. It stands for Christian Business Men's Committee. I'll tell you more about that later.

One day I got a call from a member of the Birmingham City Commission. He asked for my help. Here was his problem. Located in downtown Birmingham, about a block south of our Merrillwood Building, was a large parcel of land. It bordered on two main streets and took up most of the entire block. On it was an old bus terminal that was abandoned. It was terrible looking, a real eyesore. It was owned by SEMTA, Southeast Michigan Transportation Authority. SEMTA had built a new terminal out in Troy, and they wanted to sell the old building. They had borrowed $950,000 from the federal government to build the new terminal, and they needed $950,000 from the old building to pay off the feds. The land was not worth that much, and they had no "takers."

There was good news and bad news. The good news was it was one of two parcels of land that was zoned for a fifteen-story building. The bad news was that a developer had built a fifteen-story building on the other piece in the next block. It was an ugly, all-concrete building that no one liked. So the community told the city officials if they ever allowed anything like that again in their city, they would run them out of town. The city rezoned the SEMTA property back down to two stories. SEMTA was furious. "You can't do that to us," they said to the city. "We couldn't sell the property when we had zoning for fifteen stories. How in the world are we going to be able to sell it with two-story zoning? We're going to sue you!"

Then a fellow came along to SEMTA and offered to pay them the $950,000 if he could get his business plan approved by the city. His plan was to leave the buildings as they were and open a flea market. The city promptly rejected his plan. They wanted the buildings torn down. So SEMTA said to the city, "We're going to sue you now for sure! You not only rezoned our property down to two stories, but you have stopped a legitimate sale."

So a city commissioner called one day and asked to meet with me. He came and asked for my advice concerning the property. That was a real compliment. I had good relations with the city. I had built three very attractive buildings in the city and remodeled a couple more, but I hardly considered myself a consultant. After listening to his dilemma, I suggested that the best use of the property would be for a bank or some user who wanted a prominent location and didn't care how much the land cost, because there was no way anyone could build a two-story building on it and rent it out at market rates and afford to pay $950,000 for the land. Economically, it wouldn't work. The commissioner was convinced that we were telling it like it was. But what to do? The city was about to be facing a lawsuit. In desperation he asked, "What would it take? How high would a building have to be to make it work?" I said, "I don't know but let me do some calculations." I couldn't believe it. Here I was advising the city. I was impressed that they had that much confidence in me.

So at my own expense, I contacted an architect whom I know very well and who had designed the Merrillwood Building, and we made some sketches and corresponding calculations. If the building was to be all apartments, which was the best use for it, we determined that it would have to be twelve stories to be economically feasible. When the city official heard that, he was in a quandary. In view of that other tall building and its negative history, he wasn't sure the city would approve another building that tall, even twelve stories high, no matter how attractive it was. He thought ten stories would be the most, and even that would be difficult to get approved. We went back to the drawing board literally and came up with a ten-story building. But, to make it work, it would have to have two floors of offices and six floors of apartments and three levels of parking. The offices were necessary to produce higher rents per square foot.

When it was presented to the planning board, it got mixed reviews. Some thought it might work, but others thought it was still too tall. But when the opposition began to prevail, some others would say, "If we don't approve this building, we could have a lawsuit on our hands from SEMTA." If SEMTA prevailed in the lawsuit, the city would be forced to accept fifteen-story zoning plus perhaps damages. Keep in mind that all this time we were only acting as consultants. Then the official said to me, "If we can get this building approved by the city council, would you build it?"

At this point, I was pretty much out of the building and development business. We were just managing our properties, and I didn't have much motivation to take on another big project. In fact, it would be the largest one we had ever done, and it could be quite risky. I didn't want to risk all that I already had. So as I prayed about it, I decided that if I could get an adequate mortgage and some investors who would be willing to put up the equity money, I would do it.

The project was to cost sixteen million dollars. We found a mortgage company, New York Life Insurance Company, that agreed to a $12 million mortgage, so we had to raise $4 million in cash. Besides, we had to get SEMTA to wait until we could get all our city approvals before I would commit to give them $950,000 for the land. That turned out to be a story in itself. SEMTA was being pressured to sell the property, but they had no prospects willing to pay anywhere near the $950,000 price. But they wanted to proceed anyway. Being a governmental agency, they couldn't sell any properties without competitive bids. They decided to open it up for bids, which had to be public and out in the open. The day the bids were due, I went downtown to their offices, along with the mayor of Birmingham who, at that time, was a woman. They opened the bids in front of their board of directors and anyone else who wanted to attend a public meeting. The chairman read the bids. There were only two. The first was for $750,000 with no stipulations or conditions. Our bid was for $950,000, but it was subject to us getting all the approvals necessary from the city of Birmingham. Some members wanted to take the $750,000 as a sure deal and be done with it. Others said, "But where are we going to get the other $200,000 to pay the feds?" At that point, the mayor spoke on our behalf and told the board that she was pretty sure that the city would approve our project. The board argued back and forth; and finally the chairman asked for a vote. Someone made a motion to accept the $750,000 bid. The vote was five to four against. Then someone made a motion to accept our bid on an "if come" basis, and they voted five to four to accept it. So that was one hurdle. I thought maybe the Lord was in this deal. Now all we had to do was to convince the city to approve our plan and to raise $4 million in cash. The city people pretty well carried the ball for us, and after many meetings and with the threat of the lawsuit hanging over their heads, they sort of reluctantly approved it with some saying it was the lesser of two evils.

I thought I had enough friends and former happy investors that I could raise about $2 million. The plan was to sell shares at $100,000 each. About that time we had just finished building a cluster of condominiums for a very wealthy client out in Bloomfield Hills. He sold all the condos and was a happy camper. We told him about the project, and he said he would like to put up two million dollars and be a 25 percent partner. I thought it was going to be easy to raise the $4 million with one fellow taking half of it. Incidentally, this deal was to be like some of the others. I would do all the work, and others would put up all the money, and we were to be fifty-fifty partners. But I wouldn't get any of the income until the money partners had received all their investment back. But I would be the boss and make all the decisions.

So he wrote us a check for $2 million and took a copy of the prospectus (the business plan and details) home with him. About a week later he called and was all agitated and said he wanted his money back. When I asked him what was wrong, he said he had read the prospectus and it said that I was not putting any money into the deal. I said, "That's right. I told you from the beginning how it was structured." He said he wanted me to put in the same amount as he was. When I told him that wasn't the deal, he wanted his money back and said he was going to get a lawyer and sue us.

Well, he had already signed a paper saying he understood the arrangements, and actually we were entitled to keep his money. But I didn't. I said, "Come on over and we will give you your money back." He did and we did. Now we were back to zero in the way of investments. I remember asking the Lord, "Are You sure this is what I should be doing?" Somehow it seemed the right thing to do, so I went ahead. I called my friends and other investors and, indeed, we raised about $2 million fairly readily. Then we hit a wall. No more investors were coming, and the whole project was in jeopardy. I was continuing to pray, "Lord, I need a sign or some assurance that I should go ahead with this." We were already committed for the land. The city had given us the green light. We had $14 million of the 16 million required, but how was I going to find $2 million more? I was out of friends with money.

About then a fellow I knew called me and asked if he could come over and have me explain the details of the deal to him. Then he asked if it would be okay if he brought along his financial advisor. I said, "Sure. Bring him along." They came, and I explained the entire concept to them. During the explanation, I noticed that the advisor was getting a little antsy. He acted like he was in a hurry and had somewhere else to go or something to do that was more important. Finally he said, "Let me get this straight. You are not charging a finder's fee or a development fee?" I said, "Yes, that's right."

"And you are not going to make a profit on the construction? You are building it for the partnership at cost?" I said, "Yes, that's right." He said, "Well, I never heard of such a fair deal." He looked at his client and said, "I don't know about you, but I'm going to buy a share." And with that he picked up his coat and hat and started to leave. He said, "How soon do you need the cash?" As he was putting his coat on, he said, "By the way, do you have any more shares left?" I said, "Yes, as a matter of fact, we do." "Good," he said, "I have several clients who need to diversify their portfolios. They need some real estate to balance their stocks and bonds. If I send you some investors, will you pay me a commission?" I said, "No. We just went through the prospectus. All the money goes into the project. No fees or commissions. Sorry."

He abruptly put on his hat and turned back to me and said, "When my clients call you, they will use my name for identification." His name was Roy Belknap. I'm sure he was sent from the Lord. Within a few days the phone began to ring with his clients calling, and we soon sold out all the shares and we had our $4 million. In fact, people were still calling wanting to invest after we had sold completely out. The Lord was paving the way, and we had what we needed to get started. But we still had a long way to go.

The top six floors of the building had 159 apartments: studios, one-bedroom, two-bedroom, and a few three-bedroom units. Floors three and four contained 80,000 square feet of office space, and the main floor had about 20,000 square feet of retail stores facing two streets. The second floor was all parking for the offices, and the basement was parking for the apartment residents. Each floor held about 180 cars. We also had about one hundred spaces on the main floor for visitors plus a few on the streets. We called it "Birmingham Place." Altogether we had 500,000 square feet of building and about five hundred cars parked inside the building that were totally invisible from the street. No one would ever guess we had any cars inside the building from looking at its exterior. It was another great success. The apartments rented up very quickly. The offices took a little longer, maybe two years after completion; but they finally filled up. It was a lot of office space to be absorbed in such a small town. The investors got their money back in five years; and for the next sixteen years, we all enjoyed a nice income. We sold it in 2005 to some fellows who converted the apartments into condos. They didn't do very well, but my cup of financial blessings was really getting full.

Paul and Marilyn, About Age Fifty

Birmingham Place

42

A PUSHY LADY

There are a lot of interesting stories about Birmingham Place and the people connected with it. But I'll tell you one that you might enjoy. But first, a little background. We had owned and operated the Merrillwood Building in downtown Birmingham for over twenty years before we got involved in Birmingham Place. Our resident manager had kept us informed of the market and what features people especially liked about the various apartments and which ones were the most popular. As you may recall, we had a good mix of studios, one-bedrooom and two-bedroom units, and we only had four three-bedroom units, out of fifty-four total. When a three-bedroom unit came vacant, it usually took the longest to rent. However, we were full most of the time, actually about 98 to 99 percent over the twenty years or so. She also told us that she could rent one hundred more apartments if she had them. That was part of the motivation for us to consider Birmingham Place. As a result, in the planning of the new building, we took all this into account and determined the mix of the kinds of apartments based upon our experience. The rents in downtown Birmingham were probably the highest in all of Michigan because of the high land costs, high taxes, the cost of construction in a downtown setting. We had to charge about $600 per month for a small studio apartment. At that time, for $600 someone could get a two-bedroom apartment in Troy or Southfield, only two or three miles away. But downtown Birmingham living was very attractive because of the many amenities within walking distance and underground parking. As a result, people were willing to pay a higher rate, and many settled for a smaller living space, especially single people. As a result, our studios were very popular. So we planned twenty-four of them in the new building. They were a little larger than the ones at Merrillwood and had a full kitchen. Then we planned sixty-eight two-bedroom units and sixty one-bedroom units but only six three-bedroom units; all based on our experience at Merrillwood. At Merrillwood our three-bedroom units were about 1,500 square feet. At Birmingham Place, they were to be 1,750 square feet.

Now to the story. Soon after we had demolished the ugly old buildings on the site, which incidentally made all the city officials jump for joy, we dug an enormous hole in the middle of town. This caused some attention, and also when folks saw the big picture of the new building on the sign at the site, it aroused interest. One day a rather loud-talking pushy lady stopped by the office to inquire about the apartments. When I came out to meet her, she abruptly said, "I want to see the plans for the largest apartment you have." I proudly showed her the plan for our lovely 1,750-square foot three-bedroom apartment. "Oh no," she said, "that's way too small."

When I explained that that was the largest we had, she said, "Well, how about putting two apartments together?" I explained that we could probably do that, but we would have to do it on all six floors because the apartment configuration had to be stacked and each apartment had to be the same on each floor because the plumbing and piping had to all line up. I told her I doubted if we could rent six apartments that large. She said I didn't know what I was talking about and that there were plenty of people out there who would rent a larger apartment in Birmingham, but none were available. So to appease her, we made a plan of combining two apartments down at the end of the hall. We shortened the corridor and relocated a stairway. The end result was a three thousand-square foot three-bedroom, three-bath apartment with its own laundry room and two balconies, one off the living room and one off the master bedroom, which had a large dressing area and a supersize bathroom. She said, "That's more like it. I'll take the top floor." "But," I said, "I'm not sure we can rent five more of these." She said, "It will be no problem." I said, "Okay, if I can rent three of them, two more besides yours, I'll take a chance on three more, and we will change the plans and build six of them." She said, "Give me a copy of the plans, and I'll show you."

She went out to her country club over the weekend and told some of her friends about the building and the coming of three thousand-square foot apartments. The rent for the apartments was to be about $4,000 per month. Within a few days, people (her friends) began to call and come in and look at the plans. We had a model of the building in our office, and we could point out on it exactly the location of each apartment. We soon rented (or took deposits on) three or four of them. In one situation a wealthy widow brought her daughter in to help her decide which apartment to take. The mother said that she thought that our original 1,750-square foot one would be plenty big enough as she lived alone. As she was vacillating back and forth between the two, her daughter said, "Aw Mom, just take the big one." She did, and it turned out to be one of the most tastefully decorated ones in the entire building. It was a showplace.

But there is more to the story. By the way, as time went on, we rented all of the big apartments, and people were still asking for large apartments. There was no other way to conveniently put two more apartments together side by side. So we decided to take two apartments above each other and put in an interior stair. Each apartment was about 1,100 square feet, so combined they were 2,200 square feet with more than adequate living space downstairs and two large bedrooms up. Of course, it also had two balconies. We took six apartments and made them into three. All of this was done while the building was still under construction, so the added cost was minimal. We soon rented all of these as well. It was kind of interesting. Since they were on two floors and with doors into each apartment on each floor, if you came home in the daytime, you would get off the elevator on floor five. If you came home in the evening, you could get off on floor six and go into the bedroom area.

The building was now finished, and it was time to sign the leases. At that point we had only deposits of $1,000. When the original pushy lady came into the office with her husband, who was a banker and a real nice guy, to sign the lease, she noticed that the lease said, "No pets." She was very unhappy. She explained that her dog was very small and that she had

had it for a long time, and so on, and that we should make an exception for her. I tried to explain that if we let her small dog in, we would have to let others in; and little by little we could have Great Danes in the building. It just couldn't be. Her husband said, "Dear, maybe it's time to get rid of the dog." "No," she said; and they left, with the husband agreeing with us and shaking his head.

We had no trouble renting her apartment. A few years later, I met her husband on the street one day. He said, "Guess what? The dog died." He said his wife would soon be in to see me. Well, she didn't come to see me. She went to see the manager of the building, inquiring about the availability of large apartments. She was told that all of the largest units were occupied, with no prospect of vacancies in the foreseeable future. She was unhappy. They did tell her that one of the two-story units was coming up on floors five and six. She asked for a floor plan and she said it was too small. Then she said, "How about that one plus the one next to it on the sixth floor?" They told her that one was occupied but that there was an identical one down the hall, but it was not contiguous to the one she was interested in.

A few days later, she came back to the rental office and said, "Okay, I'll take the two-floor apartment plus the one next door to it on the sixth floor." When the manager reminded her that that one was not available, she said, "Well, it is now." She had paid the tenant in that apartment, a single man, the cost of moving him down the hall into an identical apartment and paid his rent for six months as an incentive to get him to move about sixty feet down the hall. I'm sure he thought it was a good deal. One day he went to work and when he came home all his furniture and belongings had been moved. He hardly knew the difference.

But the story doesn't end there. She came to see me with a plan as to how she was going to take the two-bedroom two-bath apartment next door and make it into a luxurious master bedroom suite. This involved removing the kitchen and making it, along with the living and dining rooms, into the new master bedroom. Of course, it would have a balcony. One bedroom became her dressing room, and the two bathrooms were to be combined into one large bath with marble finishes. The plan was very nice, and she was going to do all of this at her own expense. I said, okay, but under one condition. Since no one is going to want an apartment like this in the future, you must pay to put it back like it is at the end of your lease, which was for five years. She said okay. I recommended a contractor to do the work for her. She hired a decorator from New York, and the place was beautiful. The contractor told me later that the cost of the remodeling alone was over $450,000 plus decorating and furnishings. One day I met her in the lobby, and she said to me, "Now do I have the largest apartment in the building?" I said, "Let me see. You have the equivalent of three 1,100 feet apartments, or 3,300 square feet. The other large ones are 3,000 square feet. So, yes, you have the largest one." She said, "Good! That's what I want." I thought to myself, such vanity!

But the story goes on. After about three or four years, they moved to Florida and one of their sons, who was single, lived in the apartment until the lease ran out. Just before it did, I got a call from her husband. He said they wanted to give up the apartment at the end of the lease and how much did he owe us to put it back the way it was. We did some calculations and told him $117,000. He said, "Okay," and sent us a check.

As we were contemplating the process, I was up in the apartment admiring all of the beautiful work they had done. I thought what a shame it would be to tear all of it out, particularly the gorgeous large marble bathroom. So I decided that we would make it into a large one-bedroom, one-bath apartment and take our chances on renting it. It was easy to put the kitchen back, as all the plumbing was still there. We enlarged the bedroom by including the small dressing room and closet that she had allocated to her husband. We came up with a wonderful one-bedroom apartment with sitting room space in the bedroom and a most luxurious bath. While we were in the process of reconstruction, a lady tenant from down the hall stopped in to the apartment and asked what we were doing. The maintenance man showed her the work in process. She thought it was beautiful! She said she lived by herself and asked what the rent would be for this apartment. He said he didn't know, but since it was the size of a two-bedroom, he assumed it would be the same price. She said, "If so, I'll take it and move down the hall." She did, and she had the nicest one-bedroom apartment in the entire building.

This is how one lady influenced so much of the activity at the building. Without her, I doubt if we ever would have built the large apartments that became so attractive to so many people. She was a "pill" to work with, but we wound up with a larger variety of apartments with something for everyone, all sizes and prices. Did the Lord send her along? Maybe! I don't know. What do you think?

43

GOOD PEOPLE

Altogether we built about 150 buildings in about thirty years from 1951 to 1981. Most were new construction, but some were additions or renovations. A most interesting and satisfying thirty years!

During those thirty years, many people remarked about what wonderful people I had working for me. Those people were indeed very special and accounted in a big way for my success. Most of them were believers and were honest, ethical, and forthright with all who dealt with them. They were wonderful representatives of how I felt and acted. Many were faithful and worked for me for many years. Fred Wilkinson, the CP, I told you about, worked for me and with me for fifty-five years. We are the same age, and together we saw the business grow. He was a wonderful help to me. We became the best of friends. But he was so meticulous. He had the serial number recorded of every one of our 1,300 refrigerators, stoves, and other appliances in all of our apartments. When one was moved from one apartment to another, he wanted to know which one. If a new one was purchased, he wanted to know the serial number of both the old and the new. He did everything by hand, even up to his retirement. He said, "The day computers come into this office will be the day I retire." We did get word processors for the girls but no computers for the accounting system.

Sandy Nichols was another special and long-term employee. She came to us soon after high school and her skills grew as the volume of work increased. She worked for us for a few years until she had to quit when she became pregnant. She had two girls, and five years later, she came back and picked up where she left off and replaced another girl who also had to quit to have a baby.

At one time we had about thirteen hundred people paying us rent. Sandy was in charge of the apartment operations. She talked to all the apartment managers daily and took care of all the tenant concerns and things that the managers couldn't answer. She was, and is, terrific! The first week of the month she would record by hand all thirteen hundred of the checks that came in. We collected all the money in our office, mostly by mail. Each time a tenant signed a new lease, we supplied them with a year's supply of envelopes addressed to our office. Each complex had a different color envelope. Blue for Arbor Village, green for Westland Colonial Village, pink for Burlington Apartments, etc. The receptionist would put the various colors in piles, slit them open, put the checks in alphabetical order, and give them to Sandy. The thirteen hundred came in over about a week's time. Each tenant had a card about six inches square that Sandy kept in a tray beside her desk, separated by apartment complex, and then in two sections, paid and unpaid. Each card had a record of each month's payment recorded. The second week of the month, Sandy would put together all the invoices and bills that needed to be paid in a separate stack for each complex. Fred would check them over, and then Sandy would write the checks to pay the bills, all by hand. There were usually a hundred or more. The third week she would renew the leases. Each month a total of over a hundred would come up for renewal. There was usually a day or two between the third week and fourth week when she wasn't too busy, and then the process started all over again. She was a "one-man band" (or woman band).

One day a fellow came into our office wanting to sell us a computer system to help Sandy do her job. One of his "pitches" was that with his computer system we could easily find out the age of each tenant, how many doctors we had, how many single women or men we had. It could tell us how many were married and all sorts of information about our thirteen hundred tenants. Sandy said, "Who cares? All we want to know is that they pay the rent on time." Well, he insisted that we go with him to the office of another apartment management company where he had sold them his computer system and see it in operation. Fred wanted no part of it. But out of curiosity, Pam, Sandy, and I went. While standing behind a man running the computer, Sandy said to him, "Tell me how many people have not paid their rent as of today." The fellow began pushing buttons and looking at the screen and became embarrassed, and after about five minutes' time, he said, "I will have to look at several screens and then add them up to give you the total number." Sandy looked at me and said, "I could tell you in about two minutes by counting the cards in the unpaid section of my card file." We were not impressed. Besides, he said we would have to hire an additional person who would load all of our information into the system. It could take several months, and we might want to keep that person full-time to operate the system. I guess we could be called old- fashioned and out of the loop or behind the times or whatever, but as long as we had Sandy, we would be okay.

At this writing we have sold all of our properties except for the Merrillwood Building, and Sandy still works part-time, doing the same work. It is now over forty-four years that I have been counting on her. She is one in a million and has been very special to me all these years. I have come to love and appreciate her very much. Both Sandy and Fred, along with a few others, have been well cared for financially and should have no money problems for the rest of their lives. Another blessing from God. My cup of blessings overflowed, and some of it went to them.

There are several others who have been very special to me. A few are still with me today. Rick Weingartner came to work for us as a maintenance man at Birmingham Place back in 1990. He is a very talented and gifted technician and can do so many types of work, including electrical, plumbing, carpentry. After we sold Birmingham Place, he was not too happy with the new owners. At the same time, we had an opening at our Merrillwood Building, and he came to work with us there. This building is about one-third the size of Birmingham Place. So in some respects the physical work is less, but he has expanded his management skills and now is the building manager. He has been a most faithful, diligent employee. He and his two helpers, Margaret Moss who is the apartment manager, and Betty Sutton, the office manager (along with Shirley, Nancy, and

Jackie), are all dedicated believers in Jesus Christ and do a wonderful job of representing me and my values as they interact with tenants, suppliers, and all who do business with the building. My cup continues to overflow even until today.

44

CBMC

Let's go back again to 1954, two years after we were married. On a Sunday morning after church, a gentleman whom I knew casually came to me and invited me to a weekend men's retreat to be held in a place out near Fenton, about an hour's drive from Detroit. His name was John Boyko. He said that the retreat was being sponsored by an organization called CBMC, Christian Business Men's Committee. It was made up of Christian businessmen from various churches and denominations from all over the area and was one of several groups nationwide. He said the retreat center was on a lake and that on Saturday afternoon there was always a softball game. All the speakers would be businessmen. No preachers. He said if I was available, he would like for me to be his guest. I said I would check with Marilyn and let him know. She said it would be fine, and I accepted his invitation. It was a nice weekend, and I enjoyed the whole thing, including meeting some very successful older men who were Christians and hearing their testimonies as to how God had worked in their lives.

One interesting thing was that I met Stanley Kresge, the son of Mr. S. S. Kresge who had founded the "dime stores" that later became Kmart Corporation. He was the umpire at the ball game. We eventually became good friends. Mr. Boyko kept inviting me to other meetings sponsored by CBMC, and I kept going with him. I found out that the purpose of the organization was to encourage Christian men to share their faith and the gospel of Jesus Christ with other men through luncheons or dinners where businessmen gave their testimonies. They would invite men who were not believers, who were often not involved in a church, as a way of introducing them to things of the Lord and, hopefully, a salvation experience. I enjoyed the meetings very much, and I was encouraged by hearing other men speak about Christian growth and their walk with the Lord. I was only about twenty-six at the time, and all these older men encouraged me to always put the Lord first in my life and that I did not need to be ashamed or timid about my faith. I learned from these successful businessmen that while we should not be pushy or preachy about our faith with others, we should be open and ready to share it when the opportunity presented itself.

I found over the years that many men who were successful in business still felt like something was missing in their lives. And when I gently shared with them about the fulfillment in life that was only available through faith in Jesus Christ, many were open and wanted to hear more. As a result, I had the privilege of sharing my faith and seeing many men come to faith in Jesus Christ. Sometimes it was through CBMC meetings and sometimes just one-on-one over breakfast, lunch, or dinner.

CBMC was a great help to me. I became active in the local group, and before long I was on the local board and then they made me the chairman of the Detroit committee, helping with the arrangements for the monthly meetings. I found out that there were groups like ours in most of the major cities across the country. In fact, there was an annual convention held each year in a different city. The wives were invited, and we began to attend. There were about a thousand people there from all over the United States. All businessmen. No clergy. I became acquainted with many of them and invited them to come to Detroit to speak at our monthly meetings. Many came, just sharing their faith and encouraging others to take the step of trusting Jesus Christ and having faith in Him. There was also a national board of directors made up of men from all over the United States. At the time, there were about sixteen men on the board. John Boyko was one of them, representing Michigan and Ohio. Each board member had a certain area where he was responsible to help and encourage the various local groups. When John's four-year term expired, he suggested my name as his replacement, and I was elected to the board of directors of CBMC of USA. I had seventeen local groups to watch over in Michigan and Ohio. I was expected to visit each group, or committee as we called them, at least once a year. As you might guess, it became a part-time job. I already had a full-time job. But it became a real joy. I saw men from all walks of life come to faith in Christ through the lives and testimonies of other Christian businessmen. It was a most fulfilling experience to see men's lives changed, marriages restored, families reunited with a new purpose in life, and about every good thing that you could think of. I got into the ministry with both feet. I went from being encouraged to being an encourager. Our theme Bible verse was Romans 12:11. As the old King James Version says, "Diligent in business, fervent in spirit, serving the Lord."

After being on the national board for a while, I was elected chairman; and I served a four-year term three different times. As chairman of the board, I was "up front" a lot at the national annual conventions and became acquainted with many men from all across the country. As a result of the national exposure and as chairman, I was invited to several cities to speak at all kinds of functions. It wasn't because I was such a good speaker but because I was chairman. Over the years, I have spoken in every state in the United States at prayer breakfast meetings, luncheons and banquets, and in over thirty countries of the world.

45

MEETING A GOVERNOR

I once was invited to be the speaker at the governor's prayer breakfast in Little Rock, Arkansas. It was sponsored by CBMC. I did not know who the governor was until I was on the plane heading for Little Rock. As I read the program, it said the governor was Bill Clinton. It didn't mean a thing to me. I had never heard of him. At 7 a.m. the next morning, seated at the speakers table with about a thousand people in attendance, I was seated next to the governor. He seemed like a nice fellow as we chatted during the meal. As I was concluding my remarks, I invited anyone who was sincere about trusting the Lord as their Savior to follow me silently in prayer as I prayed out loud. With heads bowed, I prayed something like this. "Dear Lord, I am sorry that I have neglected You all my life. I am sorry for my sin; and the best I know how, right now I ask You to forgive me and I invite You into my heart as Savior and Lord."

When I finished the prayer, the local committee had asked me if I would help the guests fill out a card that was by each place. I did so, explaining to them to check the various boxes on the cards as to whether they would like more information about CBMC or information about joining, etc. Of course, there was a place for their name and address. There was also a box that said, "I have just prayed to receive Jesus Christ." I said to the folks just before I sat down that if they checked that box, when I got back to my office I would send them a book that would be a help to them along in their faith. Over the years, I have sent out hundreds of those books with a personal note.

After the chairman closed the meeting, I stood up and shook hands with the governor. He complimented me on my talk and said he enjoyed it. I said, "I hope it was meaningful to you." He said, "Oh yes, very much, and, as a matter of fact, I prayed that prayer with you and I checked the box"—pointing to the card on the table. I said something like, "That's wonderful. I'm so glad." Then he said to me, "Would you like to come over to my office and see the capital building? It's right across the street." It was 9 a.m. I said, "Let me check with my hosts here (there were two of them) and see. My plane doesn't leave until twelve o'clock." The governor said, "Bring them along." Then he said that he had a brief meeting right then but to give him about forty-five minutes and come on over. The two guys were ecstatic. They had lived there all of their lives and had never been to the capital building, much less the governor's office. We went over and were ushered into his private office. A photographer showed up and took a picture of the four of us, which I later received in the mail.

Two things I remember about that meeting. One was that the building was not only old, it was ancient. The marble steps were worn down from use. The seats in the congressional chamber were wood. It was like being in another world. The second thing that impressed me was the governor's charisma. He was a handsome, friendly, warm, and very likeable fellow. I thought, "This guy could go places." Little did I know how far. It was a nice visit.

Later, I had the picture of us hanging in my home. Then one day, when he was running for President of the United States, I heard along with everyone in the world about his escapades with Gennifer Flowers and how he admitted on national television that he had been unfaithful to his wife, Hillary, many times. I took down the picture. Several years later, the president of CBMC, Phil Downer, was visiting in my office, and he said, "I was just out in Arkansas and I was in a fellow's office and he had a picture of you and him and Bill Clinton." I said, "Yes, I know. I have a copy of it but I don't know where it is," which was the truth. A few days later, another copy of the picture showed up. Phil had told the fellow in Arkansas, and he sent me another copy.

With Governor Bill Clinton

46

ANOTHER GOVERNOR

Let me tell you another story about a governor and future president. Jimmy Carter was governor of Georgia. We had a staff member of CBMC, named Joe Coggeshall, who lived in Atlanta; and somehow he became friends with the governor. Joe said that he thought that the governor would be willing to be a speaker at our national convention, which was going to be held in Cleveland, Ohio, that year. So the board agreed upon Joe's recommendation to invite him. We did, and he came and did a nice job. It was clear that he was a believer. He was very sincere and articulate. At the close of his speech, I asked him if he would be willing to come to Detroit for a banquet where we would have five or six hundred people. He said, "Sure. Just let me know when."

We arranged for the banquet to be in downtown Detroit at the old Book Cadillac Hotel. (It later closed down and has since been remodeled.) The banquet was on a Saturday night, and the governor had agreed to stay over and speak at our quite large Sunday school class on Sunday morning at our church. The Sunday school teacher had agreed. When I approached the pastor about the possibility of the governor speaking at the morning service, he said, "I'm coming to the banquet. After I hear him speak, I'll let you know how much time he can have. He can at least give a greeting to our congregation." At the end of the banquet on Saturday night, our pastor came to me and said, "Tell him he can take as much time as he wants and I will just finish up and close the service." The governor did a great job in all three speeches. Although our church is predominantly Republican, if that had been election day, I think he would have gotten over 90 percent of the votes from our people.

When Joe was helping us and the governor with logistics for his visit to Detroit, he suggested that the governor stay overnight with us at our home. The governor questioned the accommodations and said that he would also have his bodyguard with him. Joe assured him that he would be quite comfortable at our house and that we had plenty of room for his bodyguard. So, after the Saturday night banquet, we drove them out to our home. Mimi had remarried, and her bedroom suite was now the guest room. When we got out of the car, the bodyguard, whose name was Freeman, said to the governor, "You wait here until I check it out." He asked me to show him the governor's room. I took him and showed him. He looked under the bed, opened the closet doors, and gave the whole area a good look. Then he went outside and told the governor he could come in. Freeman was a tall, good-looking black man. He was an officer of the Georgia State Police, but he was, naturally, wearing street clothes for this trip; and except for sleeping in different rooms, he never let the governor out of his sight.

After we let the governor in, we invited him to go into the bedroom and make himself comfortable and then to come out into the family room for a cold drink. We gave him Vernor's ginger ale, which he had never tasted but thought it was wonderful. To make conversation, I asked him what he planned to do after his term was up. I knew that in Georgia the governor could only serve one term. He said that he was thinking of running for a higher office. I suggested maybe the House of Representatives or Senate. He said, "No. Maybe higher than that."

I didn't want to be wrong a second time, so I said, "What did you have in mind?" He said, "I'm thinking about running for the presidency."

I almost said, "The presidency of what?" I did say, "That's interesting. How do you plan to do it? Your name is not exactly a household word. Not many people know you."

I knew that he had been on a national television show called, "What's My Line?" It was where four celebrities tried to guess a person's vocation. They were allowed to ask the person several questions. They had no idea who he was, and they were stumped. He said, "I know all that." When I asked him how he planned to get people to know him, he said, "Just like

John Kennedy. I plan to enter every primary in the country." And then he made two statements that stuck with me. He said, "When people get to know me, I think they will like me. And although I don't know much about the politics in Washington, D.C., I think that's a plus. The mood in America is ripe for a person like me who is not connected with all the bureaucracy in Washington." He was right on both counts; and, as you know, he was elected.

I have a picture of us at the banquet that night, but I soon took it down after he aligned himself with all the crooked politicians in Detroit and other places. We wound up not voting for him because of the many compromises that he made in order to get elected. After he got elected, he did not put one believer or anyone with a Christian testimony on his cabinet. He sold out, in my opinion, and God took His hand of blessing off of him, and he became a one-term president. He was, and still is, as far as I know, a fine dedicated personal follower of Jesus Christ; but, in my opinion, he compromised his walk with God for the prize of men, popularity, and prestige. If somehow, by the stretch of our imagination, I should ever be elected to be President of the United States, the first thing I would do would be to get a group of men and perhaps women around me who knew how to pray and had a relationship with God. In all of America, there must be people like that who are also skilled and capable in all the affairs of the government.

Imagine what might happen to our country if at each cabinet meeting the president said, "Ladies and gentlemen, before we begin today's meeting, let's pause for a moment and ask God's blessing on our discussions, our decisions, and upon our country." Can you imagine God not taking note of a sincere prayer like that, asking for His help? I think He would be more than happy to answer a prayer like that. Who knows what our country could be like and where we might go if the leaders were truly asking for God's help? It might be like it was in the beginning, when many of the leaders were, indeed, men who prayed for God's help and guidance. And look what happened. The greatest country in the world was born and envied by every other country in the world. People from all over the world were attracted here to enjoy a country that was built on a foundation of a faith in Almighty God.

As you perhaps know, it lasted about two hundred years, and the slide started; and it has been going down spiritually and morally ever since. Along with that slide, we have ever-increasing problems on all sides. I hope and pray that before we totally destruct, people will come to their senses and recognize what made this country great in the first place and go back and embrace those original values and the One who started everything and still controls everything.

Another thought about famous people and even presidents of the United States. No matter how popular and powerful they become, their popularity only lasts for a time. Some last longer than others, but in time their legacies fade. By contrast, a life dedicated to Jesus Christ and His kingdom and purpose can help influence people to trust Him and receive the gift of eternal life. That type of legacy, to me, is far more important and is a much better use of our time and resources. What could be more important than eternal life and helping people find it?

With Governor Jimmy Carter

47

SOME ADIRONDACK EXPERIENCES

Lehman Strauss was our pastor in the early 1960s. He was a regular speaker during the summer months at a Christian camp called Word of Life (taken from the Bible verse in Philippians 2:16). It is located in upper New York State in the midst of the Adirondack Mountains near a town called Schroon Lake. He said Marilyn and I should go for a week and take our two small children. He said they had programs for all ages. So we went for a week's vacation with Colleen, who was seven, and Kevin, who was almost five years old. Indeed, they did have facilities and programs for all ages. As adults, we were in the "inn," which was formerly a resort frequented by wealthy folks from New York, New Jersey, and all up and down the east coast. Schroon Lake is about eight or nine miles long and with beautiful mountains on all sides. About a ten-mile drive down the lakeshore, they had a camp for small children. Colleen went there. Out in the middle of the lake, opposite the inn, is a ninety-acre island where the teenagers and college kids go. At the inn, where we stayed, they have a nursery and facilities for children too young to go to the ranch. Among other things, they had pony rides for the little kids. Kevin stayed with us and went each morning to the children's program while we went to the adults' program. He loved it! Jack Wyrtzen (pronounced "Wirtzen") was the director.

The place and the people and the program were outstanding. Each morning at the end of the service, which is about noon, the children's program also ends. They are then free to spend the afternoon with their parents. At noon one day, at the designated meeting place, Kevin came running up to us and excitedly said, "Guess what I did today!" I said, "Did you get to ride the pony?" "No," he said, "I gave my heart to Jesus." Well, we picked him up and hugged him with all our might. Both his mom and I were overcome with joy. I suppose the natural tendency is to wonder if a five-year-old really understands enough to make such a commitment. But he has repeatedly said all these years that, indeed, he did; and that was the day that he always looked back to as the day of the beginning of his relationship with Jesus Christ. Throughout his life, even in his early years after that incident, he has always demonstrated a life that has been dedicated and related to the Lord.

That was the first and probably the most significant of several incidents that happened at Word of Life. A summer or two later, on a colder-than-normal August Sunday morning, Marilyn and I were seated at breakfast by ourselves at a table for four near the big open roaring fireplace (for obvious reasons). We had only been seated a few minutes when a couple walked in and the lady was sort of hugging herself to keep warm. They were looking around for a place to sit. Marilyn stood up and motioned for them to come and join us. When they saw the fire in the fireplace, they were quite happy to join us. That was the beginning of a lifelong friendship that we are all sure God brought about. They are Jerry and Dee (for Dorothy) Miller. At the time, they lived in Richmond, Virginia, and had no idea that it could sometimes be quite cool in the mountains in upstate New York, even in August. Jerry was an executive with Texaco, and they were youth sponsors in their church. They had arrived the day before with about fifteen young kids that they had left down at the ranch for a week. They had traveled, of all things, in a converted hearse, towing a trailer. That's a story in itself for another time. As is sometimes the case, we "hit it off" real well with them, and we have been special friends ever since. Dee had brought no warm clothes, and Marilyn loaned her a sweater for the week and, as Dee says, "saved the day" or maybe the week! Although we lived some distance apart, we visited them in their various homes (Texaco moved them a lot) and later, on several occasions, traveled around the world with them as our children grew up and left.

Our association with Word of Life continues until this day. It is one of the finest organizations of its kind. I got acquainted with Jack Wyrtzen, the director; and one day he told me that he was praying that the Lord would let them have a ministry (mostly camping) in one hundred countries. At that time, they did have a camp in Argentina and maybe two or three more. I remember thinking, "One hundred countries! Jack, I think you are dreaming." Little did I know. Today I think they have operations in about sixty-five countries and growing. Jack was a man of faith, and God honored him "big-time."

Another story that I have told many times to hundreds of people is worth documenting here for you. One Wednesday evening at the inn, we were invited to sit with Jack and his wife, Marge, at their table for dinner, which accommodated eight or ten people. I was seated next to Jack. Sometime during the meal, he asked me if Marilyn and I would like to go over to the island that evening where he would be speaking at a campfire for the high school and college age group. We said, "Sure, we'd love to go."

He said, "You go into the tabernacle tonight here at the inn for the evening meeting, but sit near the back. I will open the meeting and introduce the speaker, and then I will slip out the back door and come around and meet you as you come outside." We did; and as we did, we noticed that another couple came out with us. We assumed that Jack had also invited them to come along. We were right, and Jack showed up and introduced us. We walked down the hill and across the road to the boat dock. Jack drove the little eighteen-foot ski boat across the lake to the island, about a five- to six-minute ride.

As we approached the island, we could see a big, roaring campfire off to our left down near the shore of the lake. When Jack shut off the motor of the boat, we could hear the kids singing, all seated in a small amphitheater on the hillside. As we were walking along the shore toward the campfire, Jack was in front. The other gentleman and I were walking together, and the ladies were behind. Soon after we got off the boat, the man stopped for a minute and looked all around at the nice facilities on the island, including the meeting hall, a dining room, several cabins, plus other buildings. Rather philosophically, he said, "You know, this is about all I have left."

I said, "What do you mean?" He said, "Several years ago when Jack had the opportunity to buy this island, he came to me asking if I could help him raise the money." He said, "At the time, I was in the trucking business up in Maine. I was doing pretty well. I had several big, over-the-road eighteen wheelers, and all was good. I gave him $25,000, and he bought this island.

"Since then," he continued, "our business has gone in the ditch. We lost all our trucks. We have one rig left, and my wife and I drive it up and down the east coast, and we make a living. Every summer Jack invites us back up for a week's vacation." By that time, we were at the campfire. The four of us sat off to the side while Jack spoke to the 250 to 300 teenagers and college kids. The talk was a challenge to them to consider giving their lives totally and completely to Christ and putting Him first in their lives. He asked them if they wanted to make that kind of a commitment to serve the Lord with all their hearts, to come down from their seats and pick up a little stick or wood off of a pile and throw it into the fire. He said that would be sort of an outward expression of an inward com-mitment. Like dying to their own personal desires and letting God have His way in their lives and allowing Him to direct their future in whatever way He saw fit to lead them. As he finished his remarks, the kids started coming down and coming down and coming down. It was a most emo-tional scene. They were hugging each other and some were crying as they were getting their hearts and their priorities aligned with God's will for their lives. As the meeting was concluded, they quietly started back to their cabins, still holding hands and hugging. After they were gone only Jack and the four of us remained. I remember saying to Jack, "This was a wonderful event that we just witnessed. Thanks so much for inviting us."

Then I said, "Jack, how often do you do this?" He said, "Every Wednes-day night. But of course with a different group of kids." I said, "I counted about two hundred that came down." He said, "Yes, I suppose so."

"Are the results the same each week?" I asked.

"Yes, more or less," he said.

"How many weeks during the summer?" I asked. "Ten," he said. "About two thousand kids per summer?" "Yes," he said, "more or less." At that point the island ministry was about thirty years old. I quickly calculated about eighty thousand kids had had their lives changed on that island. I remember looking at my new friend and saying, "And this is about all you have left?"

"What a legacy!" Marilyn said that night back in our cabin. "That guy made a pretty good investment, don't you think?" I guess so! The activities and campfires are still going on now, over fifty years. From that time on, I have always considered all my contributions as investments for eternity. How can I get the most "bang for the buck"? What will pay the most dividends in the lives of people who will be in heaven because of my investment? That is the question to be asked.

Another interesting story about Word of Life. Jack always had a businessman speak on Thursday evenings each week of the summer. I was privileged to be one of those for several years on one Thursday evening of the summer. One summer on my way to Word of Life, I flew into Albany, New York, which was the closest airport. A staff member picked me up, and we were driving north to the conference center. He told me that he was in charge of all their vehicles. He was on his way home from New York City where he had just arranged to purchase a used Greyhound bus. By this time, Word of Life had established a Bible institute, and the bus was used to carry the students around the country where they put on plays and concerts in different cities. He said that he had found a pretty good bus for $55,000 and that they still desperately needed another one but they didn't have the money at that time. When I got back home, I called my friend John Teets, who was a fine Christian man and was president of Greyhound Corporation, and told him the story. His response was, "Paul, if we start selling our used buses to churches at a reasonable price, there will no end to the requests we will receive. " I explained that Word of Life was not a church and how good an organization it was. He said, "Okay, let me see what I can do."

A few days later he called back and said, "How does $15,000 sound?" I said, "It sure sounds good to me. Let me call Jack Wyrtzen." I said, "By the way, John, are you sure the bus will be in good condition?" He said, "Don't worry. It will be in good condition." I called Jack. As you might guess, he was ecstatic. He said, "Paul, at that price do you think we could get two?" I called John, and he agreed to two buses. When I called Jack back to tell him, "Okay. Two buses," he was beside himself with joy, and then he said, "By the way, Paul, do you know anybody that would give us $15,000 to help us out with the buses?"

I think you can figure out who bought the first bus. When the buses came, they were like new. They had all new seats inside. They had a new motor, a new transmission, and all new tires. John asked how they wanted them painted, and they came in Word of Life colors and with the name and logo painted on the side. They were beautiful! That was probably twenty-five years ago, and a staff member told me recently that while they are getting old, they are still in use. Thank you, John Teets and Greyhound!

At a conference later on, after John had retired, he and his wife, Nancy, were at a Word of Life conference where they lived in Phoenix, Arizona, and I had the privilege and pleasure of introducing John and telling the story. As you might guess, he was warmly received and pleased. Most of the people had seen the buses—another good investment of God's resources that paid dividends for years to come.

Word of Life Busses

48

SOME INTERESTING DAYS IN THE ORIENT

In the early 1960s, a ministry called Far Eastern Gospel Crusade moved their offices from Minneapolis to Detroit. We became friends with the leaders and offered to build their new headquarters building for them at just about our cost. We did, and we became better acquainted with their leaders.

A few years later, one of their vice presidents, Olan Hendrix, invited me to accompany him and another businessman, Bill Quiggle, on a trip to Japan, Taiwan, Hong Kong, and the Philippines to visit the work that their missionaries were doing and to see it firsthand. It was a three-week trip beginning in Japan. We all met in San Francisco, and the first leg of the trip was to Hawaii. The plane was an old 707 with only about twelve seats in first class. As we boarded the plane and got settled, there were about six people in the entire coach section including the three of us. I remember stretching out in an entire row of three seats and having a nice nap. I pulled the curtain back and looked into the first class section. Eleven of the twelve seats were occupied by what looked like Japanese businessmen who had to sit up all night. Go figure!

We visited missionaries in Japan, Hong Kong, and Taiwan, about one hundred in all. Some were in groups of four or five. It was a whirlwind tour. At one point, in Japan, to spend more time with one missionary, we took him on a two-hour train ride with us and then bought him a ticket to go back home!

After visiting the three countries, we were headed for the Philippines. Olan, the tour guide, left Bill and me on our own, and he went on to some conference. He said that we would be in good hands in Manila with Frank Allen who along with his wife, Jackie, were serving as missionaries there. I knew them very well. They were from our church, and I had grown up with them. They met us at the plane and showed us around Manila and what they were doing. Frank was the head of the seminary in Manila, and Jackie worked in the library. She was a professional graduate librarian.

One day as we were having lunch, Frank, Bill, and I, in a local restaurant when Bill asked Frank if there was some way we could go up to a mountain village called Banaue. Bill said there were some missionaries from his church there; and after coming all this way, he would like to visit them. Bill was from Altoona, Pennsylvania. Frank said that if we were to go, it would be a nineteen-hour bus ride. When we asked what the bus was like, Frank said, "Quick. Look out the window. There is one stopped right there in front of the restaurant." As we looked, our hearts sank. It was a two-ton stake truck with wooden benches in the back. They were really close together. It had a 2 x 4 railing on the left side and the back, and it was open on the right side. It had a canvas top over a flimsy wooden frame, with chickens in chicken coops up on top. We said, "We don't think so!"

I asked Frank if there were any other options. He said, "Well, you could fly up, but it is very expensive and sort of dangerous." As he explained further, the landing field was the top of a mountain that had been leveled off with a bulldozer and was very short. The only kind of plane that could land there was called a "helio courier." The plane sort of had extra wings that were under the regular wings for flying but could be extended for landing in very short runways. The only plane like that was owned by a mission agency known as JAARS, and it was located about halfway between Manila and Banoue in a village called Bagabog. I could tell that Bill really wanted to go and see his friends. So I asked Frank if there was any way to get there using the JAARS plane. He said he would look into it and let us know. The next day he had made some tentative arrangements but it would, indeed, be costly. When we asked how much, he said, "Altogether about $400." Four hundred dollars back then was more than four thousand dollars today, but we told him to go ahead. The plan was that another missionary, who was a pilot, would rent a small plane at the Manila airport, and he would fly us up to Bagabog to meet the JAARS plane. We would then fly the second leg, which was the dangerous part, up to Banoue and land on the mountaintop.

At 9 a.m. we loaded the rental plane with all kinds of supplies. The missionaries had heard we were coming and had requested them. The station was a compound with about fifteen or twenty missionaries with a hospital served by several American doctors and nurses. Much of our cargo was medical supplies. As we were taxiing onto the runway at the Manila airport, the pilot, named Bill Basket, reached over in front of Bill Quiggle and picked up the microphone that was held in place by a bracket on the dashboard of the plane. I was in the backseat along with some cargo that wouldn't fit in the cargo space. Bill, the pilot, said in the microphone, "Manila tower, come in Manila tower." There was no response. He said again, "Manila tower, Manila tower, come in Manila tower." Still no answer. With that, he replaced the microphone on the bracket and said, "Well, something is wrong, but we won't need that. I know where we're going."

We taxied out onto the runway and took off. When I asked Bill how he knew where to land, he said he had been there before. At that point we were above the clouds with no land in sight. He said, "The last time I was up here, I flew an hour and forty-five minutes and then I came down and looked for the JAARS airstrip." I gave up and went to sleep. A little later he announced in a loud voice, "This is headhunter territory that we are flying over." All I saw was clouds. I went back to sleep.

Later, I woke up and looked at my watch. I tapped him on the shoulder and said, "It's now two hours since we took off." He said, "Yeah, I know. But we're bucking a little headwind so I thought we'll fly a little longer before we come down." Then he decided to come down. He said to us, "Now you guys look for a village with a river running through it. That will be JAARS headquarters."

After flying low for several minutes, Bill Quiggle said to the pilot, "You know, Bill, all these villages have rivers running through them." The pilot said, "Yes, I noticed." He flew around a few minutes longer and finally said to us, "I'm sorry to tell you fellows, but we are lost." He said, "We have two options. We can fly back to Manila. We have plenty of gas. Or we can land and ask somebody where we are."

Both of us passengers said, "Where are we going to land?" The pilot Bill said, "Oh, that's no problem. We will just land on a road." He said, "There is one right there. We'll fly down real low along the road and you guys take a good look at it and tell me what you think." So he did, and then he pulled the plane back up. "Well," he said, "what does it look like?" We both said that it was a gravel road, and, more important, it seemed to be under construction as there were piles of gravel spaced along the road. He said, "Yes, I saw that, but they are fairly small piles and they're over to one side of the road. If we land in the middle of the road, the wing will be over the top of the gravel piles." So we all had a prayer and down we came.

I don't think the wheels ever hit the road. For some reason, the plane went off to the left, between two telephone poles and under the wires into a rice paddy with about a foot of water in it. The plane was going pretty slow by that time, but it came to an abrupt stop as it got stuck in the mud, and the plane tipped up, up, up, until we were straight up with the nose in the ground and then it came back down with a bang. The pilot turned to us and said, "Are you guys okay?" We said, "Yes, I think so."

With that he jumped out of the plane and ran around it assessing the damage. He put his head back in the plane and said to us, "We're in good shape. The only thing is the propeller is bent from hitting the ground while still spinning." We were only a few yards from the road, and cars began to stop. The pilot went over to the road and started talking to some of the motorists. He soon came back to the plane all excited. "There's good news," he said. "We're only six miles from a good-sized town, and they have a machine shop that can repair the propeller. You guys wait here (as if we were going anywhere) and I will ride with this nice man into town and contact the machine shop. I'll be back in a little while."

So Bill and I pulled ourselves together and took off our shoes and socks and rolled up our pants and got out of the plane. It was about eleven o'clock in the morning and the temperature was about ninety-five degrees and the sun was bearing down. The only shade was under the wing, so we stood in the mud and sometimes sat on the strut that braced the wing, so as to get some relief from the heat. Pretty soon cars and trucks began to stop and people tried to talk to us in their language. Of course, we couldn't understand them. Once in a while there was someone who could speak English. One guy shouted out from a bus, "Anybody dead?" Then the people began to get out of their vehicles and come out into the rice paddy to see these two guys with an airplane in the middle of a rice paddy. Quite a sight to them! There was one fellow who could speak broken English. He said, "How come you land plane in rice paddy?" We did our best to explain, but it didn't seem to work. Soon there were twenty to thirty people all gathered around the plane, just looking at us and scratching their heads. One fellow started shouting and waving his hands and carrying on. I said to the fellow who could speak English, "What's the matter with him?" He said, "This is his rice paddy, and he is upset with the damage to his crop."

I told him the plane isn't doing nearly as much damage as all the people here are doing by trampling down the plants. So we decided to ask everyone to help and we picked up the back of the plane and pulled it back up to the road and out of his rice paddy. We paid him some money, and he was satisfied and became a smiling friend. We put the back wheel on the road and the front wheels were down in the ditch. There we sat. At least all the onlookers were out on the road. Soon Bill, the pilot, came back with a mechanic. He said the shop could straighten the propeller and we would be fine and on our way. He said we had come down in the wrong valley—JAARS headquarters was just over the mountain. Oh, by the way, here is your lunch. He gave us each a package of Lance crackers and a warm bottle of Coke. He and the mechanic took off the propeller. We told him that we noticed when we were moving the plane that the back wheel broke off when it slammed back down. So they took that with them also. He said, "Okay, you guys stay here and guard the plane. We'll be back in a little while and we'll tow the repaired plane into town and then out in another direction two miles to a grassy field called Gomez Airstrip."

So we waited all day in the hot sun, talking to curious travelers. About 7 p.m. they showed up with the propeller and the repaired rear wheel. They put them on, and we pulled the plane up onto the road and put the rear wheel of the plane in the back of an old army weapons carrier and towed it backwards into town.

The road was full of potholes, so we went very, very slowly. Bill and I sat in the back of the truck, watching the wings go up and down over the rough road. We got into town about 10 p.m. The chief of police met us and said that the best place to store the plane would be in the center of town in the middle of the circular grassy area with a monument in the center. It was in the middle of a small traffic circle. He took down a portion of the decorative chain that surrounded the area, and we pushed the plane in and he put the chain back up. Bill, the pilot, had arranged for us to stay overnight at a Catholic monastery, just a couple of blocks from the center of town. As we went in, we were welcomed by a very nice young priest who spoke perfect English. He had been educated in Boston. All the other priests were away at a convention, so there were plenty of bedrooms. He noticed that our clothes looked pretty bad from all the perspiration. He told us to go take a shower and come back down for something to eat. We had planned a one-day trip, up and back the same day, so we had no extra clothes. He gave us some robes and said to bring him our clothes and he would have them washed and ready to go in the morning.

He couldn't have been nicer. While we were eating and sharing our story with him, he asked where we were going to take off in the plane. When Bill, the pilot, told him the Gomez Airstrip, the priest said that would be a good idea except that there was a covered bridge between here and the airstrip. Our "no problem" pilot said, "No problem. We will just take the wings off of the plane and lay them up on top, lengthwise, and tow it through the bridge and put them back on." He said there were only four bolts that hold them on. This didn't seem too good to me, so I asked the priest if there were any roads around town that were paved. He said the only paved roads were the main ones in town, and they only went out for about half a mile from the center of town in each direction.

So we all finally went to bed about 1 a.m. and had a good night's sleep.

When we got up in the morning, we had clean clothes all ready to go. As we were eating breakfast, Bill the pilot came rushing in from outside, all out of breath. He said he had been out surveying the situation, and he thought we could take the plane off starting from the center of town, using the paved road. After breakfast, along with the priest, we all went out to take a look at what Bill was telling us. We found first of all a whole lot of people gathered around the plane wondering how, overnight, a plane appeared in the middle of their town. We all walked down the proposed runway. As we did, I noticed a motel sign that was pretty close to the road. There were some carpenters working nearby. The pilot went over to one of them and he said that for ten pesos he would remove the sign. I gave him the ten pesos, and he came out with a saw and cut the legs off and the sign fell flat. As we went on, I noticed some electrical wires that were across the road. Bill said he could get the plane up before we got to the wires. But, wait a minute. He saw some other workmen nearby, and he came back to me and said, "For twenty pesos he will remove the wires." I gave him the twenty pesos. He climbed up the pole and with a pair of wire cutters he snapped the wire and it fell across the road. He came down and rolled it up off the road. As we went on and we were nearing the edge of town, there were some trees with limbs over the road. Bill said he was sure he could lift off before he got to the trees and easily clear them.

By this time there were several hundred people gathered in the middle of town. The plan was to start right in the middle of town and try to lift off between some wires and miss the trees. We decided to take all the cargo out of the plane and put it in the priest's Jeep. We would ride with the priest out to the Gomez Airstrip and meet the pilot there. The police stopped the traffic in all directions, and Bill got into the plane. People were lined up on both sides of the road, like at a parade. Bill the pilot decided to taxi down the "runway" for one last look before taking off. As he did, all the people closed in behind him and filled the "runway." They thought he was leaving. The police got them back again, and he came back to the town center. We put our heads into the plane and had a word of prayer, and away he went, just as planned. We went in the Jeep and met him at the Gomez Airstrip. While all the activities were going on in town, we looked up and saw the JAARS plane circling and watching the unusual activities down below. He then also landed at the Gomez Airstrip. We transferred the cargo into the JAARS plane and headed off with the JAARS pilot to Banoue. Bill flew our plane over the mountain to JAARS headquarters to check out the radio. We would be back there later in the afternoon and fly back to Manila.

Bill Quiggle and I were expecting the landing and takeoff on the mountaintop to be exciting. As it turned out, that was "a piece of cake" compared to what we had just experienced. The well-trained JAARS pilot put the plane down with ease. As he turned the little crank up above his head between the two seats, the wings about doubled in size, width-wise. As he set the plane down, it was almost like a controlled crash. The plane just floated down and hit the ground with a jolt, but then it only rolled a very short distance to a stop. There were about twenty to thirty people waiting for us. They were so glad to see us . . . alive! They had gotten word yesterday, when we didn't arrive as planned, that the plane was down. They thought we were "goners." One of them said, "We can't tell you how good it is to see you. If you had died, no visitors would ever come to see us again."

Bill Quiggle had a few hours with his friends, and we got a nice tour of a very primitive but adequate hospital, way up in the mountains, with dedicated, capable doctors and nurses serving the needs of the people. They all were demonstrating the love of Jesus Christ to their patients. As usual in missionary hospitals, after a person is helped physically by loving, caring personnel, they are often open spiritually to God's message of love for them. Here we saw genuine, selfless people demonstrating the love of God. After a nice visit, we went back up on the mountaintop and into the plane. This was a little scary. As we took off going at top speed, we just flew off the top of the mountain. We were airborne, whether we were ready or not. After that, it was uneventful. We flew to JAARS headquarters and changed planes. Bill the pilot said the original plane was in good shape, with a working radio. He sheepishly told us the trouble was that the microphone cord was not plugged into the receiver, which was located under the front passenger seat! We got back to Manila fine. An interesting two days, to say the least. We concluded that the Lord had something more for us to do. At that point we were ready to do most anything.

That was a long story about the airplane fiasco, but there is one more incident that occurred while we were in the Philippines that was interesting but not quite as dramatic as the plane crash.

The very next day, after getting home safely on the plane, Frank had planned a day of relaxation and information. Perhaps you have heard of Lake Taal. It is a large lake not too far from Manila. In the middle of this big lake is a mountain. Inside the mountain is a volcano. People live all over the mountain in houses from top to bottom. The volcano had been quiet for years. Then, all of a sudden, it erupted; and the black lava came pouring down the mountain, covering the houses and killing hundreds of people. It was on national television. I remembered seeing it. There was so much lava that it poured into the lake, and the water had turned black. It had been quiet for a few years before our visit. Frank took us to the lake via car, and he had arranged for a boat to take us out into the middle of the lake to see the mountain volcano.

The boat is worth telling you about. It was like a large canoe, maybe twenty feet long. It had an outrigger on one side, and it had a motor. The motor was located about three-quarters of the way from front to back. It was exposed on all three sides. It had an exposed driveshaft going to the back of the boat that turned the propeller. My seat was way in the very back, with the motor in front of me and the driveshaft between my legs. Besides the three of us, Frank, Bill, and me, and another missionary named Don, there were three or four "crew." One of them sat right in front of me alongside the driveshaft where it went through a brace that had a bearing in it to support the shaft. His job was to dip a can into the lake and fill it with water and pour it on the bearing and shaft to keep it cool. When he did, the water would hit the shaft and spray in all directions. When we saw the boat, we were a little apprehensive. But, hey, we'd been on a plane without a radio. What's wrong with a boat without a cover over the motor?

We made it out into the lake and over to the mountain while constantly pouring water onto the shaft. When we stopped, Frank pointed out to us the tops of some houses on the mountain that were covered with the black lava. The whole mountainside was black, from the top right down to the lake. Actually, the black water in the lake was hot—I'd guess ninety to ninety-five degrees. Frank and some of the "crew" actually went swimming in the hot bathwater. After our observation and swim, the crew tried to start the boat for our return trip home. But it wouldn't start. They tried and tried, but no luck. It was starting to get dark. Someone said that on the other side of the mountain there were still a few houses, and they must have a boat. So, since we were fairly close to shore, two or three of the crew got out of the boat and, with a long rope, began to pull the boat along the shore. Two or three more of the crew kept pushing the boat out into the water to keep it away from the beach. It was quite an operation! A boat with a bunch of teenagers came within shouting distance, and Frank yelled something to them as they discussed the terms of rescuing us and towing us home. Pretty soon, the kids took off. I said to Frank, "What happened?" He said they wanted way too much money. Later I found out it was twenty dollars. I could have killed him! The crew kept pulling and pushing, and we saw a boat on the beach. They made contact with the owner, and he came and hooked on to our boat and we started for home. By now it was pitch-black dark. After a little while we saw a light coming toward us on the lake. It turned out to be the mayor of the village on the shore from where we started. Don, the missionary, lived in the village. We were supposed to have dinner with him and his family after the boat trip. When we didn't come back on time, his wife sent the mayor out looking for us. We changed boats and got back safely for a nice, but somewhat delayed, dinner. Two interesting days in the Philippines!

49

WINONA LAKE

My friend Waldo Yeager lived in Toledo, Ohio. He had been one of several mentors to me in my early days in CBMC. In fact, he was chairman of the board of CBMC when I was elected to the board in 1960. Waldo was in the chicken and egg business, with his operations on the outskirts of Toledo. He was also on the board of the Winona Lake Bible Conference, located near Warsaw, Indiana. Winona Lake Bible Conference was a large, well-known conference center that operated only in the summertime. It was the home of the famous evangelist Billy Sunday, who was as popular during the first two decades of the twentieth century as Billy Graham was in the last half of the twentieth century. There was a large tabernacle that could seat five thousand people and an air-conditioned auditorium that would hold two thousand. In its day, it was well attended and had all kinds of accommodations including two hotels, a motel, and a variety of other facilities. However, by this time, its popularity was declining. People still came, and they still held meetings and conferences, but Winona Lake wasn't as it once was.

One day I got a call from Waldo telling me of a situation at the conference. He told me that the conference director, Gordon Beck, had died suddenly and that he, Waldo, was going to retire from his business and become the director of the conference. His two sons, Wally and Gus, were going to take over the business.

The board of directors of the conference consisted of men who were also the heads of the various organizations that used the conference center. They included, among others, the president of Youth for Christ International, the vice president of Moody Bible Institute, the president of

Grace College, which was located nearby, the president of Christian Life Ministries, and other similar leaders of Christian organizations. They were all mostly ministers, preachers, etc. Waldo had been the only board member who was not a minister. I wished him the Lord's best in his new role as full-time conference director.

It wasn't long after that when I received another call from Waldo, inviting me to join the board of directors to take the place he had vacated to become the general director. He said he really needed my help, as all the other members, who were clergymen, didn't totally understand the business problems, and he needed my support. He said the board only met two or three times per year and only for one day. I agreed to help out my old friend Waldo Yeager Sr. Then, one day he called to tell me when the next board meeting would be held. He also said, "When you come, please bring a copy of your financial statement with you. I'll tell you why later." He also asked me to come a day before the board meeting. When I got there, he explained that the conference was in a little financial trouble, but that he had a plan to fix it. But in order to fix it, they needed to borrow $60,000 from the local bank for a year or two. He explained that the conference needed a cosigner, which was me. He assured me not to worry, that he knew what he was doing. So I signed the note. As I did, I remember saying to him that my association with the conference was all because of him, and when he left, I, too, would be leaving. He understood, and he did do a good job of running the conference center, but it was an uphill battle financially. The Bible conference ministry movement, in general, was declining and people were not attending as they used to with all the new means of communications. The operating expenses were right at one million dollars per year, and the income was about $950,000, or a loss of about $50,000 per year. Oh, incidentally, at the first board meeting, Waldo suggested that I be elected chairman to fill the spot he had also vacated. The other members were all too happy with that, as they were all too busy with their own ministries and they all trusted Waldo, his judgment and recommendation.

The first year, a lady who was an old friend of the conference, died and left us $50,000. So we broke even financially. The second year, Waldo was going through some old files and papers, and he found the deed to a piece of land that someone had donated to the conference and had been forgotten about. He located a realtor, sold the land, and we received $50,000; and we made it a second year.

The third year was coming to a close and we were short the same $50,000. There was talk of closing it down. Pat Zondervan, of Zondervan Publishing House and the bookstore chain of the same name, was on our board, and he had a big, popular Christian bookstore at the conference. It was where they sold new books, but also where they sent all the books that were out-of-date and unsold, and they sold them at big discounts. But it was a big help to his business, so he said he would donate $25,000 if the other board members would collectively match his $25,000. Looking around the room, getting $25,000 from the other board members was not likely. So perhaps you can guess who put in the $25,000 to get the matching $25,000 from Pat. Fortunately, Waldo had paid the bank the $60,000 loan, and I was "off the hook" on that one.

I remember saying to Waldo that while business was improving slightly under his leadership, it had a long way to go. People's vacation plans no longer included a week or two at a Bible conference, at least not in the volumes that used to be. Also, we had dozens of buildings and they were all old and needed a lot of repairs and, in some cases, replacement.

At the next board meeting, when we broke for lunch, I was sitting directly across the table from Dr. Herman Hoyt, who was the president of Grace College, whose campus is about two or three blocks from the conference. Out of the blue, it just came to me and I said, "You know, Dr. Hoyt, what we should do is just give the Bible conference to you and Grace College." He said, "What? Are you serious?" I said, "Think about it. You could run it during the summertime, as usual, and in the other nine months you could use the facilities for your college purposes. You would have extra dormitory space, another auditorium, and I'm sure you could figure out how to easily save $50,000 per year by eliminating some duplication in staff. Therefore, with combined management, the conference would break even and maybe even be in the black. Your ministry goals coincide with ours, and I think it would be a win-win situation." He was flabbergasted and didn't know what to say.

When the board meeting reconvened, I introduced the idea to the entire board, and they thought it was a good one. Dr. Hoyt said that he would speak with his college board. A few months later, he brought a list of new members that he would like elected to the board. The board voted them on, and then we all (old board members) resigned; and the Winona Lake Bible Conference was now under the control of the board of directors of Grace College.

My friend Waldo was also very pleased with the new arrangement, as he now could retire for sure. The conference is still going on today, but on a smaller scale. It was an interesting three or four years and another experience that the Lord brought into my life, along with the opportunity to be associated with some of God's choice servants.

50

MY INVOLVEMENT WITH A KOREAN HOUSEBOY

During the Korean conflict, there was a fifteen-year-old Korean boy who helped the American soldiers in their barracks doing things like laundry, cleaning, shining their shoes, etc. The soldiers called them "houseboys." One army sergeant took a liking to him and nicknamed him "Billy." Since almost everyone in Korea is named Kim, they called him "Billy Kim."

His life is a story of its own. It is most remarkable how the soldier got Billy to America and helped him get a college education in a Christian university. After marrying an American girl named Trudy from Pontiac, Michigan, Billy and Trudy went back to Korea as missionaries. During his college days, he met two brothers from Toledo, Ohio, Wally and Gus Yeager. They were the sons of Waldo Yeager, the friend I told you about who got me involved with Winona Lake.

Waldo became very impressed with young Billy Kim and wanted to help him and Trudy with financial support as they went back to Korea as missionaries. He formed a new ministry called "Christian Service." It was registered with the IRS and was a tax-exempt organization. Waldo asked me to be one of five or six board members. I agreed.

Billy had a phenomenal ministry in South Korea. He started a church and began to hold evangelistic meetings all over the country. In fact, after a while, he became better known in South Korea than Billy Graham was in the United States. His personality and reputation was amazing. He was, and is, one of the most respected individuals in South Korea.

One time when he and Trudy came to the United States for a visit, there was a reception for them and some of Trudy's family attended. One was her younger brother, Herb Stephens. I was introduced to him, and we had a nice visit. Sometime later, out of the blue, Herb showed up at my office. He said he had a problem. Herb owned several "mom-and-pop" type motels all along I-75 from Pontiac, Michigan, to Sault Sainte Marie in the Upper Peninsula. His problem was that he had purchased a motel in Pontiac on a land contract and he was behind in his payments. If he didn't pay $40,000 by Friday, he was going to lose the motel.

I looked over the situation, and it was obvious that it was worth more than $40,000 so I loaned him the money with a recommendation that he go and get a long-term mortgage and pay off the land contract holder. He insisted that I become his partner in the motel. I really wasn't interested, but he gave me a 50 percent interest anyway.

A little while later he got a mortgage and paid me the $40,000. I thought that was the end of it all. A year or two later, he showed up again at my office. I thought, Oh no. He wants to borrow some more money. Instead, he said, "Guess what? I sold the motel." I said something like, "Good for you." Then he told me to sign some papers, and when he closed the deal, he would bring me my portion of the proceeds.

So I signed. A few weeks later he came back with a check for $75,000. After I thanked him, I went back into my office and I remember just sitting there all alone and looking at the check and thinking, this is a gift from God! I really didn't do much to deserve this. So let's put it to work for the Lord. Let's see, Herb Stevens is Trudy's brother. Trudy is married to Billy Kim. They are missionaries in Korea. That's the connection. Let's send it to them.

I called Billy in Korea and told him that I had just come into some extra cash and asked him if he had any need for it. He said, "In fact, we do." He explained that they were building an "old folks home." He said there were none in Korea at that time and that there was a great need to care for the elderly. When I told him, "Okay," he asked me how much I had. I said, "$75,000." There was a long silence on the phone. I finally said, "Billy, are you still there?" He said in a very weak and broken voice, "Yes, I'm still here." He went on to say that $75,000 was exactly the amount they had been praying for as that what was needed to finish the project. I said, "Okay. The money will be on its way to you tomorrow." That was maybe thirty or forty years ago. The project was finished, and they called it the Paul and Marilyn Johnson Old Folks Home.

But the story doesn't end there. About five years ago, I got a phone call from Billy from Korea. He said, "Guess what? We sold the old folks home." I said, "What? You sold the old folks home?" I asked him how much he got for it. He said, "$9 million." He said the location had become very strategic and valuable, and BMW, the German company, wanted to build their new headquarters building to serve all of Korea on the property. When I asked Billy what he was planning to do with the $9 million, he said they were going to go out in the country, where land was less expensive, and build a new bigger and better multilevel old folks home. In November 2012, Pam and I and Colleen and Drew got a tour of it as we visited Billy and Trudy in Korea. It is a state-of-the-art, five-story building with two towers; one for the patients who can still walk around and one wing for the ones who are bedridden. The main floor houses the chapel, dining room, and other facilities. It is a lovely structure and well used to ease some of the pain and suffering that comes with old age. It is amazing how God makes **much** out of a **little** when we let go and let Him have control!

51

A MODERN-DAY
MEDICAL MIRACLE

You all know my sister, Linda, and that she is fourteen years younger than me. It's like my mom and dad had two "only children" because of the difference in our ages. Linda married Dale Hebbard, who worked as a buyer for the Chrysler Corporation. As most of you know, they had two daughters, Cindy and Sheri. Cindy is married to Sean Hanson and they have two daughters. Sheri is married to Mark Janda, and they have two daughters and one son.

One day when he was in his late forties, Dale, Linda's husband, my brother-in-law, noticed a small black spot on his chest. The doctor said it should be removed. During the operation, they discovered it was cancer, and they cut him across his chest from armpit to armpit to remove cancerous lymph nodes under both arms. He recovered fairly well. But the doctors said that the cancer had metastasized and would surely come back. They said it would most likely be in one of two places: either the brain or the liver. As you might guess, everyone was devastated. They thought for sure he would be gone to heaven within a short time. The girls were teenagers at that time. So we arranged for all four of them to go on an extended trip to Europe as a family, thinking that there might not be much time left.

Sure enough, about two years later he collapsed and was taken to Ford Hospital where he was diagnosed with a malignant brain tumor. It was successfully removed. The doctor said that if you had to have a brain tumor, his was in a good place and easy to remove. Again, Dale recovered and got along for about two more years when another one showed up—this time down deeper and more difficult to remove. I remember speaking to the doctor while Dale was still in the hospital recovering and asking the doctor how many times can you do this and still have the patient survive? He said there was a young girl, twenty-five years old, down the hall, and he had just taken out number five. What a dismal future to look forward to!

Everyone had been praying for Dale for years, including many people from their church. Now the prayers increased "big-time." After more radiation, he once again recovered. Somewhere along the line, he was retired from Chrysler, due to disability. He was told to report back to the hospital after three months for a checkup. He did so, and the doctors said, in effect, "So far, so good." He went back after three more months. Same report. Six more months. Still clean. The doctors were amazed. Then it was a year between checkups. Still no sign of cancer. It has now been over twenty years, and each annual checkup has been the same. No cancer anywhere! The doctors actually call him their "miracle patient." Some of them are scratching their heads. But some of us know what God can do when He wants to. Dale's mother lived to be over a hundred. Maybe he will too. God is so good. We thank the Lord every day for Dale. By the way, before his illness he was a runner. He ran six to eight miles per day and ran in a lot of marathons. After he fully recovered, he started running again. Not quite so long. But several miles per day, and he is still doing it!

52

MY OTHER IN-LAW

I've told you about my brother-in-law, Dale, and his medical recovery. I have only one other in-law. She is Marilyn's younger sister, Ginny. As with me and my sister, Linda, Ginny is twelve years younger than Marilyn. She was a "cutie" as a baby, and Marilyn was like a second mom to her, looking after her a good deal of the time as their mother worked a lot. They were always very close, in spite of the difference in their ages.

Ginny was fifteen when her dad died. As explained earlier, Mimi and Ginny moved to a smaller house within one block of our home on Minock, so we could all be close. And close we were! Mimi and Ginny (later called Gigi) were at our house much of the time. They, along with Pam who lived across the street from them, were our built-in babysitters as well as helpers during parties, dinners, and all kinds of entertaining. In those days, there was no need for extra help or caterers. They did it all. Gigi and Pam have always been great friends and very special to each other, even today.

By and by, Gigi went to college at King's College in New York, a few miles north of New York City. There she met and later married Frank Leeds, who went on to two seminaries earning a doctoral degree and later becoming a pastor. He pastored a small church in Beverly Hills, Michigan, before being called to a church in Brooklyn, New York. That was a most interesting situation. It was a very nice old Baptist church in what was once a very lovely section of Brooklyn. The homes in the neighborhood were very nice, quite large and stately. It was where wealthy New York businesspeople used to live. However, now things had changed. There were still some old people in the area, but many of the homes were now occupied by all types of ethnic groups. There were Chinese, Hispanics, African-Americans, and folks from Haiti. It was a melting pot of different nationalities and people groups. They started attending the church, but I think Frank soon saw that they were not all comfortable with each other.

So he did a very creative thing. He got three or four assistant pastors, each with a different ethnic background, and they had separate services for each group at a different time each Sunday. I think they started at 8 or 9 a.m. and met at a different time until 3 or 4 p.m. The church grew and was very successful.

As I said, Marilyn and Gigi were very close. We used to visit them on holidays like Thanksgiving or Christmas; and it was always when the whole church met together. That was something to see, all the different kinds of people with different worship customs and personal behaviors. I'll never forget one Sunday when we were there. Right in the middle of the service while Frank was preaching, one rather large lady stood up right in the middle of the church and readjusted her dress, her hat, and her underwear, and then sat back down as if she was in her living room or maybe her bedroom. Our kids got a big laugh out of that incident!

Frank became very helpful to his church members when they had all kinds of problems with issues like applying for Social Security. He visited his members when they were in the hospital, often helping them with insurance forms. Soon the hospital authorities noticed his expertise and asked him to be a chaplain at the hospital to help others. He was good at it and compassionate as well. Soon the hospital asked him to work full-time on the hospital staff. This was an increase in salary for him and allowed his family to move out of Brooklyn into a nicer neighborhood to raise their three children, Lani, Oliver, and Janna. Gigi has the gift of hospitality and was always helping others. She was, and is, a great mom!

The hospital prospered, and Frank became second in command as the associate administrator. He was now in the health care business. Some people in Florida recognized his ability and made him the boss of several nursing and retirement facilities in St. Petersburg, Florida. Later, the ownership changed hands, and he became the director of an operation much like our "Goodwill Industries" where he hired mentally impaired folks.

They recycled various items and sold them.

In his retirement, he and Gigi live in St. Petersburg where Frank is associate pastor in a church. Among his duties, he preaches one Sunday a month. Gigi says it's getting embarrassing, as the congregation is considerably larger on the Sundays when Frank preaches.

They now spend their summers at Maranatha where they have a small cottage. Pam and I love Gigi and "Uncle Frank" and all their children.

Incidentally, Oliver is a lieutenant colonel in the air force and is married to Eriko and has two boys. Lani is married to Tony Campana and lives in Royal Oak, Michigan, with their two boys. Janna lives near her parents in St. Petersburg and has one son.

53

THE DEMOSSES

My days and experiences with CBMC were wide and varied. Through CBMC I became acquainted with Christian men in every part of the country—dedicated believers in Jesus Christ who made positive impressions on me. Men and their wives who, to this day, we still call our friends. Many now are already in heaven. I even had the pleasure of traveling overseas and speaking in thirty foreign countries. Many, many wonderful experiences and people who enhanced my life greatly. Way too many to try to tell you about.

But I will tell you about one or two. Ted DeMoss and I went on the national board of CBMC of USA together. It was in 1960. Ted lived in Chattanooga, Tennessee, and was in the insurance business. He and his cousin, Art DeMoss, owned several insurance agencies in cities through-out the eastern half of the United States. He was also the head of a Christian men's group called "Fishers of Men." After a few years, they joined CBMC, and Ted became the president of CBMC, a paid position. He was an excellent communicator and a much sought-after speaker. When I was made chairman of the board, we worked very closely together and became the best of friends. He sold his agencies, as he now had a full-time job doing what he loved best, telling businessmen about Jesus Christ.

His cousin, Art DeMoss, was also a devout Christian. Both of them were men of passion and conviction. Art, who also had an insurance background, came up with the idea of selling insurance by mail. It was a new idea. He knew that the commission on the sale of an insurance policy was equal to about half of the first year's premium or payment. Therefore, the insurance companies were paying big money to agents that brought them business. He also reasoned that if somehow the agent was eliminated, the policy could cost less to the insured. So he came up with the idea of advertising in Christian periodicals offering insurance policies without an agent. He went to Mutual of Omaha and asked how much they would charge per month to insure one thousand people who did not drink or smoke for a certain amount of life insurance. Mutual of Omaha, like every insurance company, knows that folks who don't drink or smoke live longer. Therefore, they pay more in premiums over the years so their monthly payments could be less because they live longer and there was going to be more premiums paid. Mutual of Omaha did their research and, as an example, said eight dollars per month for a certain amount of insurance, if there were one thousand people involved. So Art, in his ads in the periodicals, offered that insurance for ten dollars per month.

Well, the response was amazing. People clipped the ads out of the magazines or newspapers and sent them in to Art, many with ten-dollar bills attached, or checks. He had one thousand in no time. So he went to Mutual of Omaha and had them issue a policy to each of them. Obviously, Art made two dollars on each one, or $2,000. More people responded, and he widened his advertising and his margins. Soon he was on television. Some of you may remember Art Linkletter, who was his spokesman. His business expanded like wildfire. He was the first ever to do this. The leaders of the conventional insurance industry sued him, but he prevailed. He wasn't doing anything wrong. Just different. Soon he didn't need Mutual of Omaha. He established his own insurance company and called it "National Liberty Life Insurance." His original headquarters were in Valley Forge, Pennsylvania. Later, he moved it to the Philadelphia area near where he lived. Very quickly the business grew, and he became a multimillionaire. He and I were good friends when he was just an insurance salesman and became better friends as time went on. In spite of his wealth, he always had the same main interest in life: to see businessmen and others come to know Jesus Christ. He believed God gave him the idea and the concept of selling insurance by mail and that as a result of his success and wealth, he now had more resources with which to serve the Lord.

There are so many stories about Art. He was a little absentminded and he had a poor sense of direction. One day, way before cellphones, he bumped into another car. He pulled out his tape recorder and speaking to his secretary, Barbara, said, "I just had an accident with my car on the corner of Main and Oak Street. My car won't run. Will you please send someone to pick me up?" And then he put his tape recorder back in his briefcase. One time he came to Detroit to speak for us at a CBMC meeting and stayed overnight with us. He came to breakfast, and when he got up from the table to go back upstairs, he went the other way and opened the door to the garage.

But let me tell you about his evangelistic efforts. In CBMC in his hometown near Philadelphia, some of the members were complaining about the cost of the meal at a luncheon—ten dollars. And to bring a guest, which was the whole idea, it would cost twenty. So Art said to the members, "Just go get all the guests you can find, and I'll pay for them." Many did, and Art paid for all the guests. But he thought the members of the Philadelphia committee near where he lived were not serious enough about reaching their friends. So he and his wife, Nancy, came up with another new idea. They decided that they would invite their neighbors to their home for dinner and have a well-known businessman come after dinner and give his testimony and share his faith. Nancy told me of going up and down the street, getting the neighbors' names off the mailboxes to send them a very nice invitation in the mail. This was in a very wealthy community in Bryn Mawr, Pennsylvania, where they lived. Well, people came; and after a nice meal, they were invited into the large living room where Art introduced the guest speaker, who would share something about his business and then give a positive testimony for Jesus Christ. At the end, Art would lead them in a prayer, much like the one I told you about with Governor Clinton. Then he would say to them, "I want you all to take off your name tags and fold them together so there is nothing sticky on them. As you leave tonight, if you prayed the prayer with me, just slip me your folded name tag as you say good night." The response was most encouraging. He and Nancy would take the folded name tags and invite those folks to come back for what they called a small dinner party and encouraged the folks to join a weekly Bible study that they held in their home. Actually, there were two; one for women during the daytime and one for men early in the morning before work. More people were coming to faith in Christ than in many churches. The group grew until they actually started a church and called a pastor. It is called, "The Church of the Savior." As a result, a whole new ministry was born called "home dinner parties," and people from coast to coast came to the De-Moss home to learn how to do it.

Marilyn and I were invited to one of those meetings. There was an interesting incident that happened. The DeMosses had a large backyard, and they invited a large group of friends and acquaintances to a Sunday afternoon barbecue. The guest speakers were Roy Rogers and Dale Evans, of Hollywood fame. There were perhaps two hundred people there. After the dinner, Roy and Dale each gave a testimony of their faith in Jesus Christ. Art closed the meeting in prayer, as usual, asking any guest who wanted to pray with him to do so. If they did, they were to let him know as they were leaving by giving him their name tags. Later, after everyone had left, he had an assistant take all the name tags and the next morning record them on a piece of paper for Art and Nancy to look at.

Art had invited Marilyn and me to stay overnight and the next morning come by his office about ten o'clock for a tour. I came and saw hundreds of telephone operators with headsets sitting in front of screens on their computers. They were selling insurance from mail responses and over the telephone. It was quite a sight. As I came into Art's private secretary's office, a lady named Barbara whom I knew said, "Go ahead in. He is expecting you." As I looked into his office, I had an experience I don't think I will ever forget. He looked up and saw me and said, "Hey, Paul, come here. Look at this." And he handed me a copy of the list of the people who had prayed with him the night before. He was so excited. He said, "Look at this! This fellow is a doctor and my next-door neighbor." And, "Look at this! This couple lives down the street, and they have been having marital problems. They both prayed with me. And how about this? This guy is my stockbroker," and on and on. There were two pages of names.

I thought to myself, here is a fellow who had been out of the office most of the last week on business, and the most important thing to him on his first day back in the office was the list of people who needed their lives changed in a way that only God could do. He had a one-track mind: "Let's see how many people we can get into the kingdom." He used most of his time and his vast resources to help make that happen.

Another interesting meeting that I had with Art had to do with business. As his insurance company grew, they had a lot of money that they had to invest and keep it ready to pay their policyholders in the case of accidents or death or whatever the policy called for. They also wanted to invest the money wisely and, if possible, make it grow. As I explained earlier, my friend Paul, the restaurant owner, found that out from talking to an insurance agent years before. Art called me one day and invited me to a meeting to be held in his office. He said I was one of three or four real estate people whom he trusted and was interested in my advice. At this point, he had several vice presidents working for him. Many of them knew more about the insurance business than Art did, and he knew it. In fact, he had hired a president to run the whole operation, but he stayed informed as to how things were going and growing, and they were indeed growing.

The issue was this: traditionally insurance companies would make investments in various ways. Some stocks, some bonds, and some money was often invested in fairly secure mortgages or real estate. Some insurance companies liked homes, some liked office buildings or shopping centers or apartment buildings. They were usually fairly conservative, loaning anywhere from 50 percent of the property's value up to maybe 80 or even 90 percent of real safe properties (or at least what they thought were very safe). Art had a couple of young vice presidents who reasoned that if they were the ones loaning all the money that made these projects possible and hopefully successful, why not put another 10 or 20 percent of the money into the deal and own the entire project. They could cut out the developer and get all the benefits that he was getting and, in short, become developers and owners instead of just being lenders. Actually, some insurance companies had done that but with mixed results.

Art brought us into his headquarters in the Philadelphia area, and I remember sitting around an enormous round conference room table. There was probably room for twenty or more people. Art explained the proposition that two or three of these young executives were suggesting. As his friends, we listened. All of us were developers. One fellow from Miami was one of the biggest real estate developers in the state of Florida. In the end, we all suggested to Art, "Don't do it." Real estate developers are entrepreneurs willing to take risks, but they are also motivated by personal gain. So they get up early in the morning and work until late at night to make sure that every little detail is covered. Their attitude is, "If I don't do it, it won't get done and it might fail." Employees of larger corporations don't always have those motivations and commitments. In conclusion we all agreed. Just loan the money in conservative mortgages. Keep on selling insurance, which is what you know best. Leave the developing to developers. He thanked us, and we all left.

A few months later, in talking to Art, I said, "What did you and your fellows decide to do about getting into the development business?" I'll never forget his response. He said, "Oh, it worked out fine. We only lost $2 million." I said, "What?" He said, "Yes, those young guys talked me into a project where we were to be the owner. It didn't work, and we lost $2 million." I said, "What's so great about that?" He said, "If it had worked, we had $20 million more set aside for those kinds of deals. When we lost the $2 million, I never heard any more from those guys about real estate developing." Keep in mind $2 million back then was probably equal to $10 or 15 million today.

Art DeMoss was one of the most godly men and one of the most successful I ever knew. He had a lot of friends who were more successful and wealthy than I was, but we had a similar desire of wanting to see people come to faith in God. Art and Ted, his cousin, were so alike in their purposes but quite different in personalities. We were the best of friends. I'll tell you more about Art and his legacy later on.

54

FIVE FRUITFUL YEARS

After we finished the Birmingham Place project, I was finished with the construction part of my life. We were now strictly in the property management business, and our income was sufficient for retirement. I was fifty-six. I was at a convention for CBMC, and my good friend Ted DeMoss, who was president of CBMC, said that Nancy DeMoss wanted to see me. She was also at the convention. At this time she was a fairly young widow. Our good friend, her husband, Art, had died of a heart attack while playing tennis. He was in his midfifties. Art had left most of his assets in a private Christian foundation. Nancy was chairman of the board and the board members were the adult children plus Ted. The question was how best to use the millions of dollars in the fund to further the cause of Jesus Christ. As they pondered the question, they often asked themselves, "What would Art do?" They continued to discuss and plan the future activities of the foundation. They came up with a very ambitious undertaking. Art always thought big and, therefore, so did they. The plan was to put the plan of salvation, the gospel message, clearly explained in a new book that they would authorize and print. It would start with the testimonies of ten Christian celebrities, including Art. It would also have a second section in it that would tell a new believer how to take the first steps in developing his life with Christ. The book would be free of charge to anyone and everyone.

The question became, how do we distribute it? They thought, if we go around just handing them out, many people will just throw it away. Maybe we should let people know that it is available and then have them ask for it. That at least would show some interest. Then they thought, how do we let people know it is available? They concluded, "Let's do it like Art did. We'll advertise in newspapers and magazines and on television, and we will offer it free." As they continued, they decided to take out a full-page advertisement in every major newspaper in every city in the United States. They would put a full-page ad in every respected magazine in the United States. And they would create ads for television and put them on in every market in the United States. This indeed was a major undertaking. It is reported that one of them said, "This will cost millions." Someone else said, "We have millions! The question is, will this work and be effective?"

The book was called *Power for Living*, and they did roll out the campaign and it indeed was very successful. The people could ask for the book in two ways: one by calling an 800 phone number given on the screen in the television ads and in the print ads, or by filling out the coupon in the print ads. The ads all said, "No contributions are solicited nor will any be accepted." This was to put down the skeptics who said that they were building a mailing list to later offer to sell them some product. That attitude had little basis, because you can buy names for a mailing list for a lot less than spending the millions that they spent. Their motives were pure. They simply wanted people to know and understand how to have a personal relationship with God by simple faith.

As I said, the plan worked. Thousands of responses came in. In the back of the book was a response card for anyone who said that they prayed to receive Christ and wanted a second book that explained more about how to continue on in his faith and grow as a new believer. If they sent in the card and got the second book, the campaign ended. No one got the response cards so no one was able to contact those new believers. In the follow-up material, they were urged to find a good Bible-believing church and to get involved, but it never said which one or what kind. As the campaign ended and they received millions of response cards, they determined that while it had cost millions of dollars, it was one of the most efficient ways of reaching people with the gospel. The cost per person who prayed to receive Christ was a lot less than that of the average church or missionary activities or even a Billy Graham crusade. There is nothing wrong with all the other ministries. In fact, the foundation was also helping many of them with sizeable contributions. But most of them could not do a national ad campaign like *Power for Living* because they didn't have the millions of dollars to do it.

Now back to why Nancy DeMoss wanted to see me. The foundation was so pleased with the success of the US campaign that they wanted to take it to other countries, and she wanted me to head up that division of the foundation's ministries. She knew from Art's cousin, Ted, that I didn't have much to do in business anymore. I was excited about the opportunity and overcome and humbled with the confidence in me. But I was concerned because I had never done anything like this before. My job would be to go to a foreign country and find nine Christian celebrities who had a good clear testimony and get them involved in the project by allowing their picture and testimony to be used in the beginning of the book. That's the way it was done in the United States, and it gave the book a lot of credibility as one started to read it. They also used these celebrities in the advertisements. For instance, in the United States, one full-page ad in newspapers and magazines featured a picture of Tom Landry in the whole top half of the page. Under it was the caption, "Is football the most important thing to Tom Landry?" The copy that followed said, while Tom Landry is one of the most successful football coaches in history with the Dallas Cowboys, he says there is something even more important in his life than football. Then the copy described something of his faith in Christ, and then announced that there is a new book out called *Power for Living* that tells more about what he believes and that you can have a copy free if you send in the coupon or call the 800 number.

Not only would I have to locate nine Christian celebrities (as Art was number ten), I would have to get the book translated into the local language and arrange for the printing. Also, I would have to arrange for a telephone answering service to answer the phones and a mailing house to send out the books. I had to arrange the whole project, except for the advertising. The advertising company that handled the US campaign had offices all over the world. The agent, Ned McDonald, who worked out of their New York office would travel with me and arrange all the advertising. Quite a job!

Nancy wanted me to move to Philadelphia and work full-time in their office. As I thought more about the job and all the overseas travel, I convinced her that I could do just as well working out of my own office. She finally agreed, but she said she wanted me to come to Philadelphia twice a month for progress reports and meetings. I agreed, and Pam agreed to help me with the correspondence and clerical work.

At our first meeting, Nancy said that she had a burden to try to reach the people in France, and she would like to start there. I asked her if maybe we could start in a country where they speak English. There were enough new things to learn in this job without the complication of a different language. She and the board agreed, and they settled on England for our first campaign.

Even there we had to have the book redone and the words Anglicized. So I started out. I called everyone I knew who might know someone in England who could help. I went over and met people who knew people, and so on, until we had the people that we needed to do the job. It took about six months and four or five visits to England to arrange all the details. The Lord went ahead of me and arranged for a wonderful Christian celebrity who agreed to serve as our main endorser. His name is Cliff Richard. He is a popular singer and is as well known in England, as was Frank Sinatra or Elvis Presley in the United States. His picture was in all our advertisements and on posters all over London and throughout England. There are a lot of ads in the subway system. Real large posters, maybe forty feet wide and ten feet high, are used down in the tunnels where the trains run. They are located on the wall across the tracks from where the people wait for the trains. Cliff Richard's picture took up about half of the poster, and we had them in every platform in every station in London. He didn't need the exposure, but he got a lot of it anyway. I found a fairly well known female singer, Sheila Walsh, whom Cliff knew. She agreed to write her testimony to be used in the book, plus several lesser-known people but Christian people in prominent positions. Sheila later came to the United States and is an anchor host on the 700 Club television program. I made all the other arrangements for printing, telephone answering, mailing, etc. We rolled out the program, which lasted about six weeks. It was a success, but not like the United States. There were some real interesting stories connected with the program but too many to mention here. But I will tell you one.

An Englishman named Angus Hudson was a big help to me. He was in the publishing business and knew a lot of people. One day after the campaign had been in progress, he sent me an article from a newspaper in Nottingham, England. An Anglican pastor was telling the story of a couple in his parish who were divorced, but after reading the book, *Power for Living* they were remarried. I called the minister and told him who I was and my connection with *Power for Living* and asked if he would give me the phone number of the couple. He did, and I called on the phone. At first, the lady couldn't believe that I was calling her from the United States. I asked her to give me a few details of her story. After listening to it, I asked her if she would be willing to come to London a few weeks later and share it with a few people at a banquet we were going to have. The campaign was winding down, and we planned to have a small dinner party in London, inviting all the people who had helped us with the project. We wanted to thank them and have them meet each other. Nancy DeMoss would be in attendance to personally greet and thank them; and I would give the results of the campaign. The guests would be the advertisers and the agency people, the printer, the telephone people, and mailing house executives, the celebrities, including Cliff Richard. About sixty to seventy people in all.

When I invited the lady from Nottingham, she said she could not afford the cost to come to London. I assured her that we would pay all the costs for her and her husband and son for an entire weekend at a first class hotel in London. She couldn't believe it! But she agreed to come. The dinner was on a Saturday night. I met her in the hotel lobby about 3 p.m. and asked her again to share with me her story. Afterward, she said that she had never before in her life spoken in front of sixty to seventy people. I said, "You have no problem. Just tell them exactly what you just told me, and you will be fine." She was still a little nervous, but she agreed.

That evening after dinner, I was the MC, and I welcomed and introduced everyone. Most of them were not believers and had no idea what we were really about. They only knew their part, and many wondered what we were really doing and why. I introduced this lady, and this is what she told them. She said she was a very selfish, angry, and controlling person. So much so that her husband couldn't take it any longer and there was a divorce. Then she said that one day she saw an ad in a magazine with Cliff Richard's picture and the offer of a free book. So she called and asked for it. When it came a week or so later, she opened and glanced through it and said to herself, "Oh, this has something to do with religion," and she tossed it on the bed in her bedroom. Later that night, as she got into bed, she picked up the book and started to read. And she read the entire book and prayed the simple prayer, asking the Lord to come into her life and change her. She had a ten-year-old son who went to visit his father from time to time. One day the dad asked the boy, "How is your mother?" He said, "You know, Dad, something has happened to her. Lately she is so nice. It's hard to believe how she has changed. She is not angry anymore and she is so nice and agreeable and easy to get along with. She is like a different person."

As time went on and the boy's reports about his mom's behavior got better and better, the boy said, "Dad, you should come see for yourself." So he did, and he was impressed but still skeptical. Then one time he asked her out for dinner and she told him about the book and how God had changed her life. His response was, "I'd like to see that book." She shared it with him, and he became a believer and soon they were remarried. As she was concluding her remarks, she looked at Cliff Richard and said, "You know, Cliff, if it hadn't been for you, I never would have ordered that book, because I know that you would never be involved with or endorse anything that was a gimmick or a fake. So it's because of you that I have this new life in Christ." It was the best endorsement for *Power for Living* that anyone could give. As I looked at Cliff, I could see tears running down his cheeks. I then introduced Cliff, and he said something like this to her. "Thank you so much for the compliment, but really, I had nothing to do with your decision to trust the Lord. It was simply your time. The Holy Spirit was working in your life and it's all God's doing. Not mine." It was a wonderful night and such a blessing. Nancy had invited

Marilyn and Pam to come along because both had been so involved in all the details, particularly Pam.

Now Nancy was ready to go to France with the campaign. We had a preliminary meeting in Philadelphia with her and her staff and the advertising people from New York. All plans were put in place, and we were planning to go to Paris and get started. Later that evening, after I got home, I received a phone call from one of her staff members that changed our plans. The person told me that that same afternoon, while we were still in the meeting, an accident had taken place. Nancy's son David was a student at Liberty University, and he was home for the weekend. It was a Friday afternoon. It seems that while he and his girlfriend were driving on a two-lane road in a small convertible car, a truck coming toward them swerved and hit them head-on. They were both killed. Sometime later I got a call to come back to Philadelphia for a meeting. Ned McDonald, the advertising agent, came down from New York also. Nancy said, "Let's put France on hold. As a tribute to David, let's go to Brazil."

David had been preparing to go to Brazil as a missionary after he graduated from college. His roommate was a Brazilian, and he and David had big plans for their work in Brazil. She said, "Let's go to Brazil and pull out all the stops for a major campaign in that great country." So we did. Ned and I went to Sao Paulo and began the process. I won't go into all the details, but it was one of the most fruitful campaigns that we had. We spent seven million dollars. We had telephone banks of one hundred operators each in both Sao Paulo and Rio de Janeiro. Ned did a massive television ad blitz, and the results were overwhelming. Outside of the United States, it was the biggest and best. It was, indeed, a tribute to David. I should tell you that what motivated Nancy DeMoss was love. We did all this work and went through all these activities and spent all that money because she had a love for people. She wanted to see people come to know Jesus Christ and receive the gift of eternal life. She was such a humble person. She didn't care how much it cost, just be sure we were efficient in our decisions but get the job done. We must tell the whole world. That was her mindset and her passion. Much like her husband, Art.

As time went on, I traveled to ten countries altogether for *Power for*

Living. They included Ireland, Brazil, Hong Kong, the Philippines, Mexico, Canada, and a second campaign in the United States. The stories of how God worked in all these countries and all the details would make a book of its own. I did this for about five years, and we saw twenty-two million people respond positively, saying that they prayed the simple prayer to receive the Lord Jesus. It was probably the most fruitful period of my life when it comes to ministry. After I stepped down, the advertising agent, Ned McDonald, was hired full-time by the foundation. I helped him learn to do my job, and I went with him to several more countries as his "helper" in Chile, Argentina, Spain, and Italy.

In conclusion, I think it would be fair to say that while *Power for Living* cost millions of dollars, it was one of the most cost-effective evangelistic campaigns that ever was. The cost per person reached was a little over one dollar per person. Art DeMoss's legacy lived on and is still living due to his wife, Nancy's, faithfulness and wisdom. I counted it a great privilege to be associated with this wonderful ministry and never accepted anything except out-of-pocket expenses.

Drew Melby

55

MARANATHA

It was in the midsixties. Colleen was in junior high school, and her mother became concerned about some of the friends she was making. She didn't believe they had the same values that we did. Summer was coming. She was going to be out of school, and what she was going to do with her time was being discussed. About that time, Marilyn was talking on the phone with her lifelong friend, Marilee Dufendach. Marilee was telling Marilyn about the amenities of Maranatha Bible and Missionary Conference in Muskegon where Marilee and Bill had a summer home. Marilee said we should come and visit them and, by the way, there was a lovely, almost new, cottage for sale. It was about a three-hour drive from Detroit, and I was not too keen on the idea of a three-hour drive to go to a cottage. But Marilyn insisted that we go and visit the Dufendachs for a weekend.

So one Saturday morning we started out. By the time we got to Grand Rapids, about a two-hour drive, I thought that was far enough to drive for a summer home. But we went on. When we arrived, Marilee took us to see the cottage that was for sale. It was beautiful, overlooking Lake Michigan. Marilyn had been to Maranatha as a young girl, and she knew something of its history and ministry. She loved both the place and the cottage. It was owned by a doctor, and it was only one year old. It had been designed by an architect and built by a professional builder, unlike most of the others. It was by far the nicest on the grounds at the time. The doctor lived in Muskegon and had the cottage built for the summer months. After living on the lake for one summer, he liked it so much that he purchased a lakefront lot in a public subdivision a mile or so away and built a year-round home. So he then sold both his in-town home and the cottage.

Marilyn loved it and was sure the Lord had provided it just for us. At first I was a little skeptical, especially because of the long drive that I would have to make each weekend. After all, I had to keep working. I couldn't take the whole summer off. But I could see that she really wanted to buy it. She was such a wonderful wife and mother. If she thought that it would be best for our family and that was going to make her happy, maybe that's what we should do. So we did. By and by, I saw that she was 100 percent right (as usual).

It was one of the best investments we ever made. Maranatha is home to about one hundred families all summer, from mid-June to Labor Day. Many husbands commute on weekends, as I did. Besides the residents, there are all kinds of facilities for families who want to come for a week; hotel rooms, apartments, cottages. The conference has a different Bible teacher each week, and a different mission agency is also represented each week. Besides one-quarter mile of white sandy beach, it has an Olympic swimming pool, lighted tennis courts, indoor and outdoor basketball courts, and just about every kind of activity that any family could want from nursery facilities to activities for senior citizens.

Our kids loved it, and at this writing we have been residents for forty-two summers. We seldom miss a week at Maranatha during the summer. I was soon taking Fridays off, leaving the office about 3 p.m. on Thursday afternoon and arriving at Maranatha for dinner by 6 p.m. or so. I would then get up early on Monday morning and leave about 6 a.m., and I was in the office by 9 a.m. I had three full days and four nights with the family and almost four days at the office. I became very well acquainted with I-96 from Detroit to Muskegon. The spiritual environment for our three children all summer was priceless. As they grew up and were married, they all wanted to come back. They eventually got their own places for their families.

During our years at Maranatha, we have seen dramatic changes in the facilities, as many new buildings have been built and others upgraded. Many say that it is the finest facility of its kind in the United States. I don't know about that, but I do know that it is a wonderful place for spiritual growth and physical renewal. Again, God has been so good to provide this wonderful place for us, our children, and now our grandchildren.

56

MOODY

Karen was about to graduate from high school, and she was contemplating college. Her sister, Colleen, had gone to Wheaton College and her brother, Kevin, had gone to Taylor University. But for some reason, she didn't want to go to either one. Her aunt Ginny had gone to King's College in New York, and she suggested that maybe Karen would like that. Karen applied and was accepted, but she didn't seem too enthusiastic about it. When I asked her what she really wanted to do with her life vocationally, like a nurse or teacher, she said, "I really don't know. But I would just like to be able to teach the Bible like Betty King."

Betty King and her husband, David, were good friends of ours and attended our church. Betty was a well-known Bible teacher to ladies. She had a weekly Tuesday morning class at our church with about a hundred ladies in attendance, plus she was also a popular retreat speaker at various women's meetings all over the United States. When I heard Karen say that, I said, "Sweetie, if that's what you want to do, you should go to Moody Bible Institute in Chicago." The school had a wonderful reputation, and several people from our church had attended there. So she and her mom and a girlfriend, who was also looking for a college, took a trip to Chicago. They were given a tour of the campus, and they loved it. Karen applied while she was there, and within a few days she was accepted. In mid-August we loaded up her luggage and drove to Chicago where she would begin her studies at Moody. It was a hot and humid day. The temperature was about ninety. Her dorm room was on the sixth floor, and the elevators were not operating. Her mom and I and Karen carried all her stuff up the six floors during the hottest part of the day. Not only were we physically exhausted after making several trips up the stairs, when her mother saw the dorm room, I thought she was going to cry. It was so small and bland-looking. She said, "This is only slightly better than a jail cell."

This was not a good beginning at Moody. Before we left home, I had asked my secretary, Pam, to make us a hotel reservation near Moody. As I was leaving the office, she handed me an envelope and said, "Here is the information regarding your hotel." I asked her if it was a nice place. She said she thought I would like it. I put the envelope in my pocket and never looked at it until we had gotten Karen's stuff up into her room. In the process, we met her roommate there at the dorm. By this time, it was late afternoon and time to think about the hotel and dinner. We were all sweaty and tired and in need of a shower. We invited her roommate to join us. So the four of us went down to the car, and I opened the envelope with the hotel details.

Indeed, it was only a few blocks away and we found out it was the Ritz Carlton. As we all four entered the hotel room, it could not have been a greater contrast to the dorm room. Karen said, "Hey, Dad. How about we just stay here? It's only a few blocks, and we could walk to school each day." The next day the four of us went to a store on nearby Michigan Avenue, and Marilyn bought drapes and bedspreads for both beds to match for the dorm room and a rug plus all kinds of pictures and accessories. By the time we left the room, it was totally transformed and looked like something out of *House Beautiful* magazine. I think when it was all over, Marilyn was happier than the girls! The next day we went to the registrar's office to get checked in and to pay the fees. The nice lady told us about the costs of room and board and books, etc., and gave me a total, and I paid her. Then I said, "What about the tuition?" She said, "There is no tuition." When I inquired as to how that could be, she said that it was possible because lots of people made donations to the school. She also said there was no endowment fund. They just lived from month to month through the donations. When I asked how much it cost the school to educate a person for a year, she said, "I think it is about $8,000." (It is now about $18,000.) So I said we're able to pay our fair share and did not need others to pay for us, and I remember writing out a check for

$10,000. She seemed surprised but very grateful.

As time went on, we visited Karen and Moody regularly for various events and activities. She loved the school and its teachers. At that time, George Sweeting was the president, and he was good friends with Jack Wyrtzen from Word of Life. I think Jack told Dr. Sweeting about us and our relationship with him. On one of our visits to Moody, Dr. Sweeting called me aside and asked me if I would pray about becoming a board member. It was in 1984. After I found out that it only required three meetings a year, I agreed and was elected to the board.

The chairman at that time was Bill Mitchell from Florida, whom I knew. He was also active in CBMC in his area. Also on the board was Dr. John MacArthur, the well-known pastor from California. For the first several board meetings I just listened and became acquainted with the amazing ministries of the institute. Not only was it a Bible school with about fourteen hundred students, it owned and operated about thirty radio stations, a publishing company called Moody Press, and a flight school that trained most of the pilots who flew small planes for mission agencies all over the world. If it had been a secular organization, it would have been called a conglomerate. At that time the school was almost a century old and still doing what its founder, D. L. Moody, did a hundred years earlier but now even bigger and better.

At one of the early meetings, one of the board members was talking about the lack of athletic facilities at the school. The only place to play basketball was in a gymnasium about two-thirds the size of a regular court. The outside lines were about three feet from a brick wall on all sides. Less than adequate, to say the least, and actually dangerous. However, one board member responded that these students were here to study the Bible and that they didn't need recreational facilities.

I was appalled. I knew kids were kids, Bible students or not. It took several meetings to convince some of the "old-timers" on the board that every other Christian school had an athletic facility and most even had sports teams. I had one other board member on my side. It wasn't until we came up with a fair amount of money (mostly from Paul Wills) to get it started that the other board members began to warm up to the idea.

When the students got wind of the talk about a new facility, they were ecstatic, even though they wouldn't get to use it themselves, as it would most likely take several years to plan and raise the rest of the money. They would probably be graduated by the time it was built. Soon President Sweeting and later Joe Stowell were behind it, and a committee was appointed to look into it. I was put on the committee. As time went on and money was committed, the project was expanded from just one basketball court to two and then to three and with a running track around the top. When the Solheim family (Ping golf clubs) made a significant donation, the project was expanded and an Olympic-sized swimming pool was added. Today it is one of the finest and most complete facilities of its kind. It has weight rooms, exercise equipment room, handball courts, and just about everything one could want. It has been very well used by students and faculty and other employees now for many years. For several years it was used for practice by visiting NBA basketball teams before playing the Chicago Bulls at the United Center. It was one of several projects that I was able to help promote and see accomplished.

Moody's life and history is well documented in several books and biographies, but one amazing thing that was present in his early days still exists today in the "no tuition" policy. A more accurate terminology would be a "paid tuition" policy, as someone, after all, has to pay. It seems that when the school began, Mr. Moody, who was a businessman and part-time evangelist, had a group of street kids in a Bible class. He shared with some of his business associates how some of the kids in his Bible class had expressed a desire to know more about the Bible, but they had no money for an education. Some of Moody's friends said, in effect, why don't you start a school and we will pay the costs of operating it. Moody got some people together who would run the school and teach the kids and in a small way the school started. That principle of tuition-paid education is still in effect today. I don't know of any other school in the world of this size where this principle is in operation, and at this writing for over 125 years. Surely God has had His hand on this institution in a remarkable way.

I hadn't been on the board very long when Dr. Sweeting announced his retirement, to be about two years in the future. At each board meeting, he gave us his idea or criteria for his successor. He first said he thought he should be a pastor. The next meeting he said he thought he should be from a fairly large church. The next time he said he should be fairly young, maybe in his forties. After a while I remember saying to Marilyn that he was slowly describing our pastor, Joe Stowell. Sure enough, one day Sweeting announced that he had identified five young pastors for the board to choose from. He gave us a two-page, typewritten description and background on each of them. He said the board should start the interview process because it could take awhile. Because he lived the closest to Chicago, of the five, Joe Stowell was invited first. The only question the board had asked me about him was, did I think he could do the job. My response was, while the job would be quite different than that of a pastor, I thought he could and would do a good job.

After Joe came before the board for an interview, all others were put on hold and never interviewed. The board was so impressed with Joe that he was unanimously elected. His selection was announced at Founder's Week in February as "President Elect" but he would not take office until August so that Dr. Sweeting could finish sixteen full years as president.

I took a lot of flak from my fellow church members for taking our pastor to Moody. I had been chairman of the search committee that brought him to our church. But the truth is, I had very little to do with it. I was just a bystander and observer with one vote along with the eleven other trustees. Actually, I had mixed emotions of losing my pastor versus seeing him have a bigger job and a greater opportunity for service, as he had a tremendous opportunity to influence thousands of young people who had decided that they wanted to give their lives for service for the Lord Jesus Christ.

During those months, Joe took some courses in management and how to read a financial statement, in preparation for a very different kind of position. He was an excellent preacher and communicator, and Moody gave him a platform to become one of the most sought-after speakers, worldwide. I am so pleased to call him my friend for all these years. One thing impressed me about Joe early in his days at Moody. Actually, a lot of things impressed me about him, too many to mention here. But while he was president elect, many people (faculty and staff) would come to him, asking him for his opinion or help or advice or whatever, as they wanted to make inroads or a good early impression with the new president. His response, to his credit, always was, "You need to be talking to Dr. Sweeting about this issue, as he is still the president."

The same thing was true about Dr. Sweeting after he stepped down and became chancellor. People would come to him, asking for his influence with the new president. He also said, "Dr. Stowell is the president. You should be talking to him about this." Both great statesmen and humble servants of the Lord Jesus Christ.

The longer I served on the board and the more I learned about the school and its operations, the more impressed with it I became. After a few years, I was elected vice chairman of the board. Little did I know that the practice, while not a written policy, was that the vice chairman would eventually become chairman. After a few years, chairman Mitchell resigned, and I became chairman. It was most humbling, to say the least. It was a high and holy responsibility and one that I took very seriously. I constantly asked the Lord to help me and guide me. To be the chairman of the board of the most prestigious Bible school in the world was way beyond my ability, background, or training. However, with the help of my good friend and former pastor, Dr. Joe Stowell, I served for eleven years as chairman. I served with Joe until he resigned after seventeen years of service and through the election of Michael Easley as his successor. After Dr. Easley was in place, I resigned as chairman. In fact, I had to get off the board at that point because the age limit was seventy-five. At age seventy-five, retirement was mandatory.

I was giving my little resignation speech to the board, telling the members what a pleasure and honor it had been to serve with them for about twenty-four years. The new chairman asked me if I would please step out in the hall for a minute. I did, and soon he came out to get me and said that they had established a new position on the board for me. He said it was called "board member emeritus." This was news to me. I had never heard of it before. When I asked what it meant, he said it means two things: first we want you to come to all future board meetings but, in order to have some distinction, you will not be able to vote. I think it was the highest honor I have ever received. To think that I will still be able to be a part of the Moody Bible Institute, the school that I love and appreciate so much, was so satisfying. I was not looking forward to retiring from that board and fellowshipping with such a godly group of men. To think that they wanted me to continue to be one of them was overwhelming. And to think that I was the only person in over one 125 years to have that position was, indeed, one of the greatest blessings in my life. A few years later, they gave me an honorary doctor's degree, one of only three or four in the history of the school. But to me, to be asked to stay on the board was even more impressive. I think my friend Michael Easley had something to do with both honors.

The present board of trustees are some of God's choicest servants and include Jerry Jenkins, chairman, the famous author from Colorado Springs, Colorado; Bervin Peterson, vice chairman, Chicago real estate developer and chairman of the elder board at the famous Moody Church; Kit Denison, yacht dealer from Ft. Lauderdale, Florida; Randy Fairfax, financial planner and counselor, Akron, Ohio; Tom Fortson, former president of Promise Keepers from the Denver area; Dr. Paul Nyquist, president of Moody Bible Institute; David Schipper, another real estate developer from Akron, Ohio; Paul VonTobel, retired from the lumber business in Valparaiso, Indiana; Mark Wagner, president of Walgreen Drug Stores, also from Chicago; Rick Warren, industrialist, my neighbor and fellow church member, Bloomfield, Michigan; Dr. Richard Yook, ophthalmologist, Northridge, California.

It's not easy to put twenty-seven years of service into a few words when it concerns Moody Bible Institute. To me, the big picture is always important. One of the privileges of the board member is to sit on the platform during the graduation ceremony on the second Saturday of May each year. At least that was the situation when we used to have the ceremony in the Torrey-Gray auditorium at the school, where the stage is quite large, but the auditorium only seats about two thousand. This obviously limits the number of family and guests of the graduates.

In later years, we moved it down the street about a mile to the Moody Church, which has about four thousand seats. At the Moody Church, the trustees all sit in the front row because of lack of space on the platform. As chairman, however, I sat on the platform between the guest speaker and the president. My job, after the opening hymn, was simply to greet the guests, mostly the families of the graduates, and to thank them for supporting and encouraging their children or grandchildren or whoever, and to lead the entire group in an opening prayer. After the music and the commencement speaker, the awarding of the diplomas would begin. The graduates would line up on my right side of the platform, and the provost would read their name. They would then walk to the center of the platform, shake hands with the president, receive their diploma with the other hand, while having their picture taken, and then walk off. Then another, and another and another—in those days about four hundred graduates. Today it is closer to six hundred. At an average of four hundred per year and for twenty-five years I have seen at least ten thousand young people graduate. We believe that about 85 percent of them go into some sort of full-time service in ministry—pastors, missionaries, youth workers, and more. If each of the eighty-five hundred served an average of forty years, that is three hundred forty thousand life years of ministry. And that is just in my time on the board. Over the 125 years, it is many times more than that. Think about that for a minute. Over three hundred thousand life years of service for the gospel of Jesus Christ. If each person influenced ten people per year, that would be over three million people per year or over forty years, 120 million people. Actually, it is probably many times that number.

Speaking of the big picture, I don't know how I could have used my time and my resources in a more productive way than helping all those young people to receive the best training possible for a lifetime of service for the Lord. I look at it as having made the very best investment of time and money that I could possibly make. The dividends will be paid throughout all eternity in the lives of millions of people who will be in heaven. How I thank the Lord for Moody Bible Institute and my opportunity to be a part of it. Indeed, my cup runneth over.

57

THE FUND-RAISER

We got word that the Billy Graham organization was considering a crusade to be held at the Pontiac Silverdome. They had an advance man by the name of John Corts who came to Detroit about two years ahead of time. As he was making plans for the crusade and mobilizing the local people and starting prayer meetings and so on, one of his first jobs was to select a local chairman. They usually chose a person who was fairly well known in the community and with a prestigious position and, of course, with a clear testimony and a good reputation. After considering several, they selected Harold MacDonald, who was a vice president of Ford Motor Company, in charge of all engineering. Harold told me one time that when Henry Ford II gave him that job, he said, "Okay, Harold, it's up to you to see that the cars look good and ride good. Someone else will be in charge of building them and selling them." Quite a responsibility!

Harold and his wife, Elizabeth, lived right across the street from us and were members of our church and good friends. Incidentally, when they bought the house, it was not the best-looking house in the neighborhood, but it was a nice big house on a lovely lot with a pool. They were hesitant about buying it, and they asked me if we could fix it up. I assured them we could. It had sort of an Oriental decor inside. In fact, it was awful. So, fix it up we did! We almost gutted the entire first floor. We put in a new kitchen, new doors and trim, and more. We put on a new front porch with tall square columns, Colonial design. When we were finished, it looked like a completely different house, and they were very pleased.

So, when Harold was asked to be the chairman of the local committee for the Billy Graham crusade, he asked for a few days to think and pray about it. He came to me and said that the only way he would take on the job was if I would agree to be the chairman of the finance committee. When I asked what that entailed, he said, "Let's have a meeting with John Corts." At the meeting, John explained that the budget for the campaign was to be $800,000. When I asked about more details, he said that their history showed that they would get about half of it, or about $400,000, from offerings during the crusade. He said the local committee or, more significantly, the finance committee was responsible to raise about $400,000 before the crusade began. When we asked how others before us had done this, he said that they mobilized all the churches and started mailing information to them requesting donations along with prayer. A financial commitment on the part of the local group was necessary before they would agree to come to a city for the crusade.

So Harold looked at me as if to say, "Well, what do you say?" Without thinking too much about it and surely not wanting to become the reason for possibly not having the crusade, I said, "Okay." And the wheels went into motion for the crusade. If I would have said no, I'm sure they would have found someone else. I know I am not indispensable, especially in God's programs. As I began to think about my new job, I began to think what a lot of work this was going to be. All those churches had their own budgets, and with gifts from individuals of $25.00, $50.00, or maybe in a few cases $100.00, and in even fewer cases $1,000.00, it was going to take a lot of promotion. With the campaign two years away, there was not much need for urgency. It was going to be an uphill battle. Now I knew the Lord can do anything. And if He's in it, it could happen. So I began to pray, "Lord, what have I gotten myself into? I need Your help." One day I got an idea. I concluded that through my contacts with CBMC, I knew a lot of businessmen in the Detroit area, from one end of town to the other. So I decided to contact ten of them from all different churches and denominations and ask each of them to be responsible for $40,000. I called them together and explained the program and the challenge. They could get as many people as they wanted to help them. I even suggested that maybe they could each get ten people who would be responsible for

$4,000. They liked that idea; and with an act of faith, they all said okay, and we were off. Naturally, I was one of the ten. But I had just gotten my responsibility reduced from $400,000 to $40,000.

Stanley Kresge, the son of the founder of the Kmart organization, was a regular member of a men's Bible group that I attended every Tuesday morning. There were usually about ten or twelve of us each week. One day I was telling the group what I had just done, and I asked them to pray for my nine helpers. A few days later I got a call from Stanley. He said he was coming into Birmingham and he had something to give me. But since parking was so difficult in town, would I just come down and meet him in his car on the sidewalk in front of my office? He said he would be there about 12:15 p.m. So I did, and he drove up right on time and handed me a check for $100,000 for the crusade. He said he didn't have time to mobilize others, but that he and his wife, Dorothy, wanted to have a part. Well, as you might imagine, that was a great day! I spent the rest of the afternoon calling my nine helpers telling them the story and thereby reducing their responsibility from $40,000 to $30,000. Of course, they were delighted.

When I first told John Corts about my idea of raising the money through ten people, he was skeptical. His response was, "You are going to place this financial responsibility on just ten people?" I told him that I knew all these guys, and I was confident that they would come through. He was still nervous. "What if they come back empty-handed?" was his attitude. So, to satisfy his anxiety, I decided to call a meeting of all the helpers. I even asked them to invite anyone that had agreed to help them. We had a dinner meeting and altogether we had maybe fifty people. After dinner, I introduced John so they could meet him. After that, I gave a little devotional, thanking these guys for what they were doing. Then I went around the room, calling on each of the nine captains to give a progress report as to how they were doing in their efforts. As they each stood and gave their reports, they were all 100 percent positive. They would say something like, "So far, I have received $15,000 in commitments, and I'm sure I will get the balance." Some would say that even if they didn't get the $30,000, they would personally make up the difference. Well, John was blown away. He couldn't believe how well this plan was working and how easy it was. It was like a lot of tasks in life. If you have the right people helping and they all know their individual jobs, the project is usually a lot easier. In fact, John was so impressed that in future crusades they used the "Detroit financial plan."

Actually, my job was accomplished without a whole lot of energy on my part. Some of the other committee chairmen worked a lot harder and a lot longer than I did. There was the usher chairman who had to locate dozens of men to serve as ushers and be sure that they were in place each night of the crusade. There were several other committees such as the follow-up committee and the prayer committee and the publicity committee. Just about everything, except the program itself, was the responsibility of the local people.

58

THREE FRUITFUL DINNER PARTIES

With my job pretty well in hand, I said to Marilyn that we should probably do something personally to get our friends to attend the crusade. We surmised that Billy Graham would probably never come back to Detroit again because of his age and the many other places that wanted him to come. So we decided to invite fifty people on three different nights to be guests in our home for dinner and then in a chartered bus go to the Silverdome for the meeting. The reason we invited fifty was because that was the capacity of the bus. We did it on Monday, Wednesday, and Friday nights of the one-week crusade. We had a wonderful Norwegian woman named Signey, who was a great cook, who agreed to come to our house and prepare a gourmet dinner for the guests who were seated at tables all over the house. I think the dinner was at about 5:30 p.m. in order to give us enough time to get to the Silverdome in time for the meeting. I knew the usher chairman, and he held fifty seats for us in a very strategic location in the stadium.

All of our guests were not believers, as far as we knew. If we knew someone was a believer, it was for sure that they would not be invited. One night was "neighbor night" when we invited our neighbors. One night was "civic night" when we invited the mayor and the city commission members and city employees that I knew. We included the owner of the local newspaper and a few others. The third night was "business night" when we invited people with whom we did business and a few tenants. In getting the house ready for the dinner parties, Marilyn had her decorator come and put in some new drapes for the dining room.

When he saw some of the preparations in progress, he inquired as for what occasion she was preparing. When she told him, he said, "What about me? Could we come?" He was Jewish, but she said, "Sure, Jack, we would love to have you and Gloria attend." He said he thought it would be part of his education to go to a Billy Graham crusade. Indeed, he and his wife did attend. As a matter of fact, most people who were invited accepted. We sent them real nice engraved invitations and made it a first-class event. On the way to the stadium, I used the loudspeaker system on the bus to welcome everyone and let them know that if after the meeting, they were delayed for any reason, they were not to worry, as the bus would wait for them. As I recall, we had people go forward each night indicating they wanted to put their faith in Jesus Christ. Then, when we got back to the house, our kids, with some of their friends as helpers, had taken down all the tables and chairs and Signey had re-set the dining room table with a wonderful variety of Norwegian desserts along with tea and coffee. The kids had put all the chairs in the living room for a time of fellowship and to hear some stories from some of the crusade personalities. One night we had Cliff Barrows, the song leader, and his wife. One night we had Grady Wilson, who was one of Mr. Graham's associate evangelists and good friend of Mr. Graham. They did not preach but just told some funny stories and incidents that they had experienced over the years as the "Billy Graham Team." The guests loved the stories. The third night we had Evie Tornquist come and sing and play a few songs on the piano. She had been the soloist that night at the crusade. All three nights were a success. People heard the gospel who had perhaps never heard it before. As they left our home after the evening, the "thank-yous" and comments were so gratifying. One lady who was a widow and lived in one of our apartments said to me as she was leaving, "Mr. Johnson, I want you to know that this has been a wonderful evening. My husband was a vice president of General Motors, and we have traveled the world and, on occasions, been with royalty, but I must tell you that tonight was one of the most meaningful nights in my entire life. Thank you for inviting me."

Before they left, the guests were told that those people who went forward at the crusade meeting earlier had each received a packet of information, and we didn't want them to miss out on anything, so we had one of those packets for each of them as they left our house. It was a good investment on our part in getting 150 people to have an evening to consider some of the most important questions a person can have in this life, such as, "Where will I spend eternity?" And, "How can I be sure it will be in heaven?" Is there anything more important?

59

WALK THRU THE BIBLE

It was a rainy, cold October Saturday in the early seventies. Marilyn woke up with a cold. I remembered that there was a seminar scheduled at our church that day, something about learning the entire Old Testament in one day. When I mentioned it to Marilyn, she said, "Why don't you go ahead? I think I will just stay in bed today." So I did. As the seminar started, the young man leading it said that we wouldn't need any pencils or paper, as no notes would be necessary, and that at the end of the day, we would all learn seventy-seven stories in chronological order about the Old Testament and learn seventy-seven phrases and hand signs to help us remember them. I was impressed and started to listen with interest.

About 10:30 a.m. we had a coffee break. As I was standing in the foyer, our Christian education pastor, Ken Travilla, who was responsible for arranging the seminar, came up to me and asked what I thought of it so far. My response was that I thought the young man putting on the seminar was doing a great job. He asked if I would like to meet him. With that he went and got him and introduced him to me. His name was Bruce Wilkinson. I complimented him and said that I thought he was "on to something"—a new and creative way of teaching.

At lunchtime, Ken asked, since I was alone, if I would like to join him and Bruce for lunch. I called Marilyn, and she said that she was still in bed and that I should go. I stayed for the entire seminar, and I was greatly impressed. When Bruce heard that I was a building contractor, he asked if he could talk to me about a project they were involved in, in Portland, Oregon, where their office was located. In order to talk further, I suggested that maybe I could drive him to the airport. I called Marilyn and, again, she said go ahead. We had a quick dinner before he left. He said that he wished that I could see the building that they wanted to buy and help them with the remodeling. Actually, it was an old small frame church building. I remember telling him that I was going to be in Portland in about three weeks to speak at the CBMC group there. He asked if I could stay over an extra day and look at their project. I did, and I made a few suggestions. We became better acquainted, and I encouraged him in his new ministry. At that time, he was an instructor at Multnomah School of the Bible and doing the seminars part-time.

A few months later I got a call from him saying that he wanted to come and see me. It seems that the ministry was growing and he had trained two or three others to teach the seminars. He was thinking of moving the headquarters to Atlanta to be more centrally located, and to resign as a professor and go into the new ministry full-time. Then he asked me if I would consider being on the board of directors of a new organization to be called "Walk Thru the Bible Ministries." Bruce was, and is, a visionary. He has big ideas and wants to do big things. Big things usually start small and grow slowly as the leaders learn the business, make a few mistakes, correct them, and continue on. When Bruce outlined his plans for the new ministry, I concluded that a board of directors would be a detriment to the fantastic growth that he envisioned. I suggested that he just make it his own personal ministry and forget about a board. When he asked me why, I remember telling him that with a board, he would be subject to their approval for everything he did. He would, in effect, have to be under their supervision, and, in my opinion, he personally had the future all planned out and didn't need any others questioning his programs or activities. Since I last saw him, he had gathered around him some very talented teachers and writers. Besides Bible teachers, he had engaged some excellent writers of Bible teaching and devotional materials that would be sold to churches, individuals, and other organizations in bulk. All the materials and people were of the highest quality. The material was very popular, and sales were going very well.

He thanked me for my advice and left. A few weeks later, he called again and wanted to come back. This time, he said, that in order to qualify as a recognized organization that could give receipts for tax-deductible contributions and be authorized by the federal government, he was required to have an independent board of directors; and he wanted me to be one of the members. He explained that he had contacted a few other friends who had agreed to be on the board. They included Howard Hendricks, who was a legendary professor from Dallas Theological Seminary, Bob Boyd, a well-respected attorney from Virginia, who was also on the board of the College of William and Mary. He also invited John Van Diest, then the president of Multnomah Press, who had been a classmate of Bruce's at Dallas Seminary. There were also one or two more that I didn't know. The ones I knew were a good solid group of people and their theological positions lined up with mine. Although this was to be a not-for-profit organization, there would be sales of products and materials. The plan was to sell enough materials and bring in enough money to cover all the costs of operations to the extent that very little, if any, contributions would be required. Actually, the seminars were self-supporting, as the attendees paid a fee to attend. It sounded like a good plan to me, and I agreed to be a board member.

Bruce was, and is, one of the most creative Bible teachers whom I have ever known. He makes learning the Bible so easy and clear. Many times he is even fun to listen to, and he has the ability to make the Bible stories and their purpose come alive. The purpose of Walk Thru the Bible's teaching was to produce changed lives. Over the years, thousands of people have had their lives changed through the teaching sessions and the materials produced by Bruce and his staff.

When it came time to elect a chairman, I thought it should be Howard Hendricks, the theologian, or maybe Bob Boyd, the lawyer. To my surprise, they all looked at me and said that I should be the chairman. I felt totally inadequate and not qualified to hold that position. When I expressed my feelings to them, they all said not to worry, they would help me out. So, I was elected chairman, a position I held for over twenty years.

In the beginning, we were sort of a sounding board for Bruce. We pretty much sat back and let Bruce run the ministry. We sort of reasoned that, after all, it was his ministry. He started it, and he should have the freedom to do whatever he wanted, as long as everything was in order and proper. We gave advice and tried to keep him from doing anything that we felt could later cause trouble. With the ultimate goal being to produce the finest and most creative Bible teaching materials available and to sell them, contributions would not be such a necessity, as it was with most other ministries. However, we soon found out that the sales revenue was not adequate to fund a growing organization. There was an ever-increasing need for new computers and other equipment necessary for the start-up activities.

So Bruce called a board meeting to be held off-site in a nice hotel where he said he needed our undivided attention for three or four days. The wives were also invited. At that meeting over several days, Bruce laid out the long-term plans and introduced some new material that they wanted to produce. Well, the response was all favorable. The board said, in effect, "Go for it!" Then he told us how much it would cost, and the board became silent. We soon got the picture that he was looking to us for some financial help. We all thought it would be a good investment, and the funds were committed.

That scenario for fund-raising was soon expanded, and other folks were invited who had shown an interest in the ministry. Using a similar program of vision-casting plus some excellent Bible teaching, that method of fund-raising was expanded to two such events each year. It was a very successful method of fund-raising, good Bible teaching, getting more and more people involved in having a personal part of the ministry and many in a very significant way. At one point the average gift was over $15,000 per couple. In those days we did not depend on folks contributing $25.00 or $50.00 a month as most organizations do.

As this method of fund-raising became known, many other organizations copied it and today it is widely used by many other ministries. This is another of Bruce Wilkinson's thinking "outside the box." This type of fund-raising where a relatively few number of people give large donations worked pretty well until the economic downturn occurred in 2008. At that point, the large donors were greatly affected, and donations went down dramatically. By contrast, the organizations that had a large number of small donors did better in bad economic times. As a result, Walk Thru the Bible had to downsize considerably, due to lack of income.

During the early years and good times, the organization and ministry grew and grew. At one point we had over eighty employees at the headquarters in Atlanta, and Bruce became one of America's most sought-after speakers. The ministry soon expanded overseas. The excellent Bible teaching materials were very much in demand in many countries. The problem was that so many of the people overseas didn't have the money to purchase the materials. So we had to raise more money and just give away the materials. It was seen by many of us as a good investment, and the funds came in and the ministry flourished.

It proved to be a good practice to train pastors and leaders in the foreign countries in how to teach the materials. So a seminar would be held, and sometimes hundreds of pastors would attend. The material would be taught to them, and they welcomed it with open arms. Then they would take it back to their local churches and teach it to their congregations. The material was all, of course, biblically based and often new to the people. As a result, we saw lives changed by the hundreds and thousands as the folks learned more about how to live a life that had Jesus Christ as its focal point.

Walk Thru the Bible soon had a division called "World Teach" with leaders located in various regions around the world. At one point we were in over eighty countries of the world. Teaching by video became very popular, and Bruce as the teacher became famous all around the world. In fact, he became so popular in South Africa that after twenty-five years as president of the U.S. operations, he resigned and moved to South Africa where he felt the need was so great, and he wanted to help make an impact for Christ in that area.

After he left, our new president was Chip Ingram, a pastor from California. I resigned as chairman, and my good friend Dr. John Isch became the new chairman, but I remained on the board. After five years, Chip left to go back into the pastorate, and Phil Tuttle, who was a longtime Bible teacher and trainer of teachers, became the new president. Phil is doing a great job, but because of the economic downturn and lack of income, we have had to downsize like so many other organizations.

So now, after thirty years, Walk Thru the Bible has been an important chapter in my life and another good investment of my time and resources that will pay dividends in the lives of people in heaven for all eternity. I am so happy that I went to that original seminar back in the early seventies. Another blessing from God!

60

WHAT ABOUT THIS IDEA OF "GIVING"?

My first association with tithing and stewardship as well as an example of faithfulness goes back to my mom. I've already shared how during the Great Depression of the late 1920s and '30s, Henry Ford took pity on his employees; and instead of laying off half of them, he allowed all of them to work three days a week. In those days the pay was five dollars per day or fifteen a week. My dad would come home from work every Friday and give my mom his pay envelope, which contained fifteen in cash. She believed that 10 percent of our income was to be given to the Lord's work. In the Bible it is called a tithe. That is the plan the Lord used to pay the priests and church leaders. If everyone did this, the church leaders' income would be the same as the average of ten people in the congregation. So she would take out $1.50 and put it in a small box that she hid in the linen closet. At the end of the month she had six dollars saved up of what she called the "Lord's money." She gave three to our church, and she sent a dollar to each of three radio preachers that she said were feeding her spiritually. She also believed that whoever was helping her to grow spiritually should be the recipients of a portion of our tithe.

When I got my first job in the shoe store and I came home with my first pay, she said to me, "Remember, 10 percent belongs to the Lord. It is not yours. It is holy money. Don't touch it!" As a result of her instruction and believing that that's what the Lord would have me do, I began to tithe my income.

Marilyn's folks also believed the same way, so when we got married, tithing just came naturally to us, and we continued to give 10 percent of our income to our church and/or other ministries. I think it was about a year or so after we were married that we heard a sermon on giving. The message was that we really didn't give anything out of a heart of love for the Lord until our giving was beyond the 10 percent. The idea was that the 10 percent was a requirement or like a tax for those of us who were believers and followers of Jesus Christ. And if we really loved the Lord and were thankful for what He had done for us, we would give over and above the 10 percent as sort of a love offering. After all, we believed that actually everything we had belonged to Him. He was the One who had provided everything we had. It was all His, and as His children we were just stewards, looking after whatever He allowed us to have. So, we concluded that, indeed, we did love the Lord and were most appreciative for all we had and, therefore, we would give over and above the 10 percent the following year.

We didn't want to get carried away with this concept. So we decided we would give 11 percent the following year. Not exactly a great leap of faith, but at least it was a start. Well, at the end of the year, we had more money left over than we had the year before, so we said, in effect, let's do that again. We pledged 12 percent for the next year. Again, our income increased, and we were ahead of the year before. The Lord continued to bless us. From then on we increased our giving at least 1 percent per year, and we saw our income go up, up, and up. Each year we had left over as much or more than we had the year before. We determined that it was impossible to out give God. As one person said, "We shovel it out, and God shovels it in. But God has a bigger shovel." We followed that practice all of our married life, and we were married for fifty-five years before Marilyn passed away after a ten-year fight with Alzheimer's disease. I'll tell you more about that in another place.

Let me be quick to say that I know everyone can't do what we did. Most people have a fixed salary and it usually doesn't go up, up, up like our income did. But everyone can give 10 percent. There is no excuse for not doing so if you are a believer in Jesus Christ and want to be obedient to His Word. I think many people who are having a hard time financially don't see the connection between being obedient to God and receiving God's blessing.

One time I was invited to speak at a banquet for CBMC in Kansas City. It was held in the dining room of a hotel, and I was staying overnight in the hotel. After the banquet, a couple came up to me and asked if they could talk with me for a few minutes. So we went into the coffee shop and they told me their problem. For the life of me, I can't remember exactly what it was. I think it had something to do with a problem they were having in business. But out of the blue, the idea came to me, and I asked them if they were tithing their income. They quickly responded that it would be impossible for them to give 10 percent of their income to the Lord's work, even though they knew it was the right thing to do. They said their income was $60,000 per year (this was back in the seventies) and that they gave about $1,000 to their church. To give another $5,000 would be impossible considering all the expenses they had, etc., etc.

I don't remember all the details, but the idea came to me and I asked them a hypothetical question. I said, what if you worked for a company that had twenty employees. And one day the boss called a meeting of everyone and said that business had taken a downturn and that it would be necessary to lay off 10 percent of the workforce, or two people. He also said that he didn't know which two it would be, because everyone was doing a good job and doing about the same thing. So he thought the fairest way would be to put all the names in a hat and then draw out two names to be let go.

Then, after a long pause, he said, or . . . we could all just take a 10 percent cut and we could all keep our jobs. Let's have a vote and see which way we should go.

With this, I asked the couple which way they would vote. He said that he would probably go for the 10 percent pay cut rather than risk losing his job altogether. I asked them how they could possibly make out with 10 percent less income, in view of what they had just told me. They said, "I don't know, but we would just have to figure out something." With that, the conversation stopped, and they became silent. What they had just said was that actually they could afford to live on 90 percent of their income. So it wasn't really a question of necessity. It was a question of choice. Would they be obedient to God's requirement and give Him a good reason to bless them, or would they be selfish and keep it all for themselves? When it comes to receiving God's blessings, I asked them why would God want to bless disobedient children?

When people ask me why I give away so much, the answer is very simple. But it's for three basic reasons. First, I am so thankful for what God has done for me, and I love Him so much and I'm so appreciative. Not only has He saved me and given me the gift of eternal life, but my life has been filled with His blessings. I'm thankful for godly parents, good pastors and others who have encouraged me and taught me biblical principles, the opportunity for an education and business opportunities, for a godly wife and children who love the Lord, and reasonably good health all these years. The list goes on and on. Way too many to put down here, but suffice it to say I am a very thankful person.

Secondly, I think giving is important to God. It must be. He said more in the New Testament about stewardship and money and how to handle it than any other subject including love and grace, etc. It's actually about three or four times as many verses. It seems to me that God knows how much money means to all of us; and if He can get us to recognize that it is all a gift from Him and be willing to let go of it for His sake, He is pleased and can't wait to bless us in return. I don't think we should "give to get." That's the wrong motive, and God knows our hearts. But we should give proportionately as God has blessed us. I think it is one of the most tangible acts of obedience and shows our love for Him. And God loves us so much when we are obedient.

Thirdly, I enjoy giving. It actually makes me feel good to share with others. While most of our giving is to the Lord's work through ministries, we give a fair amount to people to just help them have a more comfortable life. We call it "a cup of cold water in the name of the Lord Jesus." The more we give, the happier I am. Giving makes me feel good, and I'm sure it also pleases the Lord.

There are a lot of stories about how God has blessed people who took the step of faith and believed God and started to tithe. One I heard recently was from a fellow who said that he knew for years that God was pleased with tithers, but he just felt he couldn't afford it. Then one day he determined to be obedient, and he started to tithe. He said that he had an old car that kept costing him hundreds of dollars each year in repairs to keep it going. But it was still cheaper than payments on a new car. He said that after he started tithing, that old car never had another problem. It just went on and on. He said it was a very distinct answer and blessing from God to show His pleasure for his obedience. There are lots of stories about folks who said that after they started tithing, the 90 percent they had left went a lot further than the 100 percent they used to keep. I think all three of my children have seen God's hand of blessing on their father and mother; and I hope that they will be faithful in passing this concept on to you, their children.

People often ask me about my priorities in giving and how much to give and/or who to give to. How much to give is not really the question. I think we should give all we can. So the question should be, in some cases, how much to keep for ourselves? I believe everything I have belongs to God. He owns it all, so it's all His. I am just a caretaker or steward of His resources. Now I recognize that many people can only give 10 percent. This is the minimum and what God expects from all of His children.

But many of His children (like us) have been blessed with a lot more than we need for daily living. Everything that we don't need for reasonable retirement expenses should be used for God's work and to enhance His kingdom. I think God gives some of us more than we need, expecting us to use it for His glory. If we don't, and keep it for ourselves, I think that we can expect God's blessings in our life to likely diminish. However, if we keep on giving, as God prospers us, I think He will keep on prospering us so we can give more. I think this is what happened with us. We kept giving, and God kept giving us more so we could give even more. Think about it. How does God's work get funded? Answer: from those of us who respond to His program. It amazes me that so many of God's children can't grasp this concept. George Barna, the Christian researcher, says that the average evangelical Christian gives about 3.4 percent to God's work. Is it any wonder God is not blessing as He would like to? So, don't be selfish with God. Be obedient and watch Him bless you. I must say, however, that giving is not necessarily the key to success. Not everyone who is generous with God will make a lot of money. But I believe the opposite is more likely to be true. If you don't give (at least 10 percent), it is disobedience; and disobedience is sin. And you are not likely to see God's financial blessing in your life. Why would God want to bless disobedient children? It amazes me that so many of God's children can't grasp this concept.

Therefore, this suggestion: never dismiss a generous impulse. If you have a thought about being generous, respond to that thought, idea, or impulse. It did not likely come from the devil. It is a prompting of God. Therefore, give it serious consideration.

The next question that people ask me is "who to give to?" This is probably the most difficult of all. God calls different people to support different ministries and many are good and worthwhile. For what it's worth to you, I think our first obligation is to our local church. If you are in a good church that preaches the gospel and is feeding you spiritually, you have a responsibility to support them financially. If it is not that kind of church, you should look for another one. Some ask how much to give to the church. That depends on a few things. If your income is about the same as most people in the church and it is a reasonably sized church, then you should probably give most of your 10 percent tithe to the church. The church needs all of its members to be participants and not freeloaders. On the other hand, if your income is larger than average and you gave 10 percent to the church, it might be out of proportion to the other members and, in some cases, could cause the other members to not give their fair share. The church budget should not depend on large gifts from one or two members. It is not healthy. On the other hand, if the church were to have a special project, like a new building or special campaign, I think someone who has the money and feels like it is a good investment of the Lord's money could give as much as he or she wants.

Also, money and gifts should never be allowed to be a means of control. Once the money is given, it belongs to the Lord and should be under the control of the church leadership. Designated gifts are okay and should be honored by the church or whatever organization and used as agreed. But a large donor should never be allowed to tell the church or organization how to run things.

Sometimes if God has blessed a person and they have extra money, they sometimes ask me how to determine who to give to. I use a simple three-word grid: (1) the people, (2) the purpose, and (3) the program. Regarding the people who run the program or the organization, what do you know about them, personally? What about their character, personal lifestyle, family background, history, expertise, qualifications, etc.? As for purpose, do they do things that you would like to have done? Do they have the purpose of winning people to Christ and/or encouraging believers toward life change? What are they really trying to do, and do you agree with it? And then, the program. Do they have an efficient way to do what they do? Do they have a viable game plan? Are they using money wisely? That is why I love Moody Bible Institute so much. More than 125 years of successfully training people who give usually forty years of their lives to God's work. That's a multiplying-effect good investment.

Then, for what it's worth, my opinion is that we should limit the giving of large sums of money to three or four, maybe five ministries. The reason is that it is difficult and often time-consuming to find out and get to know the inner workings and the people, purpose, and program of more than a few organizations. That's not to say that we only give to three or four organizations. We give to a lot more than that. But the amounts are nominal, and while it is all the Lord's money, we believe it is okay to spread it around in small amounts to several ministries that appear to be good investments and trust the Lord to bless the gift. But when I'm talking about limiting large gifts to three or four organizations, I mean gifts in large amounts like thousands of dollars or, in some cases, tens of thousands or hundreds of thousands or maybe even more. I always want to be sure they are either spreading the gospel and seeing people come to Christ, or encouraging people through God's Word.

I also believe in "doing your giving while you're living, so you're knowing where it's going." To follow this thought, Marilyn and I decided that we determine our net worth and then give 70 percent to the Lord's work and 10 percent to each of the three children. We concluded that the Lord gave *us* the money and not to the children. However, since they are all wonderful and have a close walk with the Lord and are generous toward God's work, this would be a fair arrangement and pleasing to the Lord. So we did. We sold most of our properties and divided the money proportionately. We kept some to live on in our retirement years, but most of it has been distributed. My dad lived to be one hundred, and my mom ninety-one. So there is a fair chance I may live to be in my nineties. If so, and I waited until I died to distribute the money, my children would be in their seventies. And that is pretty late in life to enjoy it and maybe even to give some of it away to God's programs that they are interested in. Also, with this plan we have been able to see our family enjoy some of its benefit while we are still alive. God is so good!

61

RUSSIA AND
THE COMISSION

It was in late October of 1990 when I received a call from my good friend Peter Deyneka Jr., the head of Russian Ministries. He said that a group of Christian leaders had been invited to go to Moscow to interact with various government leaders and to possibly meet with Mr. Gorbachev, then head of the Soviet Union. Russian leaders had asked for the group to include a businessman, and he would like for me to be the one.

The last place I wanted to visit was Russia. Those awful people! The ones who threatened us with nuclear bombs and whose leader in days gone by, Mr. Khrushchev, had promised to "bury us"! Why would I want to go see them? But, with some encouragement from my family and my secretary, I decided that maybe it would be an educational trip. It was, indeed, that and a lot more. One of the others on the trip was the author, Philip Yancey, who took many notes and, when we got back, wrote all about it in a book called *Praying with the KGB*. If you want to know more about that trip, you can read his book.

We not only had visits and meetings with the new KGB, who said they wanted to reform, but also with top government officials, the leaders of parliament, ministers of education, commerce, representatives of the newspaper *Pravda*, leaders of the media and arts, and, finally, with Mr. Gorbachev himself.

That was quite an experience. We were ushered into a conference room with a long table. We Americans were on one side, and Mr. Gorbachev and his entourage on the other. We all had headphones for the interpretation. The first thing he said was that he had to meet with us because he said Raisa, his wife, had called him on his cellphone on his way to the office that morning, telling him to be sure to meet with the "American Christians." He then said, "But you know, we are all atheists here in Russia." As he said that, he turned to his aides on both sides, as to get their approval and support. He also said he was very busy, as all of the leaders for the eleven countries that made up the former Soviet Union were in the other room waiting for him. Therefore, he could only give us ten minutes. As time went on, he warmed up considerably, and after about thirty or forty minutes later, he said, "Well, after all, I guess we are all made by the same God." We heard that his mother or grandmother was a devout Christian. Amazing! The trip was an eye-opening experience, to say the least.

The country was in terrible shape. It was as if years ago people like Marx, Lenin, and Stalin shook their fists in God's face and said, "We don't need You. We will show You and the whole world how to build a society without You." And it's as if God said, "Go ahead and give it a shot." Now, seventy-three years after the revolution, we found the country to be in shambles politically, economically, socially, and spiritually. The one bright spot was that most of those we met knew they needed help. But they didn't know what it was. Therefore, they were most open to suggestions and help of any kind. I came away with a heavy heart for the good people of that great country, misled by a handful of radicals for over seventy years and now left bankrupt in every area of life. I thought of it in a business sense of having a fast-talking financial advisor taking all your assets and promising great returns, but coming back one day saying, "I guess my schemes didn't work. You have lost everything."

Actually, in the case of Russia, they lost a lot more than their money. Many had lost their lives, and the ones left had lost family, jobs, and most of all, hope. A few who had trusted the Lord through all this chaos provided the one bright spot on the horizon for their own future and for the entire country. The question was: Could it be turned around? Such an enormous task! In my opinion, only God was able to handle a situation like this.

After my first exposure to Russia, I came home educated but frustrated. I concluded that there was little I could do to help except perhaps to support financially Peter Deyneka Jr. and his ministry and perhaps a few others who were finding open and receptive hearts to the gospel. Maybe we could reach a few for Christ, but it would be a slow uphill process.

At that time I had been chairman of the board of Walk Thru the Bible Ministries for twenty years. Ours was a small group, as boards go, with only seven members. We were selected back in the early 1970s by Bruce Wilkinson, the president and founder of Walk Thru the Bible, to give him advice and counsel. We were his friends. He was a young, gifted, and creative individual with tremendous enthusiasm and potential for great ministry in the area of Bible teaching.

One day in 1991, Bruce called to say that he felt the Lord's leading to be involved in teaching the Bible in schools in the former Soviet Union. It seemed that since the wall had come down, some of the wiser leaders in the Ministry of Education believed that the only hope for survival of their society was to start over with the children. They concluded that the present Communist Party generation was pretty far gone, and that communism, with its entrenched foothold and personal value system and lifestyles, would be too difficult and would take too long to change. They doubted if the adults could be changed at all in their lifetime. After my visit, I certainly agreed.

As a result, Bruce said that a group was being formed to study the issue, because of the unprecedented invitation from the education leaders to come and to teach the nation's children in the public schools about the need for morals and ethics in order for a society to be successful. When some of our Christian leaders explained to the Soviet educators that the foundation for this system was based on Judeo-Christian ethics, God and the Bible, the Soviet educators as much as said, "So be it! Do whatever it takes to teach our children to be honest, moral, and responsible citizens." An amazing turn of events from a few months earlier.

This was to be a major challenge, but an unprecedented opportunity. As Bruce was talking to three or four others and dreaming about what could be done, he felt strongly that Walk Thru the Bible could have a key role. When our board met to discuss the situation, they asked me, as chairman, to attend some of these early meetings and to sort of look out for our interests as an organization; to be sure it was something that we (and Bruce) should be involved in, and examine what our role would be, what it would cost, etc.

It didn't take long for me to see, after a meeting or two of interesting, innovative discussions, that this was, indeed, the hand of God moving in a most unusual way. I recommended to our board that we do all we could to be supportive. The idea developed to involve several organizations, since it would be impossible for any one or two organizations to handle this huge undertaking. It would take an unusual amount of cooperation among existing agencies and a willingness to give priority to this venture, as well as millions of dollars to finance it, plus hundreds of volunteers to actually go and do the teaching.

As the discussions progressed, each agency was to take responsibility for one segment of the strategy. For example, Campus Crusade for Christ and The JESUS Film Project, under the leadership of Paul Eshleman, was the "door opener" with their convocations; Association of Christian Schools International, under Paul Kienel, would help supply the teachers to go; the Navigators, under Terry Taylor, would train the volunteers who would go; and Walk Thru the Bible would provide videotapes for training in Russia on a variety of subjects. Several committees resulted, including a prayer committee, chaired by Mary Lance Sisk; a sending committee, headed by J. B. Crouse; a training committee, headed by Terry Taylor; a mobilization committee, headed by John Kyle; an organizational committee, headed by Paul Eshleman; a curriculum committee, headed by Paul Kienel; a church relations committee, headed by Joe Stowell. Bruce Wilkinson was the general chairman; Peter and Anita Deyneka headed the Russian liaison committee, Margaret Bridges headed the cultural exchange committee; Ralph Plumb headed the relief and development committee. One organization would take on each area of responsibility and be responsible for it in its entirety, including funding, etc. Ultimately, eighty-two organizations were involved. The name chosen was the "CoMission," and the motto became, "Let's see what we can do for the cause of Christ in the former Soviet Union, and let's not care who gets the credit." As a member of the board of trustees of the Moody Bible Institute, I encouraged its president, Joe Stowell, and the board to endorse the CoMission. They did so wholeheartedly, and Joe became a member of the executive committee.

At one of the early meetings, the executive committee saw the need for an "arrangements committee." This team would be charged with finding housing for the hundreds of volunteers who would go, giving a year of their lives to teaching the Christian Ethics and Morality curriculum to the teachers who, in turn, would teach the pupils. An office for coordinating activities would be required, probably in Moscow, and a small staff would likely be necessary. Someone said, "We need a businessman to head up this committee." We all looked around the room, and it soon dawned on me that they were all looking at me!

My response was, "Wait a minute. I'm just here for a few days as an observer and counselor, and maybe to supply a little help with some organizational suggestions, etc. What do I know about the former Soviet Union and living and doing business in Russia? I'm a building contractor and real estate developer from Michigan. Besides, all of you head up large organizations with staffs, offices, budgets, fund-raising capacities, and so on. My people are all busy full-time running the real estate management business. I'm one guy with a personal secretary who would help me, but . . . hold on here! Not so fast!" But they said, "We believe you are the one for the job."

I thought to myself, "How did I get into this? What did I do to deserve this? How could things get worse?" But they did!

As the job description unfolded, it was overwhelming. I almost had a heart attack just thinking about it. They were talking about sending hundreds of volunteers for a year, in teams of ten, with two people living together in an apartment and all of them, hopefully, in the same building, or at least close enough for fellowship. Some would be married couples, others single. Hopefully, many would be schoolteachers. But it was decided that many nonteachers could do the job, with our special intensive three-week training program. It was incredible to think that I was going to be responsible for all those logistics. But how are we going to get the apartments? They are all owned by the government. I doubt if the government is going to rent apartments to a group of people who want to teach about God. Besides, I remember someone saying, "You know, some of the apartments in Moscow and other places don't have refrigerators, since the people go to the market every day to buy fresh food. So therefore, they don't really need a refrigerator." I knew that was true, but our people would be too busy teaching to go shopping every day, so we needed to supply each apartment with a refrigerator. Also, there were few apartments with washers and dryers, so we would need to supply washers and dryers as well. Now we were getting into the appliance business! While I did know something about that, as I owned hundreds of apartments in Michigan, the former Soviet Union was another story. Just buying them from other countries and getting them shipped in and installed was an overwhelming prospect.

But it got worse! They were not talking about just Moscow but the entire country: eleven time zones, an area three times as wide as the United States. "Oh, my goodness!" I thought. "I'll probably go broke and die trying to fulfill this assignment." I guess I looked as bad as I felt, when someone said, "Don't worry. We will include the cost of the rent, the appliances, and equipping the apartments in the funds that each volunteer will raise before he or she can go."

"Well," I thought, "that will help. At least I won't have to pay for everything." They discussed the difficulty of getting materials through customs, getting money into the country, dealing with Russian printers and other businesspeople where we might encounter a lack of integrity, in terms of keeping promises as to delivery and fulfilling commitments. Things that we take for granted here were not necessarily so over there. For example, it was not unusual to agree to buy a refrigerator from a local store and agree on a price and pay half down. After waiting sometimes three or four months, the delivery truck would show up and the driver would say, "Before we can unload the refrigerator, you have to pay the other half of the purchase price *plus* a $200 delivery fee." If you refused, someone else got your refrigerator, and you were out half of its cost.

These were not encouraging things to hear when contemplating this assignment. And, worst of all, I knew from my limited experience it was all true. I remember leaving the meeting saying, "Lord, how did *we* get into this? Obviously You had something to do with it, so You'll have to be the One to see me through." And, indeed, He did!

Mission societies began recruiting lay volunteers for a short-term (one year) service with the CoMission. People began to sign up and take a leave of absence from their jobs and to rent out their homes. It was amazing how some of the least likely individuals would be impressed by God to go, including my own son, Kevin, and his wife, who served in Moscow under OMS International.

One aspect of the CoMission that impressed me early on was that there would be no new organization formed. It was to be an affiliation of existing organizations banded together to accomplish a certain task and for a limited time, five years. There would be no CoMission bank account, as such. The necessary money would be raised by each agency, as required to perform their part of the task. The executive committee was simply a coordinating group, with very little authority. Guidelines were agreed to by each agency, but the only authority was what was given by the leaders of the agencies. It was sort of like the early days of our country when the thirteen states gave up some rights to the federal government, except that the CoMission never had a national treasury. This approach avoided a lot of duplication of administration and associated costs, and kept our expenses down. As a businessman, I liked this efficient arrangement.

Since each agency recruited and sent its own people, it was logical for each to provide a small salary, insurance, housing, and supervision for its own people. But all happened under the larger banner of the CoMission. This was the only way that the arrangements committee could possibly accomplish all the "arrangements." We had to have the help of each sending agency, of which there were several.

Our job was to seek and find possible apartment opportunities; then each agency would make its own arrangements. But how are we going to get the apartments to rent? We also had to coordinate all travel and activities in the former Soviet Union. It was obvious I had to find a staff and open an office in Moscow or go myself, and that wasn't too practical. I did wind up going over seven times during the five-year period, but early in the process I began to pray for "my man in Moscow."

At one of our early meetings in Phoenix, my friend Peter Deyneka Jr. said to me, "I've got a fellow here that you should meet. He may be your man." At lunch he introduced me to Andy Bishop and, as they often say, the rest is history. Andy and his wife, Beverly, were missionaries with the Christian and Missionary Alliance (CMA). They were visiting the meeting to find out more about the CoMission and the opportunities in Russia. As Andy puts it:

> Getting to Russia, for Bev and me, started with one of our CMA donors asking me to go look at a plan called CoMission in Russia. I traveled there in September of '92 with Paul Eshleman to attend a convocation for Russian public school teachers in Orlyanok. I came back convinced of the possibilities and recommended to CMA that they join, which they did.
>
> A few weeks after I submitted my report, Bev woke me at 1 a.m. She said, "I think we ought to go to Russia." I said, "But you just said after thirty years of marriage that twenty-six addresses were enough."
>
> "Every time I pray," she said, "I see Russia. We should go there too." So I spoke with my boss. "If we're going to go to Russia, we need you here to raise money," was his response. God will supply the money, was my feeling. I asked again, and the answer was, "Wait a year!"
>
> Bev wasn't satisfied. Neither was I. I was asked a week later to go to Phoenix with a pastor and layman from CMA. Russia was on the horizon big-time. After Bruce Wilkinson gave his famous "Caught in Elijah's Chariot Wheels" sermon, over nine hundred people were pledged to go. Later, my pastor friend came into the room and said, "Let's pray."
>
> "What's the subject?" I asked. His reply: "The CoMission board wants you and Bev to go to Russia to arrange for the program of CoMission there." We prayed. I called Bev. She said, "Let's go." I

said, "We have to raise our own support." She said, "Okay." We agreed to go for five years.

The next morning, after getting clearance from CMA, I met the board. Paul Johnson would be my boss, and all we had to do was raise $200,000 and open an office in Russia for CoMission by April, about ninety days away! As I was leaving, slightly challenged by all this, a donor and friend of mine came up and said, "I've just pledged half a million to one agency for the CoMission. I'm glad we have you going to set things up." "Pray," I requested, "that we find the support. We are going for five years!" He thought a moment and then said, "I'll do one-fourth of your support for the next five years."

Well, God worked, and when I flew to Moscow in March to do the preliminary work-up, we had five years of support from seven people. God is amazing!

Indeed, God is amazing! Andy was a "get it done" type of guy, if ever there was one. He could speak some Russian and was the perfect man for the job. He became the "man in Moscow" for the entire CoMission and all the agencies. One day Andy was talking to a single fellow who had his own apartment in one of the government buildings. He was paying $25.00 per month rent. Andy asked him if he would like to sub-rent his apartment for $200.00 per month. The young man said, in effect, "Where do I sign?" He said he would move back in with his parents and with $200.00 ($175.00 net), the whole family would increase their lifestyle and comfort of living standards tremendously. When another fellow down the hall heard about the sub-renting "arrangement," he also wanted to get in on the idea. Soon Andy had so many people coming to him that he had his choice of several apartments in various locations and different sizes, etc., and most of them came furnished. What an answer to prayer! Andy also helped the CoMission find washers and dryers, as well as steel doors and locks for apartments to keep burglars out. He arranged airport pick-ups, hotel rooms for temporary layovers, transportation to other cities, equipment repairs, printing, and determined where to buy just about anything. He was a "can-do" man, and he did it!

But it was soon apparent that he needed some extra help, having only a couple of office staff. He called me from Moscow and wanted to know if the Arrangements Committee (my secretary, Pam, and I) could afford a helper for him. When I found out all he was doing, I was surprised he didn't ask for two or three, and I quickly approved the added expenditure. Here is an excerpt from Andy's report about his new helper, Vlad:

In Moscow I was with Missionary Aviation Fellowship's man, Bob. He introduced me to Vladimir Gagavyshev, whom they'd met in Mozambique, Africa. We got on well, and by the time I left he had agreed to work with me. We'd rented an office that had been used by Campus Crusade, and I felt much better about how God was going to bring it all together.

By June, the office was up and running. Vlad and I were scouring Moscow for apartments, washing machines, water filters, TV and VCR units. Vlad helped do anything necessary to make CoMission work, and along the way began to take note of what Christ in a person's life meant in practical ways. He would go to airports at all hours of the day and night to help CoMissioners with problems, and he negotiated with people who smelled money on foreigners. Increasingly he gave out Bibles or Christian books since, as he explained, "these people are bringing Russia what it truly needs." His father was a KGB engineer. "But," Vlad said, "we were raised heathens, so the Bible is suspect to us. My mother was a Christian until she married my father. She could not practice her faith the rest of her life, but we buried her as a Christian."

The CoMission executive committee made an annual visit to Moscow for one of our regular meetings, but also for the purpose of encouraging the "troops," letting us see firsthand some of the activities that were taking place. Most of us looked forward to the visits, although the accommodations often left a lot to be desired. It was not unusual to be housed in a hotel with little or no hot water, and sometimes no heat.

I remember one trip where I took my grandson, Michael, up to Vladimer in ten-degree weather. In a hotel without heat, we slept with our clothes on and under so many heavy, army-type blankets that we woke up tired from the weight!

One trip with the executive committee was planned to go first to Odessa in the Ukraine to see the work going on there, meet some Ukrainian leaders, then go on to Moscow. We asked Andy to make arrangements for a charter flight, as there were more than thirty of us, including wives and families, and it would be safer than the national airlines, "Aeroflot", quicker than the train, etc. Andy had used this charter company before, with good planes and good results. His report on the trip shows the state of transportation in the Soviet Union. Here is what he said:

> When it was time to go, we went to the airport on a nice bus. Our baggage was whisked away to be put on the plane. We were served soft drinks and snacks in the VIP lounge, and after a while, a customs man appeared and stamped all of our passports. Then, with great courtesy, we were ushered out to the airplane. There sat a thirty-five-plus year Antonov 24 (similar to an old American DC3). Beside it was a pile of luggage, and standing by, a few surly looking men. I was informed they would not load the luggage without some serious cash. The plane was weatherbeaten and had small puddles of oil and fuel under the engines. The tires were bald with threads showing! On the side was a painted-over "Aeroflot." When I saw this, I said to myself, "Paul Johnson is going to fire me! These are not the kind of arrangements he likes." Paul Kienel said, "We're all going to die, but at least we'll die in good company!" I responded, "First, we load the luggage." Overcoming shock and fear, Bruce Wilkinson began to pitch bags into the cargo hold, and Joe Stowell began to stack them.

> We got on the plane, with fervent prayer, and awaited developments. The crew arrived and casually began the flight. When

the pilot came on board, we were all on the plane waiting to go. He entered from the rear and came up the aisle, which was a steep incline, through the passenger cabin and through the cargo room and into the cockpit. He was wearing a brown leather jacket with a red scarf around his neck. Before entering the cockpit door, he turned around, smiled at all of us, and said in broken English, "Red Baron!

"There was one cabin steward, a young man dressed in a unique flight attendant's uniform. He served us warm yellow punch and cucumber sandwiches. He used the loudspeaker system on all of us to practice his English. He announced everything from the weather to the time of day. After several announcements and interruptions to our sleep or conversations, he began to apologize, and each time he came on he would say, "Now I am again!" It did help to keep our minds off our anxiety of the flight. Three hours later we landed in Moscow, and after unloading our luggage, we boarded a new Mercedes bus to town for board meeting "part two." We were all still alive, and I still had my job!

The arrangements committee, with the help of Andy and Vlad in Moscow, played a very important role in the behind-the-scenes activities of the CoMission. We were the support team for the many agencies and CoMissioners who so faithfully served during the five-year period. The overall accomplishments of the CoMission effort were very impressive. We on the arrangements committee were pleased with the total results, and glad that God allowed us to have a part in such a productive venture for the cause of His Son, the Lord Jesus Christ.

The results of that five-year effort were absolutely amazing. During that time we saw over fifteen hundred Americans go to Russia for a minimum of one year (some stayed two or three years) to teach Russian schoolteachers the curriculum called, "Christian Morals and Ethics, A Foundation for Society." The teachers then taught the students. Altogether the eighty-two agencies involved spent about $70 million to get the job done. As you might imagine, hundreds of teachers came to faith in Christ and millions of schoolkids heard about Jesus Christ for the first time in their lives, and maybe the only time. Needless to say, it was a once-in-a-lifetime experience and opportunity to serve the Lord. It cost me a fair amount of time and resources, but I think it was worth every penny.

At the end of the five years, the effort ended. It was that way by design, as most of the executive committee were heads of large organizations with full-time jobs and they couldn't give any more time to the CoMission. The work has continued on in many areas but on a smaller scale and under new leadership. It was a sad day for most of us on the executive committee when it officially ended. In fact, the members had become such good friends (including the wives) during the five years that they suggested that we have a reunion at the end of the first "retirement year" just for fellowship, with no agenda. They all looked at me and said, "As the chairman of the arrangements committee, it's your job to find a place and make all the arrangements." Well, that was fifteen years ago now, and for the last fifteen years we have had a "reunion." We usually go to a nice hotel for three or four days and just fellowship and reminisce. We have also been on cruises to the Caribbean and to Alaska. The group has bonded in an unusual way. At this writing, two have gone on to heaven, and some of us are slowing down; but it is, indeed, a very special group of Christian leaders whose hearts God has closely knit together. I was, and am, so humbled, but appreciative, to be a part of the group.

For myself, I can truthfully say, "I, being in the way, the Lord led me." When I first heard about the duties and responsibilities of the task, I felt unable to do it. But, as is most often the case, the answer the Lord wants to hear is not whether we're able but if we are available. When I finally said that I would be "available," the Lord more than supplied all that was needed to get the job done. To Him be the glory!

The CoMission Executive Committee

ntric® Birmingham-Bloomfield Edition

NEWS

INSIDE:
Editorials, page 22A
PAGE 13A

ristian Bridge'

er talks religion with Gorbachev

son, the Birmingham developer/landlord, nds with Soviet Union President Mikhail l, who was "very warm, very friendly" when

they met during Johnson's visit to the Kremlin in early November.

e meeting, the group also er, which led to much media was on the 11 o'clock news, event, prayer to KGB ," Johnson said.

preter, called himself an atheist. Minutes later, Johnson said, the Soviet leader noted how "we're all made by the same God."

Perhaps more significant was the meeting with the national board of education

We have no teachers about God. We don't even have money to buy paper to print books about God.'" Johnson said.

That desire — to put religion into public

Meeting
Mikhail Gorbachev

62

A CONSULTANT AND THE BROOKLYN TABERNACLE

A fter I had retired from the construction phase of my life, I was contacted by a very wealthy and generous friend with a request. Actually, it was from his family, after he had passed away. They were interested in financially helping a fine Christian agency in New Jersey with the purchase and renovation of an office building. They asked me if I would go and investigate the situation and report back to them as to the viability of the project. When I did so, I discovered that while the purchase price of the building was fair, their estimated cost to fix it up was way too low and, therefore, it was not a good or wise investment. I also helped them find an alternative building that was much better suited for their needs and was in "move in" condition. As a result, my wealthy friends gave them the money to purchase the building. This led to several other similar situations where I would go and help other Christian charitable agencies with a building purchase and/or renovation where my friends were contemplating helping them financially. Included in my assignment was a large building in Budapest to be the regional office for one of the largest Christian organizations in the world. I made several trips to Hungary during the process.

There were several others, and they tried many times to pay me for my services; but all I ever accepted was out-of-pocket expenses as this was, after all, a service to the Lord. One of the most interesting projects was the Brooklyn Tabernacle in Brooklyn, New York. At the time, the church was meeting in a converted theater on Flatbush Avenue in the heart of Brooklyn. It could seat perhaps fifteen hundred people and was now too small for the growing congregation. The church had investigated the possibility of constructing a new building, but with the cost of land and construction and with no real good location available, they gave up that idea.

What they did find was an old abandoned theater right downtown in Brooklyn. It had been originally built as a legitimate theater, later turned into a two-screen movie theater with a wall down the middle of the building. It was now closed and deteriorating. It had seats for four thousand people with a large balcony, as originally configured. It covered almost an entire city block and was next door to Macy's department store and across the street from a twenty-story government building. It was in the middle of a very busy shopping area. Authorities said one hundred thousand people walked by it every day. It was about fifty feet from a subway entrance.

By the time I became involved, the church had purchased the property and was in the planning stage to restore the building. My friends were interested in helping them. But before they decided what their involvement would be, they asked me to go and "check it out." They thought it was an ambitious venture—it was just a church; and while they had a wonderful reputation and a great staff, did they know what they were doing? Did they have an architect who was qualified and a legitimate contractor and a viable financial plan, etc.?

I made an appointment and went to Brooklyn to begin my investigation. What I found was amazing! Not only did they have a very qualified architect and building contractor, but the church itself and its pastor and staff were a refreshing surprise. At that point, the plans were completed, very professional and detailed. They had a loan commitment for about half of the projected costs and were trusting the Lord for the balance before beginning construction. Since the pastor and staff realized that they didn't know a lot about how to handle a project of this size, they got professional help. There was a member of the church who was a professional designer and decorator named Dianne. She had quit her job and came to work for the church to coordinate this sizeable undertaking. She was, indeed, well qualified and became my original contact person.

Perhaps a little history of the church would be helpful. It was started years ago in a storefront building in Brooklyn by a graduate of the Moody Bible Institute who felt called to minister to the inner-city people. By and by, he moved on and turned it over to his son-in-law, Jim Cymbala, who at the time was an American Airlines junior executive who was helping his father-in-law at the church part-time. Under Pastor Jim's leadership, along with the help of his wife, Carol, who was the choir director, the church began to grow and prosper. Jim quit his job and became the full-time pastor.

At that point, the Brooklyn Tabernacle 250-voice choir was well known worldwide and had made many recordings that were very popular. The church had accomplished amazing growth and success.

At one of my early meetings, I asked about the church's financial situation and how they planned to pay back the substantial monthly payments that would be required. There were several people at the meeting, including the pastor, Diane, the bookkeeper, and a few others. Pastor Jim said to the bookkeeper, a very astute and qualified lady, "Go get your books and records." She did and came back and said, "What would you like to know?" I asked about the budget, giving history, etc. She opened the books and said, "Let's start with the building fund. For the past several years, it has been running at about $100,000 per month."

I remember saying, "You mean your people give $1.2 million a year just to the building fund?" She said, "Yes. That is how we paid for the new project and that's in addition to funding all the other operations of the church such as salaries, building maintenance, and the rest." She also told me how much they gave to missions each year, and that also they had no debt. I was flabbergasted! Here was a group of people, mostly African-American, Hispanic, Asian, and other minorities with a white pastor and choir director with no members who were executives or with a lot of money. They were mostly schoolteachers, bus drivers, government workers, and "blue-collar" people who were giving at a phenomenal rate to support their church and its ministry, mostly to others just like themselves. I had never seen anything like that sort of dedication and generosity by any group before in my life. I was overcome with a sense of awe as I compared what they were doing with what most other churches that I knew about.

As a result of my investigation, I wrote a report to my wealthy donor friends with a final sentence that said, "I don't know how much you were thinking of giving them, but, in my opinion, you couldn't give them too much!" Consequently, they gave them a sizeable commitment. It was equal to half of the amount that their finance company had committed on a mortgage basis and was enough to almost complete the project.

The donor asked if I would make periodic trips to verify the progress of the construction and send them regular reports as they advanced their funds to the church. Theirs was a gift, not a loan. I made several trips to Brooklyn during the time of construction and saw it through to its completion.

The final result is a fantastic facility. They restored the building to almost its original plans and specifications, including colors and many other details. This, of course, was after completely gutting the original building, which had deteriorated terribly. The roof had been leaking for years. In the process, they built a choir loft with over two hundred seats. They renovated the basement with a nursery and a full kitchen, a cafeteria and dining room. They serve meals on Sunday after church at a nominal cost, along with so many other services and helps to their people.

The construction process was most interesting, especially being in the middle of a very busy and congested part of the city. As with many remodeling jobs, there are often some "surprises." One that they encountered had to do with the plumbing under the basement floor. In the original theater, all the toilets were located in the basement, and they were quite elaborate. They had a wide ornate stairway down to the toilet rooms, and each had a large parlor before going into the actual toilet rooms. While planning to install all new fixtures, they found the pipes under the floor had all deteriorated and had to be replaced. This meant removing most of the basement floor to install new plumbing lines.

At that point, they thought that it would be helpful if the ceiling in the basement was a little higher to accommodate the uses they had in mind. One way to accomplish it would be to dig out about two feet of dirt, making the ceiling higher. With most of the floor gone anyway, why not? So they did a most unusual thing. They cut a hole in the floor of the main auditorium, about twenty feet square, and lowered a small bulldozer down into the basement. The dozer pushed up some dirt and made a ramp from the basement to the first floor. Then, load by load with an end loader, they removed the dirt and took it outside to a dumpster from which it was hauled away. A most ingenious arrangement. While it cost more than planned, it helped to make the entire building much more usable.

One day when talking to Pastor Jim, I asked him about the government of the church, and he told me an interesting story. He said that at one point they had a board of deacons or elders that were elected to help oversee the operations. He said that he realized that the church was not to be a dictatorship and that he needed other opinions to help him discern the mind of God in making decisions. But he said that it didn't work. While the board members were good and godly men, they didn't have much business experience and most were uneducated in business. When an issue came up, they would say, in effect, "Pastor, we don't know much about that stuff. We can help you with people problems and maybe spiritual situations, but not business affairs." So he said they decided that in those areas they would depend on the Lord to lead all six of the pastoral staff to agree unanimously on an issue or they wouldn't approve it.

As an example, he said when they first heard about the theater being for sale in downtown Brooklyn, the price was $9 million. All six pastors prayed about it and thought about it, but one man said he didn't feel good or comfortable with it. He thought it was too much to pay. The other five said, "Okay, let's forget it," which they did. At that time a developer was trying to buy the entire block and demolish all the buildings. He planned to build a multistory building on the site. While the theater occupies most of the block, with entrances on two streets, there are several retail stores facing the streets that he could not acquire. Therefore, his plan was thwarted. So, after several months, the broker came back to the church and said the theater owner would now take $6 million. At this point, the sixth pastor said he would approve, and they bought the theater building. Bottom line: by waiting for full agreement, the system worked and they saved $3 million.

The church today continues to be remarkable. There are way too many things to tell you about here. They have four services on Sunday at 9 a.m., noon, 3 p.m., and 6 p.m. And most of the time the four thousand seats are full. We have been to church there several times since the building was finished. One time was most significant. Marilyn and I decided to go and take our three children and their spouses to New York for a weekend and to see the church that they had heard so much about from their dad. At one point, Pastor Jim Cymbala invited me up to the platform and before the whole church thanked me for my part in helping them with the construction. It was quite a surprise. The donors did not want to be identified and, as their representative, I think some people thought I was the donor. Anyway, it happened to be my birthday (I think Colleen had tipped him off) and Jim asked that everyone sing "Happy Birthday" to me! It was the first time I ever had four thousand people sing to me including the famous Brooklyn Tabernacle choir!

I am happy to say we continue to hear good reports about the church, its wonderful people, and the growth of the congregation and how God has blessed the faithful work of Jim and Carol Cymbala and their people.

63

THE TUESDAY MORNING CLUB

Many years ago, my friend Stanley Kresge invited me to a new group of businessmen that was being organized to meet at 7:30 on Tuesday mornings for a time of Bible study. Stanley said that he used to meet with a group in downtown Detroit, but since he lived way out north on Lake Angelus and his office had moved to Troy, they wanted to start a group closer to his home and office.

I had been involved in a CBMC Bible study group that met on Thursday mornings, and I really wasn't looking for another one to attend. But when Stanley said that it was going to be held in the office of a fellow named Bill Kunnath, my ears perked up. That's a fairly uncommon name. The only Bill Kunnath I knew was a car salesman we used to deal with maybe twenty years prior. It was when we were going strong in the construction business and we leased or bought several cars and trucks from him. He worked for a Ford dealer out in Garden City. He was a rough character, loud and brassy and with a foul mouth. But he was always nice to us and was very competitive with good deals, so we dealt with him and his agency for many years. But he was the last person I ever expected to see hosting a Bible study group.

So, out of curiosity, I agreed to come on a Tuesday morning with Stanley to the new group. Sure enough, it was the same Bill Kunnath. He remembered me and gave me a big hug and a warm welcome. He was now in the insurance business and seemed to be very successful. He had his own four-story office building, which had a very plush conference room with a big table and leather chairs that would seat maybe twelve or fifteen people.

Bill introduced me to the leader or moderator. His name was Bill Bullard. It seems that some years before, Bill Kunnath, the car salesman, was going through some tough times in his life, including some problems with alcohol and a divorce. I don't remember all the details except that his life was a mess. Somehow he met Bill Bullard who befriended him and ultimately helped him to put his faith in Jesus Christ. As a result, his life began to change and, of course, all for the better. He had remarried and was now a successful businessman with a desire to follow Jesus Christ in all facets of his life. As you might guess, he was very thankful to Bill Bullard for his help, and Bill Kunnath wanted to start a Bible study group with Bullard as the leader so perhaps some more men might find what Kunnath had found.

I added Tuesday mornings to my schedule. That was perhaps forty years ago. I don't recall the exact date when it started. But it began to grow with new men attending. Then, after a few years, Bill Kunnath retired, sold his insurance business and moved to Florida. So we had to move the Tuesday morning group to a new location. Actually, we moved it two or three times to various locations, all in Troy. Then we expanded our office space in our building in downtown Birmingham, and we built a very nice new conference room and kitchen. At that point, the group decided to move to our office where it has been meeting now for perhaps fifteen years or so.

At this writing, Bill Bullard and I are the only original members or attendees left. Bill Bullard is an amazing fellow. He lives on a lake located about halfway between Ann Arbor and Jackson, and he has been driving all that way to Birmingham, and earlier to Troy, every Tuesday morning now for over forty years. The driving time is about an hour and a half in good weather, and longer when the roads are bad in the wintertime. He is always there by 7:30 or earlier.

But here is the good part. Over the years, we have had dozens of men attend the group. Quite often they were good church men but did not have a personal relationship with the Lord. Through the Bible study times, they recognized that something was missing in their lives. While Bill Bullard does not press for a decision during the meetings, many of them expressed a desire to have a closer relationship with the Lord and put their faith totally in him. So, during private meetings, one-on-one, we have seen a number of men come to know the Lord and have their lives changed. Some of them are now in heaven. In fact, many of them are. The group is still going strong with about ten to fifteen men each Tuesday.

Here is just one example. Several years ago, I was invited to speak at a men's breakfast at a very large and prestigious church out in Bloomfield Hills. There was a nice group there, but that's about all I remember. Then, maybe fifteen or twenty years later, a man from that Bloomfield Hills breakfast meeting stopped in to see me in my office. His name is Chuck Sower, and he is a commercial real estate broker with an office located about a block from mine. The visit must have had something to do with business. I really don't remember. But in the course of the conversation, he told me that he was in that breakfast meeting and that he had remembered some of the things I had said. Amazing! That was fifteen or twenty years before!

Anyway, I invited him to come to our Tuesday morning group, and he came. During this time, the commercial real estate business was all but dead, and he was having a tough time. But he showed a keen interest in the Tuesday morning Bible study group and its biblical content and teachings. As a result, I invited him to lunch one day to a restaurant just across the street from our office. After a little discussion, I asked him if he was ready to pray a simple prayer and invite Jesus Christ into his life and allow Him to take over. He said he was and, with a simple prayer right there in the restaurant, he did so. Well, he would tell you that was a day that changed his life. His financial troubles did not go away. In fact, they may have gotten worse. But his faith is now strong and he has the Lord to go through the troubles with him (as we all do who are His children) during difficult times. Chuck and I have now become good friends. This story could be repeated a dozen or more times about men who have had their lives changed through the "Tuesday morning group."

So the lesson here is that it is the Bible (God's Word) that is so important. It is through reading it (and in some cases studying it) that causes us to sec our problems and the kind of people we really area and how to do something about it. In fact, it gives us the guidelines of how to deal with every aspect of life.

So don't neglect it. Read it regularly. Even study it. There is no other book like it. It is how almighty God communicates with us, instructs us, encourages us and a lot of other good things. And of course it is through prayer that we communicate with Him. It's a two-way communication system. And it is the best! Even better than the Internet!

64

BAD JUDGMENT

A young man approached an older man one day with a question. The young man asked the older man how was it that he had become so wise and, therefore, so wealthy. The old man replied, "Very simple, son. Good judgment!" With that, the young man thought for a moment and then said, "If I might ask, sir, how did you get the good judgment?" Again, the older man responded, "Very simple, son. Through experience!" Then the young man said, "If you would indulge me one more time, sir, how did you get the experience?" The old man quickly responded, "Very simple, son. Through bad judgment!"

There have been some experiences in my life that resulted in considerable losses and always as a result of my bad judgment. Usually they had to do with bad choices concerning people. One in particular had to do with a fellow I thought was my friend. Actually, I didn't know him too well, and I guess, to be more precise, he was a longtime acquaintance I really didn't know too well. But we had always been friendly, and he had a wonderful wife who was an outstanding Christian lady. For the sake of this discussion, let's just call him Bob. I had known him for over thirty years and conducted a little business with his father years before. By this time, I was out of the construction business; and we were only in the property management business and had actually sold one or two of our properties. I was spending the winters in Florida and the summers at Maranatha. I was semiretired.

Bob's idea was to build a state-of-the-art car wash, gas station, convenience store with a food court, an oil change facility, and car detailing center. At that time, he owned an old antiquated car wash and gas station facility that was so outdated and small that he couldn't wash pickup trucks or SUVs. But he had a good location.

The plan was to buy some additional adjoining land and build this new facility. He said he knew the gas station and car wash business inside and out; and this was the "wave of the future" for these types of businesses. In fact, he said he was an officer in the car wash association of Michigan and knew all the details, related information, and trends.

At this point, I was about to go to Florida for the winter. We had no sooner got there when I noticed that a new facility, similar to what Bob was talking about, had been built about a mile from our place. So, out of curiosity, I began to patronize it; and I was impressed. It seemed to be busy. It was a Mobil station with twelve gas pumps, a convenience store with a deli, and a full service car wash. The car wash customer would drive up on one side of the main building and get out of the car and walk through the convenience store to pay for the car wash and, quite often, buy something else and then exit the other side to pick up the car. The car wash ran behind the convenience store. I told Bob about it on the phone, and he asked me to take some pictures and measure the place as best I could. I did so and sent him a rough sketch of the facility.

I agreed to help him. My motivation was not to make money. I already had enough. It was basically to help him and his wonderful wife to have some means of financial support. His present business was not doing well, but he had a good location. He was also encumbered with a lot of debt.

The plan was that he would do all the work, sort of like I used to do in my day, and I would furnish the money through a bank mortgage and a modest amount of cash up front. We were to be fifty-fifty partners, and I believe we had a provision that he could eventually buy me out at a modest profit.

So, away we went. Or, more accurately, away he went! He insisted that we use an architect in Milwaukee, Wisconsin, who was reported to be the best in the country for this type of structure—a specialist that he had met in some of his experiences in the national car wash association. The convenience store designer was from Dallas, Texas, and was also reported to be the best in the country in his field.

When I questioned these choices with the idea that I personally knew several local architects and designers who were well qualified and who I thought would do a great job and for less cost, I was rebuffed. Bob said that I might know about office buildings, apartments, and shopping centers, but he was the "expert" in this type of venture and I should leave these decisions to him. He thought he knew best what to do. He gave me a business plan that showed sales projections, costs of operations, and profits that were very impressive. So, I sort of let him alone.

Along the way, we had some discussions about some of the features of the project. One was that the plans called for a separate gas island on the site, with a small hut to house a person who would pump the gas for the customer for ten cents more per gallon. I remember saying to Bob, "Nobody uses full-service pumps anymore. Every gas station I know of, people pump their own gas." Here again, he said, "You don't know my customers. I know what I'm doing." The plan also called for the customer to stay in the car during the car wash. Therefore, he or she would not be a captive customer to the convenience store during the wash. Again, what I was impressed with in Florida, said Bob, wouldn't work in Michigan.

After a little more investigation, I determined that Bob did *not* know all he claimed to know and was using me and my money to build the Taj Mahal of car washes. By that time, it was too late to stop it. He was so intimidating and "know- it-all" and just plowed right on through with the project. Without question, it is the finest and most elaborate operation of its kind in Michigan, and maybe in the country. But it cost so much to build, it has so much debt on it that I don't believe I will live long enough to see it be a positive venture. What was "Bob's dream" turned out to be "my nightmare." While it was still under construction and I began to see the facts, I talked to my son-in-law Drew about the situation. He decided to sell his business in Wisconsin and move with my daughter, Colleen, and their family back to Michigan and to be my "eyes and ears" daily on the construction site. He later found out that the architect had sent Bob a letter saying, in effect, that with the plans and ideas that Bob was insisting upon, it would cost so much that there was no way the venture could be profitable. Of course, Bob never disclosed that information to anyone.

Early on, when we saw how much more the project was costing and we had to come up with more money, he couldn't put up his part; and his interest got diminished and diminished until he had no ownership left. At that point, I still didn't know how bad a person he was. I thought he was just making some poor decisions. So we kept him on the payroll as we opened the business; but we soon found out that not only did he not know what he was doing, but that he was deceptive with me and was using me and my money to build his ego by being able to show off this wonderful, outstanding project to his peers and friends in the car wash industry. It is, indeed, impressive!

Bob was fired after only a few months of operations, and he left Drew and me with a financial hole from which we will likely never recover. While the losses are significant, they did not threaten our financial well-being. But here is the worst part. The money that was lost was extra money that we had. Money that we didn't need to live on. It was money that would have gone to help Christian ministries and the cause of Jesus Christ around the world. It was actually the Lord's money. I hope the Lord will forgive me for using some of His money in such a poor way. I can only take comfort in the fact that we have done so well in other ventures where the Lord blessed and I knew what I was doing. As a result, a whole lot of money was given back to the Lord because of His blessing upon our efforts.

I can't finish this chapter without giving credit to Drew for his untiring efforts and dedication to helping me out of a terrible financial mess. To his credit, he saw Bob's "true colors" early on and tried to tell me. But I couldn't believe that Bob could be that selfish and bad. But he was; and Drew (and now Colleen with the Biggby coffee franchise) has kept the business thriving and doing as well as anyone could for over ten years. He and Colleen have helped meet the heavy debt requirements and, for a long time, without much or any compensation. They have been a "God-send" for me along with some key faithful employees including Terry and Cheryl Stacy.

So, what is the lesson here? To you children and grandchildren, be sure you know well anyone that you plan to be closely associated with. Know all about them. Investigate them thoroughly. Know their motive (if you can) and, above all, pray about the decision. Perhaps ask two or three godly friends to pray with you. The Scripture says there is wisdom in the counsel of many. Take your time. If you feel any hesitation or "check in your spirit," don't do it! Don't allow bad judgment and experience to teach you good judgment. Pray and trust the Lord to lead you in all decisions.

Plymouth Service Center

65

A MOST FRUSTRATING TIME

After I sold most of the properties in the early 2000s, particularly the Birmingham Place in 2005, son-in-law Scott was out of a job, as we had nothing for him to do. As a help to him, I told him that if he could find some sort of a business to go into, I would help him financially.

It wasn't too long when he and his brother-in-law, Randy Witt, came up with the idea of building a water park in a western suburb of Chicago. Randy had been interested in water parks for many years and knew a lot about them from considerable research on the industry and actually visiting several parks and talking to a lot of park owners and operators.

They had a very ambitious and interesting plan. Randy knew something about the details of the business operations, and Scott was to be in charge of putting the deal together financially, getting investors, land acquisition, mortgage money, etc. The plan on paper looked great. They acquired the land, hired a very professional water park designer, made financial projections, and obtained investors. I was one of them. They also arranged for bank financing for about 50 percent of the costs. As time went on and it was time to "seal the deal" on the mortgage loan, the lender came up with some new, last-minute and very restrictive, if not punitive, requirements. This is not unusual with unscrupulous lenders. They get you with what I call "involvement." They act cooperatively through all the early negotiations, and you get involved with them exclusively. Then, at the last minute, they "stick it to you," and by that time they believe you have no alternatives but to meet their demands. And often that is the case.

When I heard about this deal, I advised them not to go ahead with the lender. I then asked my bank if they would make the loan to the water park venture, which was to be called "Raging Waves." My bank said no, but they would loan the money to me, and I could loan it to Raging Waves. So, that's what we did, and we were off and running.

Everything looked good. They had a good location, wonderful plans for a state-of-the-art park, and all the money they needed . . . until the first setback occurred. One of their prime subcontractors went broke and bankrupt about two or three months prior to completion of the park. Randy and Scott had to move in and deal with the other subcontractors, many of which had not been paid for work done, and negotiate with them to complete the work. This resulted in considerable cost overruns. All this served to delay the opening of the park, from the original date of Memorial Day, to late June. This resulted in about one-third fewer operating days and a proportionate loss of income for the first year.

At that point, there was no money to pay the subs for the extra costs. To their credit, mostly Scott, with the help of their attorney, was able to negotiate settlements and a payout plan over a few years to keep most of them satisfied. The second year was the coldest summer in fifty-eight years in Chicago and a disappointing year financially.

However, the downturn in the economy in 2008 was another major setback—not only in revenue at the park but with my bank. The game plan was that I (and my bank) was to be the lender for a short time until the park could get up and operating at a profit. At that point, the plan was for the park to get its own financing and pay me off. I, in turn, would pay the bank.

At the time of the original loan, my real estate assets were plenty as collateral to justify the loan. However, when the market went down, the bank said the value of my assets also went down below the amount of the loan. That was really not true, but at that point the bank was making their own rules and decisions accordingly. They wanted more and more collateral until they took everything I had, including my house, as collateral. They were unmerciful.

I had been a customer of the bank for over sixty years and never missed a payment with loans in the tens of millions of dollars, and this loan should have been no different. We never missed a payment, but that didn't count. They were now making the new rules. Then one day they called to say that they were worried. After all, they said, I was eighty-three years old; and if I died, they would be in trouble. I had a meeting with them and showed them how, if I died, they were more than secure. No matter. They demanded a very large insurance policy on my life, payable to the bank. When I explained that I was in good health and that my mom died at ninety-one and my dad at one hundred, it made no difference. "Get an insurance policy or we will call the loan," was their reply.

It is the most unreasonable business arrangement that I have ever been in during all over sixty years in business. From the beginning, they have required monthly financial reports on the water park. When we tried to explain that the park only had income for three or four months, the bank said, "No matter. We want reports monthly." At one point, they wanted an appraisal on the park. It cost $12,000. They then, in effect, threw it in the wastebasket. The park has a qualified CPA firm who sends monthly reports to the bank (at added cost to the park). Then the bank said they wanted a larger CPA firm to audit the local CPA's figures to establish their accuracy. That audit cost $24,000 and proved no changes were necessary to the original report. The bank promptly threw that also in the wastebasket. It's crazy! They demand all kinds of verification of how the park is doing (at lots of costs to them), but give us absolutely no credit for the park's value.

They also demand all kinds of regular reports on all our other assets, but then they make their own decisions as to its value no matter what the reports show. It is obvious they no longer care about helping their customers or working with them to a successful conclusion.

Although the water park is now profitable, with revenue going up each year, the bank refuses to give any credence to its value. It is the largest and best park in Illinois, with rave reviews from everyone. At one point, the bank sent a representative to visit, and he came back with a glowing report. It seems that somewhere along the line the bank lost money on a water park loan somewhere else, and now all water parks, good or bad, are (in their minds) "painted with the same brush."

To get financing on a water park is not easy. It is, indeed, a seasonal business and weather related. Lenders want to see three or four years of solid operations that establish a trend before making a loan. "Raging Waves" now has had three great years and is looking forward to a fourth in 2013. If so, alternative financing is available; and we can pay off the bank. That will be a great day! In the meantime, the bank is fully covered, whether I live or die. All we've ever asked for is a little time. We know what we're doing. We have a plan. In the meantime, we have paid them over one million dollars a year and never missed a payment. Go figure!

In spite of all I've gone through with this bank, I would do it again. Because if I hadn't stepped in, the original lender would have been able to foreclose on Scott and his partner by now, and there would be no owner-ship by any of us in Raging Waves. They would have wiped us all out due to the provisions in the documents that they had demanded. So, some good has come of it. Also, Raging Waves is now doing fine and will be a very profitable venture in the future. It is just taking longer than planned due primarily to the subcontractor's bankruptcy, one cold summer, and the downturn in the economy. All beyond our control. Why the bank didn't see that or want to see that is most frustrating.

At this time, the bank has recently been paid in full by getting other lenders involved and by giving the new lenders only about 50 percent of what our bank had demanded as collateral, and with lower rates and bet-ter terms. It is ironic that they could have kept the business with a very good customer and with just a little patience and understanding and with twice the collateral.

Suffice to say, they are short-sighted. They surely don't understand basic business practices and how to deal with good, long-term custom-ers. Keep in mind that they never lost a dime with me. As I said, it has been a most frustrating time!

So what is the lesson here? I really don't know. Maybe it will be known in days to come. I keep reminding myself, like my mom said, "If you do the right thing, you will never go wrong." And as far as I know, we have always done the right thing with this bank. Also, we don't always understand the reasons for things that happen to us as they are happening. In the long run, this exercise may be just another blessing from the Lord and another "P" in our lives. Maybe for protection. Who knows? At least at this point, this pain is over!

Often times we don't see what God is doing in our lives in times of adversity. He doesn't always reveal His bigger purpose—remember God is sovereign. He will do what He will do.

The Bible is full of examples. Perhaps Job is one of the best. Job was the object of a conversation between God and Satan about faithfulness. Job in all his suffering had no idea of the "bigger picture." Likewise, I doubt if Joseph in the book of Genesis knew God's plan for him when he was thrown into prison when he was innocent. Little did he know at the time that God was planning to use him to salvage the remnant of the Jewish nation. But in both cases (and in many others), God honored their faithfulness. We don't always know what God is up to in times of adversity.

How about in my case. Why did Marilyn have to suffer with Alzheimer's for ten years? I have no idea. God must have had His reasons, because He loved her very much. But I know that then, after the worst year of my life, the Lord in His mercy brought Pam into my life and a most wonderful new relationship.

Or how about Scott Melby, who is currently the victim of leukemia? I'm sure Karen and Scott, their family, and many others may be asking why? Again I have no Idea. But we do know God is faithful and loves him very much. It may be a long time (if ever) before we know the good that may come from this illness that is most likely going to take a year out of his life. How will God be gloried? I don't know, but I believe He will.

So our job is to just trust Him, no matter what. Maybe someday we will see God's "bigger picture."

66

NEW WIFE—NEW LIFE!

When Marilyn passed away in late 2007, I thought that, for all practical purposes, my life was over. There wasn't much to live for. I was seventy-nine. I thought I would just "put in my time" until the Lord called me to Glory. Life on earth had lost a lot of its enjoyment for me. I had had a good life, a full life, with so many wonderful experiences. I had been so blessed with a great wife and marriage for fifty-five years, three wonderful children and fourteen grandchildren, and even reasonably good health. I had all that I needed financially to live very comfortably for the rest of my life, and even with some left over to share with others and to help the Lord's work. But I was so empty inside.

Colleen and Drew were living with me and were committed to looking after me for the future. And they were doing a good job. Karen and Scott and their family lived just a mile away; and they, too, did all they could to help ease the pain of loneliness by keeping me busy with many activities including family get-togethers and travel all over the world. Between my two girls and their families, all living so close, they kept me busy and occupied. Even Kevin, who lived three hundred miles away, did all he could to help. Several others joined in, including friends. Everyone did what they could; but the loss and loneliness continued. That summer at Maranatha was particularly hard, as I was really all alone in the cottage that Marilyn loved so much. I remember many lonely afternoons, sitting in the swing out on the deck overlooking beautiful Lake Michigan. It was, indeed, beautiful. But my life was not.

During that year, Colleen's oldest son, Michael, had graduated from Carnegie Mellon University in Pittsburgh. He is a very gifted and accomplished violinist. He had applied to a graduate school with the expectation of getting a master's degree. It seems that the school of his choice only took one or two students into their grad school program each semester, and he had applied too late. "Try again next year," they told him. In the meantime, he was living with us. To occupy his time he set up a big screen and theater in our basement. The screen is about ten feet wide and seven feet high and is motorized and comes down from the ceiling where it is totally invisible when not in use. He did a great job with an overhead projector, surround sound, and all the technology of a professional theater.

After a while, I think he got bored and began to look for something else to do. So he contacted three other string instrument players, and they made themselves into a string quartet. Then they signed up with the Holland America cruise line to play chamber music on one of their cruise ships. It was a six-month contract beginning October 1. The ship sailed each Saturday from San Diego down the coast of Mexico to three or four cities to what was called the "Mexican Riviera." It went down and back from Saturday to Saturday for several weeks, and then it went on through the Panama Canal and across the Atlantic Ocean, ending up in Rome, which ended the six-month contract. From Rome they would fly him home.

Colleen decided that since Michael could not come home for Thanksgiving or Christmas, she and Drew would go on one of the cruises with him. They decided on the second week of November and invited me to go with them. So she booked two staterooms, side by side.

As I began to think about the trip, I concluded that Colleen and Drew would want to be with their son as much as possible during his free time, and I would be like a "fifth wheel" and either in the way and/or perhaps alone much of the time. During the past year, Pam, my longtime secretary and friend, had been a dinner partner and a "fourth" once in a while when Colleen and Drew and I went to the symphony where we had season tickets for four. So, I asked Colleen if she would mind if we asked Pam to come along on the cruise. She said, "Sure, invite her," and she booked a third stateroom. Pam agreed to come along.

Things on the ship went along about as I expected. We listened each evening as Michael and his group played in one of the lounges before and after dinner. On two nights they actually played during dinner in the dining room. He was free most days in the daytime, and we all went ashore at the various stops to visit places that he knew about. After dinner, and when he was finished playing, he and his parents spent time together; and Pam and I were on our own. We visited the various shows on the ship and sometimes just sat in other areas, listening to the various kinds of music and other performers. Sometimes we just sat out on the deck and enjoyed the tropical night air. We had a great time! Most enjoyable!

All of a sudden, it dawned on me that I was really enjoying being with Pam. Although I knew a lot about her from our years of being together in business and at family functions, I was never alone with her like this. It was so nice and so comfortable, and she was wonderful! I had a new appreciation and different feelings toward her.

One night, out on the deck with a big full moon glistening off the Pacific Ocean, I was overcome with these new feelings toward her. The name of the ship was the *Oosterdam*, but to me it became the "Love Boat." All of a sudden, it just came out. I asked her to marry me. I think she was surprised. In fact, I'm pretty sure she was surprised. Her response was, "I don't know. I've been by myself for so long, always free to do whatever I wanted. I'm not sure how I would be in a marriage relationship." I guess it might be a normal reaction after all the years of being alone. Anyway, I asked her if she would pray about it. She said she would. From then on, every time I saw her I asked her if she was praying. She always said, "Yes."

It wasn't until three or four days after we got home that she said, "Yes!" she would marry me. That was a great day for me. I was so happy! We announced it to our family when we were all together at Christmastime, and all the children, spouses, and grandchildren clapped their hands in approval. They all knew her very well and loved her very much.

Then the questions began. People were asking when was the wedding to be? We had thought maybe in the spring, when the trees had blossomed and the flowers were in bloom. We had also decided that it would be a small wedding. Just family. That was enough. Both families alone would amount to thirty or forty people. Her family was mostly one brother and his wife, one widowed sister-in-law, and a few nieces and nephews and perhaps some of their children.

About that time, daughter Karen spoke up and reminded us of a missions trip to Kenya that was planned for mid-February. The trip was to include her whole family of husband and five children, Kevin and two of his boys, and me, along with two or three others. Karen suggested that if we got married before mid-February, Pam could come along with us.

She no sooner got the words out of her mouth when Colleen chimed in. She said, "Wait a minute. Drew and I are leaving on a missions trip to Cambodia on January 19, and we don't want to miss the wedding. So let's get on with it and do it before January 19."

This was during the Christmas holidays. January 19 was only about three weeks away. So we put things in motion in a hurry.

Soon after our decision to get married, I called my good friend Joe Stowell. I asked him if he was sitting down. He said he wasn't, but he would! I then told him the news, and he was delighted. I also asked him if he would come and marry us. He said, "If I am anywhere in the United States on the date you select, I will gladly be there." Indeed, he was, and it was wonderful!

Many of you know the details, but suffice it to say it happened on Saturday, January 17, 2009. I'm satisfied that the Lord went ahead of us and worked out the details in so many ways. It included finding a wonderful place, finding a suitable wedding dress, getting out the announcements, and many more details.

The place was the Birmingham Country Club. Our club, Oakland Hills, was closed for the winter. But other clubs had reciprocal agreements with us. The nice lady showed us a lovely room with a big stone fireplace, wood paneled walls, and leaded glass windows, overlooking the golf course. It was like a setting found in "Jolly Old England." She said it seated about sixty to sixty-five people for a dinner. The wedding time was to be 4 p.m. with a dinner to follow. It was available on Saturday, January 17, and we booked it. When folks heard of the wedding, some said, "We're coming, invited or not!" I questioned whether my sister, Linda, who had just gone to Florida for the winter, would come back. But not only did she and her husband, Dale, fly back, but she brought with her our cousin, Calistine, and her husband who were visiting her in Florida. After the number of guests got to sixty-four, we were forced to limit it, as there was no more room.

The winter day could not have been more beautiful. It had started snowing on Friday morning, the day before the Saturday wedding. It snowed all day Friday, Friday night, and all day Saturday. The snow was about six to eight inches deep by the time of the wedding. Looking out of the windows of the country club overlooking the beautiful snow-covered golf course, it was like a fairyland. Added to the enchantment were the all-white Christmas lights that were still up in the several trees on both sides of the long entrance drive into the club. It was spectacular in every way!

That was four years ago. I couldn't be happier. As I've said many times to anyone who will listen, I don't know of anyone in the whole world that I would be willing to be married to except Pam. She is the best wife any man could have. I am so blessed! She is so much like Marilyn in many ways. She has a sweet, sweet spirit and is liked by everyone who knows her. She was never married. She has a great attitude: positive and always upbeat. She has a great love for the Lord and has a close walk with Him. She is spiritually discerning and wise in all decisions. I rely on her judgment a lot. She loves all my children and grandchildren as though they were her own, and they all love her. She respects what God has given us financially and also has a desire to use it wisely. She is not personally extravagant but very generous with her own money toward others. She is industrious, never lazy about anything, and always thinking about what she can do to help others, especially me. As I said, "New wife, new life!"

After we were married, Colleen said, "Well, Drew and I will move out now and give you your house back." After a little thought, we said, "Not so fast. Let's talk about this." We decided that the house was big enough for all of us, plus room to spare when her kids came home. They were all either married or away at college. That was also four years ago, and it has been a very compatible arrangement.

Now Pam and I spend two to three months in Florida in the winter and ten weeks at Maranatha in the summer. So, with a few weeks of travel added, we are only home about half of the time. We decided at the beginning that Colleen would be the "lady of the house." She had been that for over two years already, and that wouldn't change. Pam would be her helper and do whatever she could to do to help. But Colleen would be the boss. We have help in housecleaning and caring for the outside, so the "work" is actually minimal, including planning, shopping for and preparing meals; and that is a joint effort. We, all four, enjoy the same sports and TV programs and are as compatible as could possibly be. So far, it is wonderful . . . a win-win situation for everyone. Colleen and Drew have a nice place to live; and Pam and I have extra help to assist in caring for the house. What could be better?

Paul and Pam, January 17, 2009, Another Very Happy Day

67

CONCLUSION

To you, my grandchildren, by now I hope you see and understand why I say that my cup of blessings runneth over. And I know full well, as the Bible says in Titus 3, that it is not because of works of righteousness that I have done but it is because of His mercy. Not only has He saved us, but He also sees fit to bless us. It is all because of Him and His love for us.

In my case, the blessings of God have not only filled **my** cup, but it has overflowed onto several others, including you. And I am so grateful. It is beyond my ability to express it. And let me suggest to you that there is no way to have a life that is complete, happy, and fulfilling other than the one who puts the Lord first and revolves around Him. True happiness is not found in any other way. Just trust your papa in this area. He really knows what he is talking about.

I recognize that I may have told you, my family, more than you wanted to know about Papa's life. But in case there is anything more about any of the stories or experiences that I mentioned in the book in the way of detail that you would like to know about, just let me know and I will be glad to sit down and tell you all I know or can remember.

You should also ask your parents to share with you some of their own experiences. Ask them what their experiences have meant to them; and perhaps what they have learned can be of a great help to you. Believe me, it is much better and less painful to learn and benefit from other people's experiences (particularly negative ones) than it is to go through them yourselves. So, ask, listen, and learn from other people. But most of all, stay close to the Lord. Keep short accounts with Him. Communicate regularly with Him through prayer, and He will communicate with you regularly as you read His Word. Allow the Lord to lead you by His Spirit and prompting in all decisions. He loves you and wants the best for you.

As you perhaps know by now, even though we know the Lord personally and are trusting Him for eternal life and want to be led by His Spirit, we still have the old nature (selfishness and Satan) inside of us. It is a constant battle inside of us. Who do we listen to and follow? Sometimes our own ways look so good and attractive. But even though we know better, we don't always do it. I have given you some examples of that in my own life.

So, what do we do? Someone told me a long time ago it is like two dogs fighting within us. A white dog representing God and the Holy Spirit and a black dog representing selfishness, Satan, and often wrong desires. The outcome will be determined by which dog we feed and which dog we starve. We feed the white dog by righteousness and decisions and actions that please the Lord. It is not always easy, but it is always very important. When we feed the white dog, it gets stronger and stronger. If we starve the black dog, while it never dies, it gets weaker and weaker and has less influence.

So how do we do it? Two words sum it up. Trust and obey. Trust God for what He has promised. You can rely on Him like no other. Don't doubt Him, no matter what. Remember once again, He loves you and wants the best for you.

Secondly, be obedient to what you know is the right thing to do. We have a manual for life (the Bible) that clearly shows us the way and what to do. It's really that simple. Just trust and obey. And, as my mama used to tell me over and over, "If you do the right thing, you will never go wrong!"

Also, I think you should know that for years every day I have prayed for each of you by name, and now including spouses and great-grandchildren. My prayer for you is that you will, indeed, just trust and obey.

May God bless each and every one of you and your children and grandchildren. And do be faithful to "pass it on." I hope I will see you all in heaven one day and for all eternity. (Incidentally, that's a long time.) Until then, may your cups also be full and overflowing in this life with God's blessings.

And may your cups also be full and overflowing with God's blessings.

ACKNOWLEDGEMENTS

I am certainly a novice as a writer or author. When I asked my longtime friend Greg Thornton, who is Vice President of Media at Moody how to proceed, he said "Just send me the manuscript and I will help you." Well, that was an understatement.

So with his help and guidance and with the others that he engaged, I am very grateful. They include Betsy Newenhuyse who provided wonderful editorial oversight, Cindy Hart and Pam Pugh for careful proofreading. Joe and Pat Ragont took care of the cover design and typeset all the pages, including placing the pictures with the captions. They were so patient with me in guiding me through "unfamiliar waters." All these people while associated with Moody Publishing, did their work for me apart from their regular duties at Moody. What a blessing!

Greg and his helper Karen Waddles, did a wonderful job of coordinating the production details.

There is no way all this could have been accomplished without your help. Thanks again Greg. You have been absolutely wonderful!

Then of course, the one who worked the longest on the whole project was my dear wife Pamela who typed every word of the manuscript including many changes, suggestions, and encouragement.

So, this has been a joint effort and I am so very grateful to all of you for your help with this project.

50029049R00165